Leo Laporte's

2005 Mac Gadget Guide

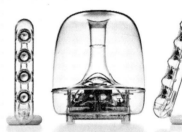

Leo Laporte & Todd Stauffer

800 East 96th Street
Indianapolis, IN 46240

Leo Laporte's 2005 Mac Gadget Guide

International Standard Book Number: 0-7897-3174-6

Library of Congress Catalog Card Number: 2004107074

Printed in the United States of America

First Printing: November 2004

07   06   05   04   4   3   2   1

Trademarks

All terms mentioned in this book that are known to be trademarks or service marks have been appropriately capitalized. Que Publishing cannot attest to the accuracy of this information. Use of a term in this book should not be regarded as affecting the validity of any trademark or service mark.

Warning and Disclaimer

Every effort has been made to make this book as complete and as accurate as possible, but no warranty or fitness is implied. The information provided is on an "as is" basis. The author and the publisher shall have neither liability nor responsibility to any person or entity with respect to any loss or damages arising from the information contained in this book.

Bulk Sales

Que offers excellent discounts on this book when ordered in quantity for bulk purchases or special sales. For more information, please contact

U.S. Corporate and Government Sales
1-800-382-3419
corpsales@pearsontechgroup.com

For sales outside of the U.S., please contact

International Sales
international@pearsoned.com

Publisher
Paul Boger

Associate Publisher
Greg Wiegand

Executive Editor
Rick Kughen

Development Editor
Laura Norman

Managing Editor
Charlotte Clapp

Project Editor
Tonya Simpson

Copy Editor
Linda Seifert

Indexer
Larry Sweazy

Proofreader
Carla Lewis

Publishing Coordinator
Sharry Lee Gregory

Interior Designer
Anne Jones

Cover Designer
Commercial Artisan

Photo Acquisitions
Jessica Kinnison

Page Layout
Kelly Maish

Contents at a Glance

Table of Contents

About the Authors

Leo Laporte is the former host of two shows on TechTV: *The Screen Savers* and *Call for Help*. Leo is a weekend radio host on Los Angeles radio KFI AM 640. He also appears regularly on many other television and radio programs, including ABC's *World News Now* and *Live with Regis and Kelly* as "The Gadget Guy." He is the author of *Leo Laporte's 2003 Computer Almanac* and *Leo Laporte's 2004 Screensavers Technology Almanac*, both of which have been bestsellers. Leo also is the author of three newly published books on consumer technology in his Leoville Press series: *Leo Laporte's Guide to TiVo*, *Leo Laporte's Mac Gadget Guide*, and *Leo Laporte's 2005 Gadget Guide*, all published by Que.

Todd Stauffer is the former host of *one* show on Knowledge TV: *Disk Doctors*, which he referred to as "Screen Savers Lite" at least once when Leo was in hearing range. Todd is author or co-author of more than three dozen books about computing and the Internet. His books for Que include *The Absolute Beginner's Guide to Creating Web Pages*, *HTML Web Publishing 6-in-1*, *Easy AOL*, and *Using Your Mac*. Todd is a frequent contributor to *MacAddict* magazine, as well as co-founder and publisher of the Jackson Free Press (www.jacksonfreepress.com), a news and culture weekly in Jackson, Mississippi, where he lives with writer Donna Ladd and an embarrassing number of cats. He can be found at www.macblog.com on the Web.

Dedication

This book is dedicated to eBay, which keeps us up at night, dreaming that our next great gadget might even be affordable.

Acknowledgments

Our thanks to the folks who make these projects happen at Que, including and in particular Rick Kughen, Laura Norman, Tonya Simpson, and Linda Seifert. Special thanks to Jessica Kinnison, who helped us find and secure permission for most of the images you see in this book. Also, thanks to the companies that provided the pictures, demonstration units, and the information we needed to tell you about all these great gadgets.

Todd would like to thank his colleagues at the Jackson Free Press who helped him manage the packages, faxes, letters, and PDFs, as well as those who put up with his late evenings and absence from daily operations for the duration of this project. And, of course, special thanks to Donna Ladd for putting up with him in general.

Finally, Todd would like to acknowledge "The Empty Hamper," which provides a vital pick-up-and-delivery laundry service that he would gladly pay for even if he couldn't afford food.

Photo Credits

All product photos used in this magazine are owned by the respective manufacturers, including but not limited to Acme Made, Add On Technology, AddLogix, Altec-Lansing, APC, Apple, Archos, Asante, ATI, Audio-Technica, Beachtek, Belkin, Bochs Project, Booq, Brother, Canopus, Canon, Inc., CMS Products, Contour Design, Creative, D-Link, Delkin Devices, DigiDesigns, Digital Dream, Digital Networks North America, DLO/Netalog, Dr.Bott LLC, Eagle Creek, Econ Technologies, Elgato Systems, Epson, Evological, First Int. Digital, Inc., Focus Enhancements, Formac Electronics, Fuji Photo Film, Gefen, Grandstream, Griffin Technology, Harmon Kardon, Hollywood Lite, Hewlett-Packard, IDEATIVE, iKelite, Infocus, Information Appliance Associates, IOGear, iRiver, Jabra, JBL, JVC, Kainhow Software, Kanguru, KeyTec, Keyspan, Kensington, Konica-Minolta, Kodak, Lexmark, Lacie, Lemkesoft, Lexar Media, Linksys, Logitech, Lowel, MacAlly, Macsense, Magma Expansion, Marathon Computer, M-Audio, Microsoft, Microtek, Monster Cable Products, Netopia, Nikon, Oiympus, Orange Micro, Perceptive Automation, Photo Control, Plantronic, QuickerTek, Rain Design, Samsung, SanDisk, Smart Home, SMC, Smith-Micro, Sonnet Technology, Sony, .Sony-Ericsson, Sumdex, Targus, TrippLite, Vara Software Limited, Video Innovators, Viewsonic, Wacom, XTremeMac, Zio Corporation, Ten Technology, YDL, XTen, and ZyXEL.

We Want to Hear from You!

As the reader of this book, *you* are our most important critic and commentator. We value your opinion and want to know what we're doing right, what we could do better, what areas you'd like to see us publish in, and any other words of wisdom you're willing to pass our way.

As an associate publisher for Que, I welcome your comments. You can email or write me directly to let me know what you did or didn't like about this book—as well as what we can do to make our books better.

Please note that I cannot help you with technical problems related to the topic of this book. We do have a User Services group, however, where I will forward specific technical questions related to the book.

When you write, please be sure to include this book's title and author as well as your name, email address, and phone number. I will carefully review your comments and share them with the author and editors who worked on the book.

Email: feedback@quepublishing.com

Mail: Greg Wiegand
Que Publishing
800 East 96th Street
Indianapolis, IN 46240 USA

For more information about this book or another Que title, visit our website at www.quepublishing.com. Type the ISBN (excluding hyphens) or the title of a book in the Search field to find the page you're looking for.

Introduction

Ah, gadgets. The plastic and glass and metal and new smell and buttons and blinking lights and the utter magic that is the technology behind the liquid crystal display.

We love 'em, don't we?

In some ways the Mac is one of the biggest gadgets there is, and certainly an important gadget that a lot of us have put front-and-center in our digital lifestyles. What with iTunes and iMovie and iDVD and iPhoto and GarageBand—just about all the applications that come with every Mac is a gadget unto itself, not to mention the design of the Mac and the slickness of the operating systems. Indeed, FreeBSD-based Mac OS X is one of the most elegant "Swiss army knives" of productivity and fun ever created. (A real geek could spend hours just playing with Terminal!)

But beyond that stuff you already know about are a number of technologies that the Mac offers which are designed to help it talk to other stuff. Those technologies range from the mundane—USB, FireWire, ethernet, and display ports—to the sublime, including fun stuff like wireless AirPort and Bluetooth support. All these technologies beg for cool gadgets to hook up to your Mac (or in the case of the wireless technologies, to simply hold in the same general area as our Macs) and, fortunately for we the Mac people, those gadget are out there.

That said, not all gadgets will work with our Macs—unfortunately. Unlike our Windows-using brethren, the Mac user has to pick and choose among a minefield of exciting products that are not always completely (or at all) compatible with the Mac. This is unfortunate for us as Mac users, but fortunate from the point of view of a book author—it gives me something to talk about and focus on in the pages that follow. The devices you'll find here do offer at least some level of Mac compatibility and, when they don't, they're discussed here because there is a solution—such as a third-party driver or application that supports the Mac. In most cases, I'll be able to discuss that solution at some length; but in every case I'll try to clearly point it out.

So, come along and enjoy the more than 180 Mac-compatible (and Mac-complimentary) gadgets in this little tome. I think you'll have a good time.

How This Book Is Organized

I've organized the gadgets in this book into 12 chapters that represent categories for these happy little devices:

- **Chapter 1, "Input Devices"**—This chapter covers different ways you'll get data into your Mac, in particular keyboards and mice, trackballs, trackpads, shuttles, and even something that just looks like a big ol' button.

- **Chapter 2, "Storage"**—You'll find everything here, from the Mac's humble origins as a little guy with a single floppy drive to today, when storage can mean anything from an ethernet-based 500GB hard disk to a pen with a hidden USB connector.

- **Chapter 3, "Video and Audio"**—The Mac's reputation as a multimedia wonder is in no way diminished by the number of audio and video add-ons you'll find for your Mac, including speakers, computer audio solutions, third-party displays, and more.

- **Chapter 4, "Printers and Scanners"**—What are the best choices for the money and features? Or is speed your need? The world of printing and scanning is wide open to the Mac, particularly if you're interested in color.

- **Chapter 5, "Networking and Wireless"**—If you've got more than one Mac (or PC) and it isn't connected in some way, then you're doing something wrong. Network those Macs, go wireless, have a party. (For instance, a LAN party, where you can play bloody games against one another for hours on end. Pop some corn!)

- **Chapter 6, "Digital Video and Accessories"**—For years it was a chore to get video into a Mac for editing; these days, Apple makes it second nature. Here we will take a good look at the different DV camcorder options, as well as choices for capturing analog video (VHS and other styles) for editing on your Mac, along with the accessories you need to shoot great video.

- **Chapter 7, "Digital Cameras and Accessories"**—For the still photographer, digital cameras get cheaper and better all the time; this is the year of the digital SLR, where pro-style cameras become more affordable and consumer-oriented cameras get smaller, lighter, and better than ever.

- **Chapter 8, "Webcams and Spy Cameras"**—Isn't it time we had videophones? That's what Apple has built into the Mac OS with iChat AV; other options for cameras include using them for security, for checking out the weather or traffic, or for the classic app—displaying a fish tank.

- **Chapter 9, "PDAs and Smart Phones"**—The Palm may no longer dominate the way it once did, but it's true that the PDA, the phone, and wireless Internet are all converging into some exciting new devices; throw in MP3 players, GPS receivers, digital cameras, and audio note-taking and you've got the modern PDA.

- **Chapter 10, "Audio Players and iPod Gadgets"**—The iPod *does* still dominate music players, but it's not the only game in town, even for a Mac. If you have opted for the iPod, though, you can only make it better by shopping some great little gadgets that extend the iPod's handiness and expand its reasons for being.

- **Chapter 11, "Gadgets for Portable Macs"**—More and more of the Macs that are sold each year are portable models, and as they become more popular so do different ways to carry, augment, and peripheralize them. That's assuming that "peripheralize" is even a word.

- **Chapter 12, "Desktop Mac and Home Gadgets"**—What else could there possibly be? We've got some gadgets aimed directly at particular desktop Mac models, as well as a few key categories we've missed until now, including X10-compatible home automation, display and keyboard-sharing solutions for using multiple Macs at once, and software that enables you to run different OSes on your Mac, either through emulation or by simply being a different operating system that can run on your Mac! (Think Linux.)

- **Chapter 13, "Home Audio/Video Gadgets"**—We end with a foray beyond the Mac and into your living room or home-theater room, if you're lucky enough to have one. Some of the gadgets discussed here interface with your Mac, while others are just cool add-ons and components to make your home entertainment system that much more, well, entertaining.

The best gadgets get their own, special label and write-up, which I call, humbly, "Leo's Picks." Each different category has a general introduction in case you're not familiar with the technology or how far it has come in the past few years, and then you can dig in and get the specifics about the particular devices I've covered.

Cool Web Sites

Along with the descriptions and prices, each gadget has its manufacturer's web site listed; a surprising number of these devices are available for direct purchase, although you should always toss the gadget's name into your favorite search engine to see whether you can come up with a better price. Most of these gadgets are available from Mac catalog retailers or from the usual suspects such as Best Buy, CompUSA, or Circuit City.

If you have a ton of fun with this book, then you should check out some of the other serious geek sites, including the absolutely priceless Gizmodo (www.gizmodo.com) and the equally fun EnGadget (www.engadget.com) blogs.

For additional reviews and Mac-centric gadget reviews by Todd Stauffer, my co-author, see www.macblog.com; to reach me, as always, stop by www.leoville.com.

Input Devices

1

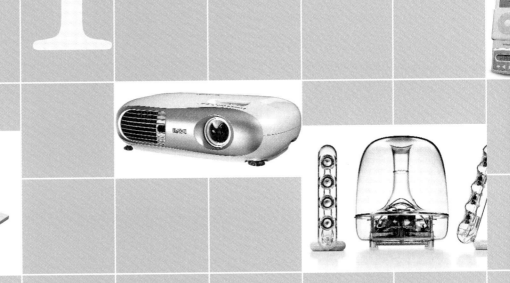

Keyboards

It's not something that you would think about day in and day out, but the technology that you use for interacting with your Mac is an incredibly important part of the experience.

Both Apple and third-party manufacturers offer keyboard solutions that you can buy off the shelf or from online retailers. For many of us, the keyboard included with our Macs is basically good enough—but there are good reasons to look into other options. For one, you're pounding away on your keyboard a good bit and you might eventually wear it out. Two, you might need to fit in a more compact space than your standard-issue keyboard allows. Or, if you're like me, you might work most days on a PowerBook, but want the luxury of a full-size keyboard when you're at your own desk.

Some keyboards offer more specialized capabilities—for instance, Apple and other manufacturers now offer wireless keyboards (and mice) that can make it a little easier to move around your input devices on your desk or control your Mac from across the room. Two general technologies are used for wireless input: RF (radio frequency) and Bluetooth. Either technology is an acceptable approach, with RF sometimes offering the capability to work over a greater distance, but requiring an external receiver within line-of-sight, whereas Bluetooth works closer to your Mac, but your Mac may have the built-in capability to receive the signal.

Aside from wireless, you might want to look into a more ergonomic keyboard offering—or, at the very least, one that offers different positioning for your hands. Or, you might look into a keyboard that offers other specialty items, such as a built-in pointing device (a trackball or trackpad) that you may find convenient.

Whatever the case, you'll find that the input devices (that aren't wireless) are almost all connected to your Mac via a Universal Serial Bus (USB) cable. The Universal Serial Bus is a standard that makes it easy to attach devices such as keyboards and mice. These devices can be plugged and unplugged while your Mac is running without any damage to the device or the Mac. USB has the additional advantage of being a *powered bus*, meaning devices can actually use their USB cables to draw small amounts of power; that means you'll see some keyboards, mice, and other devices that light up and work without being plugged into a wall socket.

   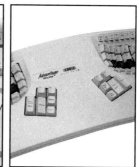 

Apple Keyboard

You can argue with the way Apple makes its name-brand mouse (and we will, later in this chapter) but it's difficult to avoid the fact that they've got some good keyboards available. Yes, they tend to be a bit pricey and, true, they're not as colorful as they once were, but Apple Keyboards are very solid platforms for the everyday typist.

The Apple Keyboard actually comes in two incarnations the way we're defining it—a wired and wireless variety. The Apple Pro Keyboard is Apple's typical USB model; larger than it once was, it still takes up a minimum of space for a keyboard that includes function keys across the top and keys for controlling volume and ejecting removable media (CDs and such). The price can be a bit tough to swallow, but the keyboard has a great feel and includes a USB hub, which means you can attach your mouse and one other device directly to the keyboard instead of filling another USB port on the side of your Mac.

The Apple Wireless Keyboard is, of course, even sexier, if only because wireless still feels pretty new. For only $20 more over the Apple Keyboard, the wireless model uses Bluetooth technology to connect to your Mac; many of today's Mac models include Bluetooth out of the box (particularly the PowerBooks), or it can be easily added with a small Bluetooth adapter to any USB-compatible Mac running Mac OS X 10.2.6 or higher. With Bluetooth you've got up to 30 feet away from the Mac to work with.

We're tempted to say that you should shop other brands first before utterly settling in with Apple because of Apple's prices—so, we will. But if you can afford the "real deal" then Apple's keyboards are well-constructed, designed to work with your Mac and may just be worth the premium price.

Model: Keyboard and Wireless Keyboard
Manufacturer: Apple, Inc. (www.apple.com)
Price: $49 (USB) and $69 (wireless Bluetooth)

Photo courtesy of Apple, Inc.

Logitech Cordless Navigator Duo

Third-party manufacturers have a tendency to bundle their wireless keyboards and mice; Logitech is no exception with the Cordless Navigator Duo package, which includes a mouse and keyboard for the price of the Apple Wireless Keyboard. The Cordless Navigator is an RF-based keyboard that's bulky compared to Apple's offerings and includes some "navigation" keys that add considerably to the size of the keyboard.

If you like the size, you'll find the "zero tilt" design may be more comfortable to type on. (Logitech touts the "zero tilt" as slightly more ergonomic—there's no angle to the keyboard from back to front like there is on most keyboards.)

Logitech makes good stuff and this little bundle is a great way to move into wireless. Because it doesn't connect via Bluetooth wireless technology, you'll still need an available USB port for the RF receiver. We've read some complaints of dropped connections that require repositioning the keyboard or recalibrating, which is a concern particularly with non-Bluetooth wireless keyboards.

Model: Cordless Navigator Duo
Manufacturer: Logitech
(www.logitech.com)
Price: $59

Adesso Tru-Form with Touchpad

When Apple switched Macs from the older style ADB ports to newer USB technology, it did a great thing for Mac owners; by choosing the PC standard, it became easier for manufacturers to build devices that support both Mac and PC. However, that doesn't mean that all manufacturers are equal in that support; many support the Mac as an afterthought. That's why a company such as Adesso can be nice to come across—it offers quality products focused on the Mac, even in an area such as after-market keyboards.

Although the company presents a number of good choices, our favorite is the Tru-Form with Touchpad, which offers an ergonomic split design and a built-in touchpad for moving the mouse pointer in a way that's similar to a PowerBook or iBook. This keyboard is not cheap, but it's a nice solution if you need to fit your keyboard in a space that has no room for a mouse and yet you appreciate the comforts of a split keyboard. (Some people can type well on them, others find that their hunt-and-peck typing style doesn't conform well to a split keyboard.)

Model: Tru-Form with Touchpad
Manufacturer: Adesso
(www.adesso.com)
Price: $99 ($79 without touchpad)

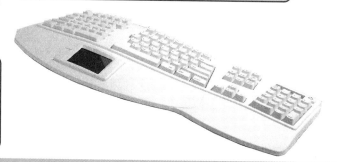

MacAlly iceKey

MacAlly offers a very interesting approach to a desktop keyboard—based on the design of PowerBook keyboards, the iceKey has relatively low "scissor" keys that don't have to be pressed as far as the keys that you typically find on an external keyboard. The result is that it takes a little less pressure and may be a little more comfortable if you happen to like that approach. iceKey also has the advantage of fitting into some spaces that might not accommodate a full-size keyboard, such as small desk drawers or keyboard trays.

Along with the potential for improved keyboarding, the iceKey is also strikingly designed and stark white to match the latest round of iMacs, eMacs, and even iBooks. This is definitely an interesting option if you like the way it feels to type on a Mac portable, and you'd like a similar-feeling external keyboard.

Model: iceKey
Manufacturer: MacAlly
(www.macally.com)
Price: $59

Mantias Tactile Keyboard

This keyboard just might be the exact opposite of the IceKey—it's designed to mimic the Apple and IBM keyboards of old by providing a tactile "click" with each keystroke. If that click is important to you, then you've probably already remembered it nostalgically; if you didn't spend much time with the original Macs, the Apple Extended Keyboard, or with true-blue IBM equipment (or high-end dumb terminals for accessing central computers), then the tactile click may not mean much to you.

Suffice to say that many people love the old Extended Keyboard, and that, to Mantias, looks like a market. They've revived the same technology but instead of the old beige, they've got it in a plastic housing very similar to Apple's current keyboards. Complete with a power key and eject (although no sound-control or other Mac-specific function keys) the Tactile Keyboard gives you a somewhat pricey solution for living the good old days with what appears to be a good quality keyboard.

And if you're not up for that, check out the half keyboard, which uses "*chording*" principles, which enable you to type with one hand. (With chording, you hit two or more keys at once to type certain letters. This lets you type with one hand, which some people are quite good at.)

Model: Tactile Keyboard
Manufacturer: Mantias
(www.halfkeyboard.com)
Price: $99

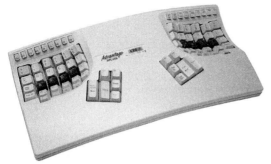

Photo courtesy of Kinesis Corporation.

Logitech diNovo Media Desktop

While we're spending a little money on a keyboard, how about going all out on the Bluetooth support? This wireless keyboard offers comfortable, full-travel keys; the wireless mouse is rechargeable via its handy cradle and it's got a nice, palm-fitting design. The real standout, though, is the MediaPad, a wireless, Bluetooth remote that you can use to control your Mac from across the room when watching DVDs or listening to music, for instance. It also doubles as a number pad for heavy number-crunching.

Model: diNovo Media Desktop
Manufacturer: Logitech
(www.logitech.com)
Price: $199

Kinesis Advantage USB Contoured Keyboard

If you're so serious about the ergonomics of your keyboard that you're willing to pay good money to try something different, then the Contoured Keyboard is such a solution. With keys in a familiar QWERTY layout, they're still grouped in a new way, by placing them in curved wells designed to keep your hands apart and to encourage proper alignment of your shoulders and wrists. The keyboards also are designed to move some of the strain from your fingers to your thumbs, which tend to be stronger but under-utilized by a typical keyboard, where the thumb is only used to press the spacebar. With the Contoured Keyboard, the thumbs are used for function keys, backspace, and many others.

Model: Advantage USB Contoured
Keyboard
Manufacturer: Kinesis
(www.kinesis.com)
Price: $299

Mice and Pointing Devices

We promised complaints about the Mac mouse, so here they are. What's the deal with the single mouse button? Of course, Apple has a theory, and that theory is that the mouse should only have one button because, er, we guess it keeps people from getting confused. Maybe that's true. But the notion that you have to hold down the Control key in order to get a "right click" command would probably be a bit hard to grasp at first, too, wethinks.

Anyway, it's not for us to say. What is for us to say is this—think about a different mouse, particularly if you're a power user. The Apple mouse is nicely designed and the latest "tic tac" models at least make *some* sense in their overall design, but for the past five years at least, Mac mice have been form over function—they're just not that handy. (Get it?) You can find a mouse with many more functions, decent design, overall mouseability, and even a little ergonomic comfort if you look hard enough. And we have.

The truth is, a mouse isn't always a mouse; sometimes there's some other pointing device that beckons to you. The old standby is the trackball—it requires less room than a mouse and allows for a different range of motion; you roll your fingers across a large ball to reposition the mouse pointer on your screen. You can then generally choose from a number of different buttons, some of which you may be able to program to do interesting things. Trackpads work on a similar theory; you pass your finger along the pad to move the pointer. And whether you go with a trackball or trackpad is based on the same decision-making process—it's totally up to you. Head to a retailer and see whether this type of mousing works for you.

We'll also quickly cover "artpads" or digitizers in this section—input devices that enable you to move the mouse pointer using something resembling a pen. That device lets you draw onscreen, which can be really cool if you can draw. For instance, Todd can't draw, and so it's less cool. But if you know what you're doing, pen-based input can be useful for a variety of tasks.

 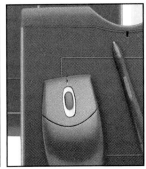 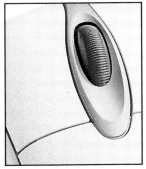  

Kensington Turbo Mouse Pro

Leo's Pick

You've got to be able to handle a trackball if you're going to go with this pick, but if you can, then this is the Porsche of trackballs. It's large size should still fit on the side of your keyboard with room to spare, allowing you to sprawl your hand over the large trackball and access the myriad of buttons. The trackball features four mouse "buttons" in the traditional sense, each of which can be programmed for a variety of options; for instance, you can program one button for a "Control+click" to bring up contextual menus; another button can be programmed for a "⌘+click" that can be used in certain applications to select an entire sentence at once. The options are numerous.

Also, across the top of the mouse are some other buttons which can be used as quick-launch controls. In other words, you can program the mouse to instantly launch (or switch to) up to six of your favorite applications. (Or even applications that aren't really your favorites but that you just have to use a lot.) And, the Turbo Mouse has a scroll control that can be used to scroll up and down in documents, Web pages, and other applications that are built to respond to a scroll control.

The key to the power of the Turbo Mouse is the software, MouseWorks, which Kensington bundles with the trackball. It's straightforward stuff that's built for Mac OS X (or Mac OS 9, depending on your preference) and gives you greater control over how you go about your mousing responsibilities.

The Turbo Mouse comes in both wired (USB or old-style ADB connectors are in the box) or wireless (RF style requiring AA batteries). There's not much point to the wireless approach unless you need to sit far from your Mac, as the Turbo Mouse isn't designed to move around otherwise; but if you want the option, it's there.

Model: Turbo Mouse Pro
Manufacturer: Kensington (www.kensington.com)
Price: $109 (USB) and $129 (wireless)

Microsoft IntelliMouse Optical

The other side of the mousing spectrum from the Kensington Turbo Mouse is the Microsoft Wheel Mouse Optical, which is essentially the mouse that Apple should be building and offering with its Macs. (A snazzier white or metallic would match Apple's stuff better than the beige and gray that Microsoft has chosen.) This mouse is basic and functional, but offers some extras, such as the two buttons (the right button automatically maps to a Control+click command when you're using Mac OS X) as well as a scroll wheel. Once in your hand, the Microsoft Wheel Mouse becomes second nature. It even has a nice contour to it, with a larger barrel at the bottom of the mouse to better fill your hand and allow you to relax your hand over it instead of squeezing the sides to keep control. Our only complaint is that it feels a little lighter than the Apple mouse, but the build quality seems good and the plastic grips a bit better than the slick Apple model.

Model: IntelliMouse Optical
Manufacturer: Microsoft
(www.microsoft.com/mactopia)
Price: $34.99 (USB) $49.99 (wireless)

Contour Design Perfit Mouse

How seriously do you take your comfort? If it's important to you, you might want to spring for a Perfit Mouse from Contour Design. The Perfit Mouse comes in different sizes—ranging from extra small to extra large for right-handers and small to large for left-handers. (Just another bit of evidence that left-handers are second-class citizens, although at least Contour Design is making an effort.) The mouse is also more ergonomically shaped than most, with a larger base for your palm and more of a slope along the buttons. Using this larger, sloped-mouse is a bit awkward at first, but the shape does seem to lead to better comfort over time. (The idea is to get more local hand muscles into play so that the tensors in your carpal tunnel aren't over-used.) You'll pay for that comfort, though, as these mice aren't cheap. The even pricier optical model is a slight redesign of the original that includes scroll wheels and a special rocker switch on the side of the mouse.

Model: Perfit Mouse
Manufacturer: Contour Design
(www.contourdesign.com)
Price: $89.95–139.95 (mechanical)
$109.95 (optical)

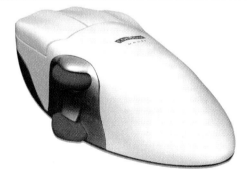

Logitech MX700 Cordless Optical Mouse

If you're going to go the cordless route, then it's a good idea to get a rechargeable model if you can—there's nothing less fun than hunting for batteries for your mouse when you're trying to get some work done. There is a trade-off—with a battery-powered mouse, you've got the option of swapping batteries and getting immediately back to work when it dies, whereas a rechargeable has to, well, recharge before it gets going again. A mouse that simply doesn't work for a while is an irritant, at best.

A rechargeable mouse generally has a small dock (like the MX700's) into which you place the mouse when you're done using it. That keeps it charged for the next session, as long as you remember to place it there when you're done using it.

The MX700 is also an optical mouse—it uses RF with a six-foot range and includes some special buttons on the side of the mouse designed for work with the Back and Forward commands in your web browser.

Model: MX700
Manufacturer: Logitech
(www.logitech.com)
Price: $69.95

MacAlly iceMouseJr

The last little mouse we'll cover is designed for the road—or for very cramped desks. MacAlly offers a number of different takes on the small mouse; this one is optical, reasonably priced, and has a cord; if the cord bothers you—or if you like to see people point and whisper about you on planes—the company has Bluetooth, RF, and even small rechargeable "mini" mice. A small mouse isn't really a good idea for day-to-day use, and we certainly don't recommend one for your desktop Mac, but when you need to make use of all the room you can get on your neighbor's tray table on an airliner, a little mouse might make the difference. Particularly if you're not a fan of your portable Mac's trackpad.

Model: iceMouseJr
Manufacturer: MacAlly
(www.macally.com)
Price: $29

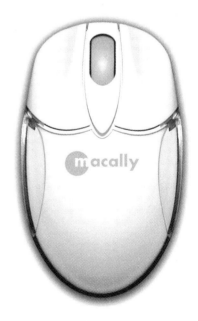

Wacom Graphire3

Wacom makes several Mac-compatible graphics tablets, including the Graphire3, which is the lower-cost model, ranging from $99–$199 depending on the size you choose. The Intuos2 offers better sensitivity and more professional-level features, but the Graphire3 is generally enough tablet for anyone below the professional level. Along with the pen and tablet, the Graphire3 includes a four-button mouse that glides across the tablet for day-to-day mousing; when you need to draw, just move the mouse out of the way and pick up the included pen.

Mac OS X 10.2 and higher includes InkWell, a technology that can actually be used for handwriting recognition and written commands. So, if you get a graphics tablet, you may find it handy to write directly on the graphics tablet, using InkWell, to accomplish some input tasks. (You may also *not* find it handy—handwriting recognition takes some getting used to.) If you have a compatible graphics tablet plugged in, you'll see the Ink control pane appear in System Preferences.

Model: Graphire3
Manufacturer: Wacom
(www.wacom.com)
Price: $99–$199

Ice Cad

If you're looking for a smaller digitizer that fits nicely next to your keyboard, this is a great solution. It's probably not big enough for day-to-day drawing tasks, although you could certainly use it for the occasional sketch or for shading and other tasks within an application such as Photoshop. Where this little guy really shines, though, is in combination with Apple's Inkwell handwriting recognition technology. If you've ever considered the possibility of entering data by writing it, plug in this device, then explore the Ink item that appears in System Preferences.

Model: Ice Cad
Manufacturer: Macally
(www.macally.com)
Price: $39

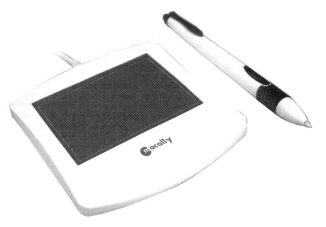

Gaming and Other Input Devices

Are Macs gaming machines or not? There's no question that the Mac tends to get games a little later than the PC world; Todd has both a PC and a Mac on his desk and will admit to turning to the PC sometimes to play a little of the latest James Bond first-person shooter or perhaps enter the Star Trek universe for a day or two. Of course, those popular games do generally end up coming to the Mac and, for Mac owners who *don't* have access to a PC, they're often eagerly anticipated. The Mac doesn't really have many advantages over a PC when it comes to gaming, but a good, modern Mac doesn't suffer many deficiencies, either, as Power PC (particularly G5 level) processors offer plenty of speed and Macs tend to have good video hardware (see Chapter 3, "Video and Audio," **p. 31**).

So, a Mac probably isn't the first machine you should run out and buy if your primary goal is gaming. But if you have a secondary or tertiary goal of gaming, and you've got a Mac, then that's not a bad place to be. Your next step is to get some good gaming input devices.

Okay, sure, you *can* use your keyboard and mouse for gaming. In fact, for some shooter-type games, that's perfectly reasonable. If you can get used to spinning yourself around with the mouse, then you can pick weapons or inventory items using the special keyboard keys. No sweat.

If you're flying a plane or driving a car or if you've simply developed a taste for, or you're comfortable with, console-style game controllers, for instance, then you may want to look into a special gaming input device for your Mac. The options range from steering devices to joysticks to gaming controls that offer force feedback—they vibrate or otherwise react to stimuli in the game.

Most of these devices are fairly simple to install; you just plug them in and go. In the case of certain devices, you may either have to install special software or use games that support the device. In most cases, you can still use a game controller that isn't specifically supported by a game (say, your high-powered flight wheel that isn't handled by a certain driving game) but you will have only rudimentary controls and certain buttons or switches won't be active.

Oh—and not all creative input devices are gaming devices. In fact, our winner is pretty much in a category by itself.

Griffin PowerMate

Even Griffin Technologies' own marketing materials are tagged with the line "What Is It?" It's a knob, and it's a button. And it looks like the simplest little control you've seen.

Leo's Pick

But, behind that simplicity is a programmable power that makes it work great in a variety of circumstances. It turns out that there are a lot of reasons to use a knob with—or instead of—a mouse. For instance, you can use it to "scrub" back and forth in video editing software such as iMovie or Final Cut Pro. Or, you might use it as an on-the-fly scroll wheel for web pages or long documents.

The trick is that the PowerMate comes with software that enables you to program it to react differently in different applications. In Word you might assign it to scroll the document when twisted left and right, then, when the button is pressed, to save the document. In a browser window, you could scroll using it and then use the button to create new windows. Of course, it also can be a volume control, and you can use it to scrub through songs in GarageBand.

The PowerMate offers more than just left, right, and click—it also recognizes discreet combinations of those (left+click, right+click) as well as a "long click." Each can be programmed to do something particular in an application; once you get one, you'll start to come up with reasons. You'll find tons of options for productivity applications; for games, you can set it to Game Mode, which limits it to left, right, and click—but those are all handy moves in games.

On top of all those things, the PowerMate is attractive—the standard model is all aluminum, and there's a limited edition black model—all the way down to its glowing blue base, which is actually powered by the USB connection. So even for occasional use it passes the most biased of gadget-factor tests—it looks cool.

> **Model:** PowerMate
> **Manufacturer:** Griffin Technology
> (www.griffintechnology.com)
> **Price:** $39

Nostromo SpeedPad n52

If we're talking something that looks and feels like a *gadget*, we've got it in the SpeedPad n52. Designed for keyboard gamers—particularly first-person shooters—this controller features a bevy of programmable keys along with easy access to a thumbpad, scroll wheel, and buttons. It's designed to fit your left hand, which leaves your right hand free to use a mouse for choosing directions and shooting. (As you might infer, the system isn't as left-handed as it is right-handed.) The benefits pretty much speak for themselves—you don't have to hunt around on the keyboard to find keys that do certain things—you can program them all into the SpeedPad. The SpeedPad n50, the predecessor to the n52, is still available, offering one less row of keys and fewer buttons, but all for a lower price.

Model: SpeedPad
Manufacturer: Belkin Components
(www.belkin.com)
Price: $49.99 (n52) and $34.99 (n50)

Saitek R440 Steering Wheel Combo

Ready to drop some serious scratch on your gaming habit? That's one of the reasons that Saitek made the R440—another is to give you the most realistic driving experience possible with some of today's Mac driving simulations. The R440 package includes a wheel and pedals, which offer a nice balance between compact design and enough weightiness to keep them from feeling too cheap, particularly for the price. The design of the wheel includes force feedback capabilities, which means that certain games can cause the wheel to shake and shimmy, which can help to make a dramatic moment in a game feel even more so. If there's a drawback, it's that there simply aren't enough driving games out there for the Mac; if you really like *Nascar 2003* (or if something even better comes along) this is a good choice.

Model: R440
Manufacturer: Saitek
(www.saitek.com)
Price: $79.95

Contour Design ShuttleXpress

If you're really serious about your digital video or digital audio editing, you may find this little input device handy. It works essentially as a shuttle knob for moving quickly back and forth along a timeline-based project, which is how most audio and video is edited. It's also handy for *scrubbing* back and forth in a media presentation. But where ShuttleXpress really stands out is the multiplicity of buttons that it makes available for quick access; those buttons are programmable, including some preprogrammed options that work really well with popular editing programs such as Apple's Final Cut Pro. (And if you're really, really serious, you'll spring for the Pro model, which is very nicely designed, a bit more substantial, and crafted to put up with constant use.)

Dual Action Gamepad

The Mac joystick and gamepad landscape is a little more crowded than you might think, thanks in part to the fact that both Macs and PCs use USB these days, so it doesn't take much in the way of manufacturing to turn out a device that works for both platforms. In most cases, they tend to work a little better for PC than for Mac; the Logitech Dual Action Gamepad works great on the Mac—just plug and go. You don't get the same game presets that a PC user gets, but it gives you the functionality you need for most games. It's a comfortable and usable controller, but it's a touch flimsy and lightweight. Maybe that's to be expected when it's less than $20.

Model: ShuttleXpress (or ShuttlePro)
Manufacturer: Contour Design
(www.contourdesign.com)
Price: $49.99 (Xpress) $129.99 (Pro)

Model: Dual Action Gamepad
Manufacturer: Logitech
(www.logitech.com)
Price: $19.95

Storage

2

Hard Drives

Okay, so maybe storage isn't the sexiest gadget category we've got in the book, but there's nothing more attractive than a good solution for more storage when you're hurting for space. And, if you've ever lost a good chunk of data due to a crashed disk or something similar, then you're probably a great candidate to find a backup solution that you can love.

By storage we're talking about a few different things. First, there's the old hard disk; we're not going to dig deep into the sort of internal hard disk that you can add to a Power Macintosh—those are, for the most part, not all that gadgety. (Is *gadgety* a word?) For most Power Macintosh models you can choose off-the-shelf ATA model

internal drives and install them in the additional drive bays that your Mac provides.

Instead, when we're talking about hard drives as gadgets, we're talking about external models. Those external models can offer a few different benefits—they're usually portable, they're often easy to hook up and, if you shop a little, you'll find some that have some fun extra features—special support for quickly backing up data, for instance—that certainly qualify them as gadgets.

Or, if you've got a little cash to burn (and a reasonably legitimate reason to burn it) you can opt for some high-end external drive systems that help with speed and redundancy, which is perfect for your second career as a videographer or movie producer.

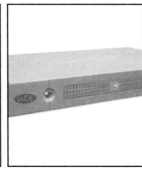

LaCie Big Disk Extreme

Leo's Pick

The point of this drive is pretty straightforward—it's designed to be big and it's designed to be fast. For the latest Macs, the drive supports FireWire 800—the newer FireWire standard that can move data from your Mac to the drive at twice the old throughput. Plus, the drive itself is optimized to bring about some blazing speeds; according to the company, the drive is rated at 88 megabytes per second as a maximum sustained rate using the FireWire 800 interface; your results might not be quite that good, but compare them to a typical FireWire 400 drive at about 40 megabytes per second—and that's using the latest and best mechanisms. Typical FireWire drives can only sustain speeds in the 30MB/sec range or lower—sometimes much lower.

The Big Disk is also, well, big—it's currently offered in capacities of 320GB, 400 GB, and 500 GB. (As LaCie likes to point out, that's about half of a *terabyte* of data.) These days those are basically breakthrough capacities; drives such as these were stuck around 180–200GB for a while, particularly for portable drives that are (at least somewhat) reasonably priced.

And, to round out things, the Big Disk offers two different interfaces, including the aforementioned FireWire 800, as well as the original FireWire 400, which means you could use it with different Macs in your home or workgroup (if you have one), or you can use it with certain Windows PC models that support FireWire, which is also called IEEE-1394 or i.Link (on Sony computers).

It's actually a somewhat attractive drive, its case is stackable, and the speed and capacity make it a wonderful option for the prosumer user of digital video cameras or camcorders, where storage is often a premium. We'd recommend it as an option for a home or small business network where storage is maxed out or where you're dealing with a lot of multimedia, but you're not interested in a RAID or network drive solution.

Model: Big Disk Extreme
Manufacturer: LaCie (www.LaCie.com)
Price: $369 (320GB), $449 (400GB) and $549 (500GB)

ABSPlus Backup Drive

The ABSPlus is an interesting drive designed *specifically* for backup. When you first set up your ABSPlus, it creates a mirror image of your Mac's hard disk; then, when you plug it into your Mac or turn it on from powered down, it will automatically make changes to the backup image that reflects any changes you've made on your Mac. The brilliant part of this approach is that you can actually boot from the hard disk if you ever encounter trouble. (The less than brilliant part is that you could lose both your backup and your main disk if you ever get infected with a damaging computer virus or worm; using removable disks to back up really important files might still be an important step.)

The drive works with its own backup software that is flexible enough to work with a number of different backup schemes, including partial backups that *don't* mirror your entire drive and other approaches that focus on quickly synchronizing your most important files.

> **Model:** ABSPlus
> **Manufacturer:** CMS Products
> (www.cmsproducts.com)
> **Price:** $209–399 depending on capacity
> (80–250GB) and portability

ComboGB

This drive from Wiebetech offers an ultimate approach to compatibility—it has pretty much every port you could imagine for a portable hard drive. It supports FireWire 400, FireWire 800, USB, USB 2.0, and it includes five different cables in the box to prep you for any situation. When you connect it using FireWire, the drive is bus powered—it doesn't require an external adapter. It also doesn't require extra driver software in most configurations—it should hook up and work fine with modern Windows and Mac machines, making it an option for carrying from office to work or on a trip when you need to transport large chunks of data.

> **Model:** ComboGB
> **Manufacturer:** Wiebetech
> (www.wiebetech.com)
> **Price:** $119–$429 depending on
> capacity and drive speed

RaidTECH 800

The "Big Disk" approach can be handy for a home or office machine, but the power of a RAID—Redundant Array of Independent Disks—can be handy when you've got to get some professional computer work done, particularly multimedia. A RAID is simply multiple drives that use software routines to use the drive in tandem; they can be used either to speed up storage (by writing data to both drives at once, called *striping*) or to create redundancy in case a drive fails (called *mirroring*).

With a hardware RAID like the RaidTECH 800 series running in mirroring mode, you can literally swap a drive that fails while the other drive keeps clicking along; the new drive will be recognized and mirrored to immediately. This redundancy helps keep critical Macs running.

Because it's a hardware RAID (a circuit board controls the RAID functions instead of software) then you get good performance and very little setup requirement; it's basically plug-in-and-go.

Model: RaidTECH 800 series
Manufacturer: Wiebetech
(www.wiebetech.com)
Price: $599–$1,799 depending on capacity

LaCie Ethernet Disk

This is pretty cool. Say you've got an ethernet network in your home or office. You need plenty of storage that everyone can access, but you don't want to install Mac OS X Server or dedicate one of the Macs to that function, since you don't need other server capabilities. That's the need that the Ethernet Disk is designed to fill. You configure the Ethernet Disk via a web browser, which enables you to share the disk via AppleShare, Windows protocols, or Web protocols. The disk can also be accessed via an FTP client for access from other types of computers or via the Internet, if your network's Internet connection makes such a connection possible. The Ethernet Disk is rack-mountable, but that isn't a requirement; it also offers a FireWire or USB port that can be used to add capacity using typical external hard disks. In some cases you can even use the Ethernet Disk as a print server for workgroup printers that have a PC-style parallel port.

Model: Ethernet Disk
Manufacturer: LaCie (www.LaCie.com)
Price: $599–$1,199 depending on capacity

Removable Drives

Hard drives aren't the only type of storage we're talking about. While most of us Mac users are generally content these days to burn CDs and DVDs when we need to back up data from our hard drives (or share that data with others or create audio CDs and so on), there are other types of *removable* storage to consider, including tape backup, Zip or even floppy drives. And if you don't have a CD-R or DVD-R or similar drive, you can consider hooking up one.

And, within the category of "removable" media is something that should probably just be called "movable" media—there are some really fun little storage solutions on the market that are worth a look if you find it convenient to carry your data from one place to another; sometimes called "key drives" or something similar, these

are small devices that come in many shapes—pens, dongles, keychain fobs, or even wristwatches—that include a few megabytes (or a few hundred megabytes) of storage. And, anyway, nothing says *gadget* like a wristwatch that stores data.

These key drives (and other shapes) use Flash RAM technology to store the data and USB or USB 2.0 for the connection, both of which make them compact, quick and cool progeny of the floppy disk and other (mostly) archaic "sneakernet" technologies. You simply plug in one of these little drives to an available USB port and it pops up on your desktop, ready for you to move files to and from it. Simple as pie and convenient as heck, not to mention stealthy.

Iomega Rev

Leo's Pick

Iomega, maker of the once dominant Zip drive, has a good idea with the Rev; it's a fast cartridge-based removable drive that's a solid substitute for a tape drive in part because it offers the large capacities that tape offers, and partly because it's a lot faster than most tape drives. It should also prove to be a boon for Mac users—at least, once the external FireWire version shows up and Iomega fully supports the Mac, which hadn't happened at the time of writing. Judging from the PC versions (a USB 2.0 version is designed for the PC but can be used with a Mac for read-only tasks), the Rev is a mix of pricey-ness and usefulness that might make it an ideal gadget for this guide.

The downside is that the media is pretty expensive (about $60 per cartridge); the upside is that you probably won't need a lot of them. With a capacity of 35GB per cartridge (up to 90GB when compressed), you can easily use the drive to provide you with what is essentially unlimited storage. The files are readily accessible as well and faster than a tape backup, so that you can, say, use the cartridges to back up data such as large images, digital video files, publishing layouts, MP3 audio files, and other files that are taking up too much space on your Mac workstation or on your local network. The media is also unproven in the marketplace yet since it's new—for mission-critical backups, it might not yet be time to replace tape (or some other approach) with a Rev cartridge.

Another upside is that the Rev drive is pretty fast compared to tape—in fact, you could easily use it for day-to-day use, with speeds that are similar to external hard disks. Because they can be swapped out, you have the luxury of storing 35GB or more on multiple cartridges and moving them around as needed. The cartridges are extremely portable, the drive is attractive, portable and with a minimum amount of driver installation can easily be used with multiple machines. If you're not interested in committing to a tape drive system for rotational backups, then a Rev drive might be just the solution to spring for.

Model: Rev FireWire
Manufacturer: Iomega (www.iomega.com)
Price: $399

LaCie USB Floppy Disk Drive

From the expensive to the sublime. The LaCie USB Floppy Disk Drive gives you compatibility with those old floppies (at least, the 1.44MB "high density" floppies) and enables you to access files stored on them either by you and a Mac in a former life, or by some crotchety old PC user who still finds the things useful. The LaCie model is bus powered, so it doesn't require an external power supply; just plug it in and it's ready to move little tiny bits of data around.

Model: USB Floppy Disk Drive
Manufacturer: LaCie (www.LaCie.com)
Price: $49.99

Iomega Zip 750

The Iomega Zip 750 is the company's fastest and most versatile Zip drive, particularly in the Mac-compatible FireWire version. Throughput on the drive tops out at 7.3MB per second; not the speed on an external hard disk, but a respectable alternative to the time it takes to burn CDs. Capacity is about the same as a CD-R, although the cost for the media is not; each 750MB disc is about $15, or a little less in bulk. That means you'll want to use them for swapping with friends and colleagues; but you'll want to get those discs back.

The biggest reason to go with Zip 750 is that you've always gone with Zip. As a backup option, it's behind the times because capacity is so limited and CD-R discs (which store only a little less data) are so cheap. But the Zip 750 will also read from Zip 100 and Zip 250 disks and it will write to Zip 250 and Zip 750 disks, which is handy if you've already got a slew of them and want to stick with the removable drive that brung ya. The typical Mac buyer's choice is the FireWire version, although an internal Mac-compatible ATAPI model is also available for those Power Mac G4 models that shipped with mirrored drive doors.

Model: Zip 750
Manufacturer: Iomega
(www.iomega.com)
Price: $149 (FireWire or ATAPI)

LaCie USB Data Watch

The data watch is no longer a brand-new concept, but it's still a pretty cool gadget. The idea is that you get somewhere between 128MB and 256MB of storage that fits into a reasonably attractive wristwatch; the best models include a small plug built into the strap so that you don't have to carry anything with you. Sit down at a computer (PC or Mac), plug in and you'll have instant access to your documents.

We like the LaCie model because it has a USB 2.0 connector—making it faster than most competitors—and the company specifically supports Macs.

Model: USB Data Watch
Manufacturer: LaCie (www.LaCie.com)
Price: $69.95 (128MB model) and $99.95 (256MB model)

Edge Memory DiskGO! USB Pen and Watch

Well, it's not a pen and watch set, but either would make a great gift for dad or grad. Instead, we're tossing both types of USB storage into this pick because Edge offers a slightly different take on both.

The watch is currently just USB 1.1, so it's slower than LaCie's, but Edge offers one advantage; a slightly more attractive steel silver design that makes it work as a dress watch and a tech toy. It does not, however, have a cable built-in, meaning you'll need to keep the extension cable with you.

The pen is a neat little contraption designed to do the same thing as the watch—store a few megabytes worth of data—and write in ink at the same time. It's a bit hefty—call it fat—but if you don't mind a well-rounded little pen for writing, you'll find it's handy to pull apart into pieces, which reveals the USB connector.

Model: DiskGO! USB Watch, USB Pen
Manufacturer: Peripheral Edge
(www.edgememory.com)
Price: $89.95–$139.95 (USB watch, 128MB–256MB) $34.95–$89.95 (USB ink pen, 32MB–256MB)

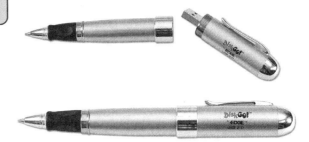

JumpDrive Secure

It feels like there are thousands of key drives available and, truth be known, it's tough to pick the perfect one. The name "key drive" is something of a misnomer; the idea is simply a USB flash drive that happens to be about the size of a key, or at least about the size of something that reasonably fits on a keychain.

How to pick? On sheer reputation we went with the Lexar Media series of "JumpDrives," because Lexar Media has been in the flash RAM business for a quite a while. The JumpDrives come in many shapes and sizes, including the nicely crafted "Elite" model or the JumpDrive photo that specifically guards against overwritten images. Our favorite is the JumpDrive Secure, which can store up to 256MB. The drive offers a "public zone" for storage that anyone can access and a "private zone" that, once configured, can only be accessed with a password. The 256-AES encryption offers good protection for your secure file in case you lose the drive or it falls into the (ominous music here) wrong hands!

> **Model:** JumpDrive Secure
> **Manufacturer:** Lexar Media
> (www.lexarmedia.com)
> **Price:** $39.99 (64MB), $49.99 (128MB),
> $79.99 (256MB), $129.99 (512MB)

Sandisk Cruzer Titanium

Sleek looks and one of the fastest throughput speeds thus far makes this USB key drive one that the chicks really dig. The device offers 512MB capacity and the ability to write quickly to and from this drive; reading at up to 15MB/sec (and writing data at up to 13MB/sec) when connected via USB 2.0. The company makes the claim that the drive is "virtually indestructible"; we're simple enough that we just think the little sliding USB port connector is cool.

> **Model:** Cruzer Titanium
> **Manufacturer:** Sandisk
> (www.sandisk.com)
> **Price:** $199

Optical Drives

The world of removable media—once dominated by the Zip drive and, before that, the Syquest and similar cartridge drives—was forever changed with the popularity of the writeable compact disc. That was truer in the Windows-compatible PC world than it was in the Macintosh world, at least for a time, because it took Apple a few years to figure out that write-able discs were the future. After removing the floppy drive from the iMac and subsequent Mac models, there was a gap there where a lot of Mac users turned to Zips or external CD writers. Then, eventually, Apple "got it" about CD-R.

The result was that the company added CD-R writing capabilities directly to the Mac OS, making is possible to write data to CD-R media (and erase and rewrite to CD-RW media) from within the Finder and associated applications. These days, many Mac users create and "burn" CD media as a matter of course. It's still a two-step process (first you tell the Mac what files you want to copy to a disc, then you tell it to "burn" those files to that disc, which can take a little while), but at least it doesn't require third-party software.

When Apple added the burning capability to the Mac OS (which, incidentally, was creatively named "Disc Burner" in early iterations), the company also began to offer writeable disc drives as options on its Mac models. Later, Apple would introduce the SuperDrive, one of the earliest consumer drives capable of writing to DVD-R and DVD-RW media. That capability went hand-in-hand with Apple's iDVD software, which makes it possible for regular folks to build movie DVDs that can be played back on a typical consumer DVD player. Of course, you need a compatible DVD drive to make that happen.

Probably the main advantage of writeable CD technology is that the media is cheap. The fact that you can pay a few cents for a CD-R that holds nearly 700MB of data is a huge boon for Mac users who need to physically move data from one place to another relatively inexpensively. (For a few dollars, you can get a DVD-R or DVD-RW disc that can hold up to 2.7GB of data.) So, if your Mac didn't come with a CD-RW or DVD-RW drive, you might consider adding one. The latest on the market are cheap, fast and offer some bells and whistles.

    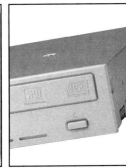

Pioneer DVR-10x DVD Recordable Drive

Leo's Pick

It's kinda boring to look at, but the Pioneer DVR-10x series of drives (the current model at this writing is the DVR-108) is the mechanism used by Apple for its SuperDrive. So, if you've got a Power Macintosh that's currently SuperDrive-challenged, you may well be able to fix that by replacing your current optical drive with this Pioneer model. (On some Power Mac models, you may have an extra drive bay free, as late-model Power Macintosh G4s, for instance, support two optical drives.)

The trick, of course, is that you're going to have to install this drive. In a Power Mac, that's usually pretty easy—the Power Macintosh G4, in particular, is easy enough to open and slide the drive in. Depending on where you order the drive (one recommendation is www.macsales.com) you should be able to get some instructions for the replacement surgery. Apple also has documentation available for certain "Customer Installable Parts" via its knowledgebase, for instance the article at http://docs.info.apple.com/article.html?artnum=26262 covers installing items in the Power Macintosh G4/800 model.

One thing we haven't answered is this: *Why* do you need an original Pioneer mechanism? Because it's the one that's most readily recognized by your Mac's software. And that means two important things in particular—it can be used to playback DVD movies and it can be used to create DVD movies with iDVD or DVD Pro from Apple. With an external DVD-R drive, you can burn data or even audio files to recordable DVDs, but playing back DVD movies is essentially impossible and burning DVD movies is much more difficult—it, at the very least, requires additional non-Apple software.

And if you don't have an internal upgrade bay available? In that case, an external DVD-RW drive is still a great deal if you need to do some serious backup or if you just want the most flexibility. And prices are such that getting a DVD-RW drive is cheap enough that you might as well opt for it over the cheaper CD-RW options, unless you want something ultra portable. To round out this entry, the Pioneer mechanism is often put into external enclosures by third parties such as Other World Computing (www.macsales.com).

Model: Pioneer DVR-108
Manufacturer: Pioneer
(www.pioneerelectronics.com); Other
World Computing (www.macsales.com)
Price: $109 (IDE/ATA internal)
$175 (FireWire external)

EZQuest Boa Slim

Need an external DVD+RW drive that's portable and easy on the eyes? This one can be handy for offering rewriteable DVD technology to your SuperDrive-challenged iBook or PowerBook, or you might just find it's nice to pick up and move around in your home or office. At 2x for DVD burning and 8x for CD-RW creation, the drive is relatively slow compared to the fastest drives on the market. (EZQuest offers DVD-R/+R speeds of 8x and CD-RW speeds of 10x on their Fast Boa, which is designed for high speed.) But, the portability might make up for some of the finger tapping you'll have to do while you create your discs.

What do the speeds mean? For a DVD drive, the "8x" and "10x" readings mean "the number of times faster the drive is" than the original DVD drives way back when. Those drives could move data at 1.385MB per second, so an 8x drive can move data at about 11MB per second, or 660MB per minute; that means it takes them about 8 minutes to write an entire 4.7GB DVD full of data. (For CD-based drives, the original speed was a lowly 150KB/sec, so a "10x" drive works at around 1.5MB per second.)

> **Model:** Boa Slim
> **Manufacturer:** EZQuest
> (www.ezq.com)
> **Price:** $249

Formac Devideon

The bulbous, white Devideon DVD recorder *sorta* matches many Mac models, and it's designed specifically to work with the Mac OS, so it has a leg up there, too. (In fact, it's essentially an external enclosure for a Pioneer DVR drive.) While it doesn't integrate with iDVD, it offers its own DVD authoring software that, although perhaps not as slick as iDVD, it does offer many of the same basic options. It's also designed to work closely with Formac's TVR solution, enabling you to capture television shows (or other video input) and record them to DVD.

> **Model:** Devideon
> **Manufacturer:** Formac
> (www.formac.com)
> **Price:** $199

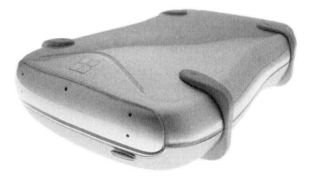

Video and Audio

3

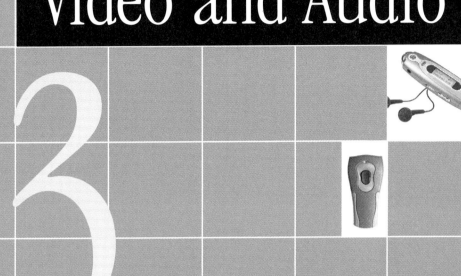

Monitors and Displays

The future—indeed, the present—is flat. The liquid crystal display (LCD) "flat panel" computer monitor has completely infiltrated the Mac world, so much so that Apple itself hasn't designed a standalone cathode-ray tube (CRT) monitor in many years and the only Apple product that still sports any of that old-school technology is the low-priced eMac. Today, it's safe to say that the LCD is king.

There is, however, a difference in LCD displays, starting with the type of connection. While Apple's displays all use digital connectors, an analog connector—good old VGA, also called HD-15—is possible on third-party displays. That makes for a slightly less-crisp image on the screen, but it has the advantage of being more compatible with older systems and a little more affordable. For connecting third-party displays to digital Macs, you may need an adapter, depending on the Mac—the DVI port is standard, but the ADC (Apple Display Connector) is proprietary and, hence, a little pricier of an option. Which type of connection you use depends in part on your Mac's video card and port.

Apple has made Power Macintosh models that had either ADC ports or DVI ports; ADC was popular with the company for a while, but they've lately moved toward DVI. iBooks have tended to have VGA ports or small, specialized video ports that can accept adapters that make them work with VGA displays or DVI displays. The latest PowerBooks have DVI or "mini DVI" connectors. Connecting a non ADC-compatible Mac or video card to an ADC display is expensive; all other solutions (connecting a DVI display to an ADC video card or similar feats of translation) are relatively less so.

If you want one good reason to buy a CRT—other than the possibility that a CRT is simply your preference—then you might look into a high-end color-calibrated CRT. For much less than a state-of-the-art LCD, you can get specially designed CRT displays that include tools to help you calibrate the color on the monitor, with the end goal being color that's true to your final, printed product. While most often this is the domain of professional designers and publishing folks, color-corrected CRTs are inexpensive enough to be interesting to any photo hobbyist or other power user.

   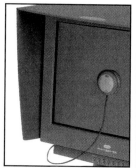 

Apple Cinema Displays

C'mon. Whose your daddy? When you find him, hit him up for a few grand and see if you walk home with one of Apple's fine little (little?) LCD displays. Apparently bent on dominating the market for displays that are larger than some of our televisions, Apple offers Cinema Displays in three sizes: 20-inch, 22-inch, and 30-inch. All of the displays have a wide-aspect ratio, making them not only large, but wide—any one of these displays make it easier to have multiple applications open and working at the same time. Similarly, these displays are great for applications such as Final Cut Pro, which can take full advantage of all the screen "real estate."

The aluminum enclosure helps the display to match the Power Mac G5 and PowerBook models, but it also adds some strength, according to Apple. It also enables Apple to build it with a thinner housing than was possible with the last generation, so the displays can more easily be pushed up next to one another and used in tandem. Yup, you read that right—Apple recommends you go ahead and purchase *two* Cinema Displays. All we can say is...of course they do.

The latest Cinema Displays eschew the ADC connector for the more standard DVI connector, which is overall a good thing. Although the ADC connector was nice because it required only one cable for your monitor (which carried both power and video signal) it was expensive to workaround if your Mac didn't natively support ADC. Now, with DVI connectors, you've got to plug in the display, but the upshot is that it's much more compatible with older Macs, PowerBooks, PCs, and so on.

If there's anything Apple gets dinged for (over and over and over again) is the price that they put on things; the 20-inch model—as the cheap-o entry—is $1,299, which is high considering a number of name-brand 19-inch displays can be had in the $700–900 range. Apple's displays are impressive, good-looking, and almost universally appreciated for their quality—even if the prices can be a little tough to swallow. Of course, the saying is that you "get what you pay for," and a lot of Mac users swear by that saying.

Model: Cinema Displays
Manufacturer: Apple
(www.apple.com)
Price: $1,299 (20-inch model),
$1,999 (23-inch model) and
$3,299 (30-inch model)

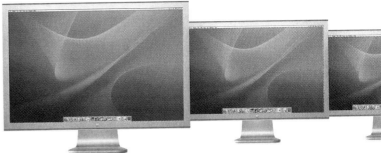

Photo courtesy of Apple, Inc.

Samsung Syncmaster 192MP

Choosing the runner-up displays is much tougher than choosing the winner, because the Apple displays are so well designed and rated. The Samsung Syncmaster 192MP is not only a very sturdy and attractive 19-inch computer display, it also happens to double as a TV tuner, complete with remote control. Perfect for a spare room or a dorm room, it's also priced very nicely considering the features. Most of the reviewers who know what they're talking about give it a thumbs up, particularly for brightness and contrast. The only negatives we've seen have to do with response time—there's a little bit of a "ghosting" effect when you're playing a fast-moving game.

Model: Syncmaster 192MP
Manufacturer: Samsung
(www.samsung.com)
Price: $949.95

Formac Gallery Displays

So maybe we're a little taken in by the name of the company, but Formac happens to make some decent displays that rate well with reviewers. With a look that is similar to Apple's previous generation of floating plastic displays, the Formac models blend well with Macs. They also offer good brightness, good response, and they're reasonably priced, if not inexpensive. Another nice treat is the Formac Calibrator that can be used to color-calibrate your display. It's not cheap, at $250, but for the cost of an Apple 20-inch Cinema Display you can get the Formac Gallery 1900 and the Calibrator, which might end up being a better option for a budget-minded professional setup. All three displays support an ADC connection; the two larger displays also support DVI without an adapter.

Model: Gallery
Manufacturer: Formac
(www.formac.com)
Price: $649 (1740), $799 (1900), $1,299 (2010)

Wacom Cintiq

This book is about gadgets, not hardware you say? Even displays can be gadgety if they want. The Wacom Cintiq is not only a touch-sensitive graphics pad, it's also—wait for it—either a 15-inch or 18-inch LCD display. The 18-inch is particularly nice (as you knew it would be) with a decent response time, support for DVI, and, of course, the ability to draw *directly on the screen*. How cool is that? The 18-inch display isn't as bright as the 15-inch, which is a decent bargain when you consider what it's capable of, particularly if you have some professional (or prosumer) freehand drawing needs.

Model: Cintiq
Manufacturer: Wacom
(www.wacom.com)
Price: $1,499 (15-inch), $2,499 (18-inch)

KeyTec MagicTouch Displays

You can't draw on this one, but you can touch it to move the mouse pointer, which is pretty gadgety, too. Useful for kiosks or demos or just for being able to show off a bit, the MagicTouch series of converted NEC monitors respond to your finger thanks to an overlay on the display itself. The displays run from 12-inch to 19-inch LCDs and less-expensive CRTs are available, as well.

Model: MagicTouch
Manufacturer: KeyTec
(www.magictouch.com)
Price: $525–$1,035, depending on style and size

Lacie electronblue IV

If you need serious color matching capabilities and you're willing to put up with a CRT, then Lacie's fourth-generation of flat-screened CRTs might be the right mix of budget friendly and high-end. The displays feature a non-glare tube and a specially designed hood that keeps the display uniformly shaded, regardless of the time of day or the state of the window blinds. These displays work hand-in-hand with the pricey Blue Eye Vision calibrator ($399), which can be stuck to the screen and used to adjust the display's color output for the best possible matching to your output devices or to your ultimate printing destination.

Model: electronblue IV
Manufacturer: Lacie (www.lacie.com)
Price: $379 (electron17blue), $699 (electron22blue)

ViewSonic G90FB-2

Okay, so the LCD is king. But there's still at least one good reason to turn to a CRT—you can get a big screen for cheap. This particular display offers a very flat screen that gives you a good bit of screen "real estate"—about 18 inches of viewable space measured diagonally. Various technologies have been put together to make the experience with this CRT a good one—an anti-reflective coating, special onscreen controls and what ViewSonic calls "SuperClear" technology. If you opt for a CRT, check out ViewSonic in a store if possible and put a few extra dollars into a larger display, as long as it'll fit on your desk.

Model: G90FB-2
Manufacturer: ViewSonic (www.viewsonic.com)
Price: $269

Video Cards

Depending on your needs, you may end up looking into new video hardware to push the pixels around on your new display. (How much money do you *have*, anyway?) The latest and greatest video cards are designed for gamers, but that doesn't mean the rest of us can't take advantage of them; the faster your video, the faster your Mac will seem to run, assuming it's not running into massive bottlenecks in terms of processing power or RAM. (If you're running Mac OS X on a "blue" Power Mac G3 with 128MB of RAM, then you've got issues that a video card can't address.)

Why does a good video card speed things up? Because it can free up the main processor by offloading a lot of the math that's required to draw complex moving and three-dimensional images on the display. In fact, such a video card includes its own processor, it's own RAM (often a lot of it) and a great deal of expertise that's gone into optimizing the software routines that the card goes through to generate those effects.

The result, for gamers, is increased *frame rate*, or the number of frames of gaming animation that can be seen in a second. More than 30 per second and you're in good territory, as that's how many frames you're seeing on television when you're watching a show. Even more frames than that and you know your Mac is sitting in good shape for some serious "fragging."

The world of after-market video is pretty limited for Macs—only ATI offers store-bought video card upgrades, while nVidia offers upgrades that you can buy with build-to-order Macs directly from Apple—unless you're shopping eBay or an aftermarket dealer.

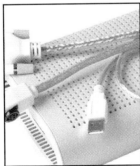

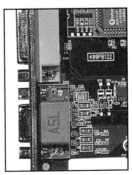
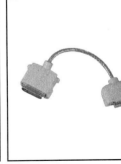

ATI Radeon 9800 Pro (Mac/Special) Edition

This is a great aftermarket card to add to your Mac, even if the offerings out there for Mac are basically ATI, ATI, and ATI. nVidia, which also makes graphics circuitry for Macs, doesn't offer them as aftermarket options, but only as "build-to-order" options via Apple's online and retail outlets.

Still, even if ATI is the only game in town, the Radeon Pro Mac Special Edition is a good option for Power Mac G5 users who really want to squeeze the most gaming or 3-D performance out your Mac. Just be ready to offer your current video card up for auction on eBay, because you're going to need to replace it to use your Mac's one AGP slot.

We're talking about two cards here, by the way. The "Mac Edition" has 128MB of RAM and works in any Mac that supports AGP cards. The "Mac Special Edition" works only in G5 machines.

The Mac Special Edition card also improves on the original Radeon 9800 Pro Mac Edition by offering a full 256MB of high-speed memory (instead of 128MB) to augment the dual 400Mhz graphics processors. Just to give you a sense of what those processors are capable of, here are some telling statistics: 3 billion pixels per second, 380 million transformed and lit polygons per second, and over 18 billion anti-aliasing samples per second. As you can see, those sorts of stats speak for themselves. (Er...)

Actually, for the sake of comparison, many gamers will use the polygons per second number; the lesser Radeon 9700 Pro, for instance, can do 300 transformed polygons per second. (The 9700 Pro is the high-end option in that last round of Power Macintosh G4 models.) The 9800—in whatever flavor—is a serious gamers card, and pretty good for professional applications as well, considering that it can drive two displays at once. The cards come with DVI and VGA interfaces; if you need to connect it to an ADC (Apple or Formac) display you'll need an ADC-to-DVI adapter, as discussed later in this section.

Model: Radeon 9800 Pro
Manufacturer: ATI (www.ati.com)
Price: $399 (Pro Mac Special Edition — 256MB), $349 (Pro Mac Edition—128MB)

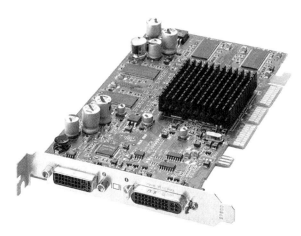

ATI Radeon 9000 Mac Edition

For something a little more affordable and a little less drool-worthy, the Radeon 9000 Mac Edition offers a quick-and-easy way to spruce up an aging Mac, particularly for gaming. (This is particularly true if you have enough RAM in your Mac; if you don't have a lot of RAM in your Mac yet, that's the first step to a speedier Mac for gaming before worrying about upgrading the video card.) This card also has an ADC adapter built-in, which makes it great for connecting an older Mac (say, an earlier Power Macintosh G4) to an Apple display that requires ADC. Indeed, it's a lot cheaper than an adapter for ADC would be. This card also supports dual monitors and includes a DVI-to-VGA adapter so that you can connect to an older display if you've got one.

Model: Radeon 9000 Mac Edition
Manufacturer: ATI (www.ati.com)
Price: $149.99

Dr. Bott DVIator

When Apple changed the way to connect displays—by creating the Apple Display Connector (ADC) cable, which carried the video signal, USB, and power to displays—well, there was sort of a thud. It's not a bad idea, as it means there's only one cord going to a display; nice and neat. But Apple eventually abandoned ADC because it was costly to implement and non-standard; now, Macs support DVI for digital connections and Apple displays support DVI for connecting to Macs (and PCs).

The upshot, though, is there are still a lot of ADC-only displays out there made by Apple (and Formac Electronics) that need to be connected to DVI-based Macs and PCs; indeed, your new G5 may no longer support your older ADC display. That's a bummer until you get an adapter; Apple offers its ADC-to-DVI adapter, but another option that's been on the market is Dr. Bott's DVIator, which does the job nicely for a few bucks less.

Model: DVIator
Manufacturer: Dr. Bott LLC
(www.drbott.com)
Price: $94.95

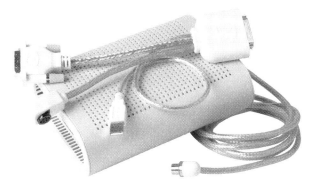

Dr. Bott's DVI Extractor

The flip side of this ADC wonderland that Apple created is when you need to connect a DVI display to a Mac that has only an ADC adapter; that's a little easier (and cheaper) to accomplish. The DVI extractor connects to the ADC port on a Mac's video card and gives you a DVI connector into which you can plug your display's cable.

Some of the video circuitry built in to late-model Power Macs can actually support displays connected to both ports, as can the ATI cards discussed in this section. In that case, an adapter might not seem so silly; if you've got an ADC and DVI connector on your video card, and you've already got the first DVI connector filled with a display, you might need to use that ADC port for a second DVI display; hence an ADC-to-DVI adapter is necessary.

> **Model:** DVI Extractor
> **Manufacturer:** Dr. Bott LLC
> (www.drbott.com)
> **Price:** $37.95

VGA-to-ADC Adapter

The folks who are really left in the cold on the whole ADC thing are those of us with aging Mac portables—even though you may have a PowerBook G4 that can handle dual-display support (using the PowerBook display and a second, external display)—who wants to use an Apple display with an ADC connector. First, our suggestion is *don't do that*. It isn't cost effective. But, if you really have a good reason—for instance, your uncle gave you a 23-inch Apple LCD display with an ADC cable and you only have a PowerBook 12-inch with a VGA port—then there is a solution. The VGA-to-ADC adapter from Gefen is an expensive one-trick pony, but it does let you do something that you might be craving; you can look at a PowerBook display on a nice, pretty Apple ADC display.

> **Model:** VGA-to-ADC Adapter
> **Manufacturer:** Gefen
> (www.gefen.com)
> **Price:** $299

TV Devices and Projectors

Back in the day—"the day" being the late 1970s and early 1980s—a television was an integral part of the computing experience, if only because you had to hook one up to your Atari or Commodore or TI or Apple II computer in order to see what was on the screen. With the advent of the IBM PC and the Macintosh, however, the move was to dedicated computer monitors, which is a place we remain to this day.

But the TV has always had a flirty relationship with the computer, particularly over the past decade or so. Various options exist today, as well, for hooking up your Mac to a TV to display an image or a presentation or perhaps a DVD

movie. Or, maybe you'd like to project your Mac's screen image onto a wall or screen for presentations or—if you're among the lucky few—for an impromptu movie theater for DVD playback.

The flipside offers devices that enable you to view a television picture on your Mac's screen. The latest of these not only enable you to watch a little TV—which is already kinda cool—but they work as a DVR (digital video recorder) to store television shows on your Mac's hard disk. How cool is that? You could then turn around and connect your Mac to the TV again to display television on your, well, television.

Elgato EyeTV

Leo's Pick

Elgato's original EyeTV was a hit with Mac gadget freaks who liked the idea of not only watching and recording television on their Macs, but also were geeky enough to think it was totally cool to use their Macs for recording and managing shows instead of a device like TiVo. And with today's larger displays, you might find it convenient to have these TV capabilities for your Mac.

With that caveat in place, the EyeTV is a very cool series of products. The original EyeTV used USB and recorded a less-than-perfect image using MPEG-1 compression; the modern version uses FireWire for the connection and records video using DVD-quality MPEG-2 compression. The difference can still take up quite a bit of room on your Mac (2GB per hour versus 650MB per hour for the USB version), but the theory is that your Mac has some hard disk space to spare or you're not likely to be a great candidate for the EyeTV.

With any DVR, which includes the combination of EyeTV and your Mac, the device records a buffer of whatever it is that you're watching at the time. That enables you to simply press the Pause button at any moment, which can pause what appears to you to be live television. The image is paused but the DVR keeps recording, so that when you play the image again, you can continue to watch the show from where you left off.

Using an Internet browser you can connect to the schedule service and choose the items that you want to record; the EyeTV is automatically programmed to do so. Once you've got a show recorded, you can move through it much as you would a program on tape—rewind, fast forward—but, because you're working on a Mac, the EyeTV (FireWire edition) also includes software that lets you edit the show, archive it to DVD-R or CD-R media and so on.

The EyeTV devices include built-in tuners or other devices that are necessary to connect to the various options you have for television service; the EyeTV 200 is the FireWire version, which includes a built-in cable tuner; other versions support different types of television signals. Bringing up the tail end is the EyeTV USB, which is still available and pretty cheap, to boot.

Model: EyeTV
Manufacturer: Elgato Systems (www.elgato.com); EyeTV 200, EyeTV USB
Price: $349 (EyeTV 200 with remote); $169 (EyeTV USB)

Elgato EyeHome

Another Elgato product? What this one does is act as an interface between your Mac and an actual television set or home theater. The box includes all sorts of output options for TV—composite video, S-video or component video—as well as an Ethernet port for connected to your Mac or to your home (or office) network. Once connected, the EyeHome can be used to play multimedia items from your Mac to your TV—it specifically ties into your iLife applications and plays back movies (from iMovie), songs (from iTunes) and photos (from iPhoto) that you have stored in your home folder on your Mac. And, it can be used to surf the Web (via your Safari bookmarks) and access Web radio. Coupled with an EyeTV, you can use the EyeHome to watch shows on your television that were recorded using your EyeTV.

Model: EyeHome
Manufacturer: Elgato Systems
(www.elgato.com)
Price: $249

Formac Studio TVR

Formac's TVR is similar in function and implementation to Elgato's EyeTV; the TVR is designed to work as a 125-channel tuner, which you can connect to your Mac via FireWire. You then use the included software to watch and pause live television, schedule shows for recording, and catalog your recorded shows or movies for playback. The TVR can also be used to digitize any other video source, such as playback from your VCR or DVD player, or audio from cassettes or CDs. The TVR software also offers a direct link into Apple's iMovie, enabling you to edit the video you record; and, you can export your television shows to the video out ports—so that you can watch them on a connected television— or you can export to QuickTime. The TVR will also work with Formac's external DVD-R device for recording DVD movies from your television shows.

Model: Studio TVR
Manufacturer: Formac Electronic
(www.formac.com)
Price: $299

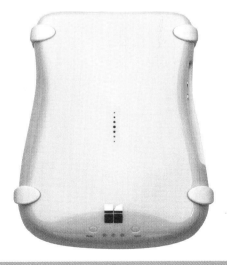

Focus Enhancement
I-TView/Mac

The I-TView/Mac is a scan converter, which is simply a device that can take a standard VGA-out connection and display that connection on a TV or similar video component (such as a VCR). This Mac specific model is designed to work with typical Macintosh display resolutions; the device includes a feature that scales display of the Mac's desktop so that it appears proportional on the TV screen. If you've got classes to teach or presentations to give and your Mac doesn't include its own video out port, then a scan converter is a necessary option.

Model: I-TView/Mac
Manufacturer: Focus Enhancements
(www.focusinfo.com)
Price: $119

Apple Video Adapter

Certain models of the iBook, PowerBook G4, eMac, and iMac offer a mini-VGA port that can accept this adapter; the other side of the adapter is an S-video and composite video port that you can use to send the video image from your Mac's display to a television or compatible video device. (Note that some iBook models have a special AV port that requires the Apple AV Cable instead of the Apple Video Adapter; it's the same price.)

Model: Apple Video Adapter
Manufacturer: Apple (www.apple.com)
Price: $19.95

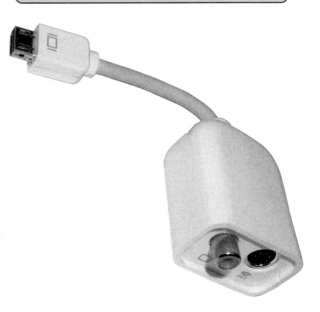

InFocus X2 Projector

The X2 model from InFocus is a good double-duty projector according to the company—it integrated well with your Mac for playback of either computer presentations or DVD movies; you can also hook it up to other components, such as a standalone DVD player or your home entertainment system, in order to get the most out of it for movies and television. The X2 offers 1,500 lumens, an important measurement of the brightness of these projectors; according to their spec sheet, the InFocus X2 can be used for images over 17 feet in width; just imagine what a good action movie will look like!

One thing to watch out for before you take the plunge with any multimedia projector is the bulb or lamp—for the InFocus X2, for instance, the lamp is about $299 and it's designed to last about 3,000 hours. If you watch 20 hours of TV per week, you might be looking at a new bulb every three years or so.

Model: X2 Projector
Manufacturer: InFocus
(www.infocus.com)
Price: $999

Epson PowerLite Home 10+

The trick to a home projector is the 16:9 aspect ratio, which can make DVDs look particularly good; these units are often designed to throw up a larger image with less distance from the screen; for instance, the PowerLite Home 10+ is designed to put up an image that's 100 inches wide with only eight-feet between the projector and the wall. Although not as bright as some multimedia projectors, the PowerLite is designed to work from closer distances and can be used in a variety of lighting situations, including a relatively well-lit living room or a fully darkened home media setup. (The lamp for the PowerLite Home 10+ is about $200 and rated at 2,000–3,000 hours.)

Model: PowerLite Home 10+
Manufacturer: Epson America
(www.epson.com)
Price: $1,299

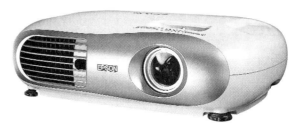

Audio Gadgets

The Mac has always been big with sound people—even during the odd little time of the Mac's existence in the late 1990s and early 2000s when Steve Jobs decided to drop audio inputs from the back or side of the Mac. (What was *that* all about?) Anyway, they're mostly back, along with some renewed interest in both professional and amateur audio production thanks in part to software tools from Apple such as SoundTrack and GarageBand.

There are really two types of audio to discuss when you bring the topic up around Macs—digitized audio and MIDI audio. Digitized audio is an entire class of recorded audio that takes sound waves and turns them into 1s and 0s that computers recognize. These files are stored in formats such as AIFF, WAV, MP3, and AAC. These "music files" can be downloaded, edited, and played back.

Most of that editing and playback is done in software or using devices that are at least

tangentially iPod-related, so we'll cover some of those in Chapter 11, "Gadgets for Portable Macs," and Chapter 12, "Miscellaneous Gadgets." In this section, we'll focus on hardware that gets digital sound into and out of your Mac—microphones, digital audio input devices, and speakers.

The flipside of computer audio is MIDI—the Musical Instrument Device Interface language. The MIDI language is essentially the computer version of a player piano's tape; a MIDI file is not recorded digital samples of audio, but rather *instructions* that tell a MIDI instrument or application how to playback a particular song. MIDI has always been immensely popular with many musicians and Mac users, and it has experienced a slight resurgence thanks to GarageBand. These days, you'll find a lot of USB-to-MIDI devices and adapters, which can be used to "play" songs and record those songs as instructions that can be edited and fed back to MIDI devices for automatic playback.

Harman Kardon SoundSticks II

Harman Kardon—one of the top names in designer audio products—created SoundSticks to augment the design of the iMac flat panel and other Apple models; they still look good next to pretty much any Mac model. They also work as a nice proof of concept for Apple's digital audio connection over USB. The theory is that the all-digital connection results in less "noise" creeping in than usually happens with the metal-to-metal connections of miniplugs; the USB connection also means the speakers are more completely integrated with Mac OS X.

That said, USB isn't the only choice; the SoundStick II model also offers a miniplug jack for compatibility with most any audio-out plug, meaning they can be used with a PC or iPod as well.

SoundSticks don't just look good—the setup includes an integrated subwoofer, which can go a long way to improving your computer's sound—the 20-watt subwoofer provides bass and low-range sound that's often missing from the typical computer's slightly more tinny sound. The 10-watt SoundSticks don't offer amazing volume—they're designed primarily to be heard by someone working at the computer, not to shake the foundation of your home—but they do offer high-quality sound that hits most ranges. And the stereo effects can fill a room with sophisticated sound, not just brute volume.

Model: SoundSticks II
Manufacturer: Harman Kardon
(www.harmankardon.com)
Price: $199

M-Audio Sonica Theater

This one comes in two different versions—the M-Audio Sonica Theater is a USB device for any compatible Mac and the Revolution 7.1 is a PCI card for Power Macs. Both are designed to add to your Mac's bag of audio tricks the capability to support 7.1 Surround Sound for DVD or other audio playback. The small box (Sonica Theater) or card (Revolution 7.1) offers eight analog-out ports for the various speakers—left and right center speakers, center subwoofer, etc.—as well as a digital output designed to work with surround sound speaker systems, including those sold by M-Audio.

Model: Sonica Theater (USB) and Revolution 7.1 (PCI)
Manufacturer: M-Audio
(www.m-audio.com)
Price: $119

Creative Gigaworks S750

Here it is—something in approaching the ultimate in Mac audio. The Creative Gigaworks S750 system is Surround Sound 7.1 compliant, featuring a 210-watt subwoofer and seven 70-watt satellite speakers for a total of 700 watts of audio power. The system connects to a Surround Sound 7.1–compatible sound card (like those from M-Audio described in the previous review) and can dramatically alter your notion of computer audio, from DVD playback to gaming to music. It's pricey, and other options can offer similar results, but if you really want to go to the top of the line for Mac audio, this is a good choice.

Model: Gigaworks S750
Manufacturer: Creative
(www.creative.com)
Price: $499

Plantronic DSP-300 Headset

This USB headset is a must-have if you're spending any time audio chatting using iChat; I use iChat to talk to one of my frequent co-authors in France and save an extraordinary amount of money on long distance. The DSP-300 is nice in that it offers its audio in stereo, meaning it also works well for gaming audio or music along with voice solutions such as iChat. (If you're shopping for a headset, you'll need a USB headset; most analog PC headsets don't work with Macs.)

Model: DSP-300 Headset
Manufacturer: Plantronic (www.plantronic.com)
Price: $89

Jabra Freespeak 250 Bluetooth Headset

If your Mac happens to have Bluetooth capabilities either built in or added on (see Chapter 5, "Networking and Wireless" **p. 69**) then you can use a Bluetooth headset with your Mac for those same gaming or iChat tasks; that can be handy, as the headset is wireless and it can be used with your Bluetooth-compatible mobile phone, too, if you have one. The Jabra Freespeak is designed to fit comfortably in your ear with a short microphone stalk that only reaches about to your cheekbone, yet can hear you well at a regular tone of voice. (Note: To use a Bluetooth headset with your Mac, you may need to update your Mac's Bluetooth software or firmware; check http://www.apple.com/support/bluetooth/ for details.)

Model: Freespeak Bluetooth
Manufacturer: Jabra (www.jabra.com)
Price: $99

USB MIDISport Uno

Got your own keyboard or similar MIDI device? Then you'll need a connector to hook it up to your Mac; once it's connected, you can use it with GarageBand or another MIDI-compatible application. One simple way to connect a MIDI device is using a USB-to-MIDI adapter, such as the USB MIDISport Uno. Connect to your keyboard (or other MIDI controller) and plug in to USB, then install the software drives and launch your music application. In most cases, it's a straightforward connection that quickly gets you up and playing music.

M-Audio Keystation 49e

The Keystation 49e is a MIDI controller, making it possible for you to play songs in Apple's GarageBand or any other MIDI-compatible software. When you use the Keystation to play notes, you either cause your Mac to sound an instrument "voice" that you've selected in the software application, or you can "write" music by playing notes on the keyboard that are translated by the software application. The Keystation 49e connects directly to your Mac via USB, making it simple to set up and use.

Model: Keystation 49e
Manufacturer: M-Audio
(www.m-audio.com)
Price: $129

Model: MIDISport Uno
Manufacturer: M-Audio
(www.m-audio.com)
Price: $39

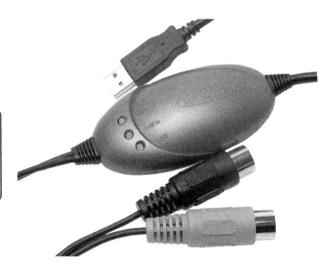

Digi 002

This is a fun one. The Digi 002 is a hardware sound mixer board that connects to your Mac via FireWire and works directly with Pro Tools LE software to enable you to mix multiple audio inputs at once. Call it a studio in a box; you can produce your entire band with a single Digi 002. It's got eight inputs that you can use for microphones or line-level inputs (guitars, keyboards) and four of those include some digital effects that are built in to the mixer. Once you have all those elements in your computer at once, you're ready to mix, fix, and change up your creations, thus producing the best sounds you possibly can. True, this is a little more costly than a USB keyboard and GarageBand (by about 2,400 bucks!) but if you've got your own garage band and a bevy of musical talent and you're serious about music editing with your Mac, this is a great little bundle to grab. (If you don't need that many inputs, DigiDesign also offers the MBox, with 2 channels over USB about $499.)

Model: Digi 002
Manufacturer: DigiDesign
(www.digidesign.com)
Price: $2,495

iMic

When Apple removed the microphone/line-in port from Mac models in the early 2000s, it left a lot of people scratching their heads. The ports are back now, but you may still find use for the iMic, regardless of whether or not your Mac has a line-in port. That's because the iMic not only connects to your Mac using USB, it enables you to plug in a standard mini-plug style microphone to it and use the microphone for speech or recording. That's a good thing, because Apple's own line-in port only supports special "Plaintalk" style microphones that have a longer plug.

Model: iMic
Manufacturer: Griffin Technology
(www.griffintechnology.com)
Price: $39.99

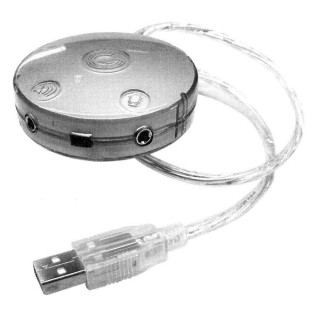

Printers and Scanners

4

Laser Printers

A laser printer works by fusing dry toner to the page in a process that's similar to a photocopy machine, including the fact the paper is heated up quite a bit. This is different from most inkjet printers, which use wet ink shot through tiny nozzles to create letters and images.

In terms of speed and cost-per-page, the laser printer is still king, even if the inkjet in recent years has gained steadily. Indeed, for a number of years now the equations have remained relatively the same—laser printers are often quicker and sometimes quieter than inkjets and, because they use toner cartridges that tend to last for significantly more pages than do ink cartridges, a laser printer's costs can be a little lower over the long haul.

At the same time, some things are changing about laser printers and inkjets. It used to be that only inkjet printers could be "multifunction" printers—those that can print and fax and copy and so on. But more and more laser printers have come along that are capable of such multitasking, and their prices have come down tremendously. The same basic thing is true of color printing; there was a time when color was only found on inkjet printers. Then, laser printers came along that could do it, but they were expensive. Today, those color laser printers are even affordable, at

least compared to what they have been, and that makes them downright amazing.

Another thing we've noticed about laser printers is that they've gotten a bit more "personal"—the market seems to have quite a few small, inexpensive laser printers that simply are connected via USB and allow you to crank out the pages at 15 pages per minute or better. That's handy if you're the type who is always printing articles from the Web or research for your books. Wait. That's us.

Students, teachers, professionals—if you don't need the color and you do need the speed, consider a small personal laser. Small business folks can consider a multifunction laser. Or if you're really ready to print some pages that impress your clients, opt for a color laser printer and start making those impressions happen.

While you're shopping, it's worth noting that Mac OS X and most Mac applications are fully compatible with PCL-compatible laser printers (the PC standard, developed by Hewlett-Packard), which hasn't always been the case. You'll still find that there's an advantage or two to buying a printer that's PostScript compatible, particularly if you use high-end page design applications (InDesign, QuarkXPress) with your Mac. But for most daily tasks, a PCL-based printer works great.

Color LaserJet 3500

The Color LaserJet is a true color laser in the sense that it isn't a whole heckuva lot slower when it's printing in color than in black and white. Both crank out at a respectable 12 pages per minute (ppm). And, it's considered a workhorse by HP, which rates this printer at a maximum 45,000 pages per month; that's somewhere just shy of 2,000 pages per work day. Yowza.

The printing quality for both black and color ink is pretty good—the native resolution is 600×600 dots, although HP's resolution enhancement technology (called imageREt), gives it a virtual 2400 dpi resolution which, were it true, would be something approaching the quality of a glossy magazine. The image quality is good, and the color is relatively cheap.

There's no question that color laser printing is more expensive than black-and-white printing, if only because you've got to buy so much more toner and additional consumables. A laser printer uses three color toner cartridges—cyan, magenta, and yellow—along with the black toner to create a color page. When one of those cartridges runs out, it must be replaced in order to continue color printing; and the color cartridges are rated at fewer pages (about 4,000 pages per cartridge versus 6,000 pages per cartridge for the black toner). They're also about $120 a pop.

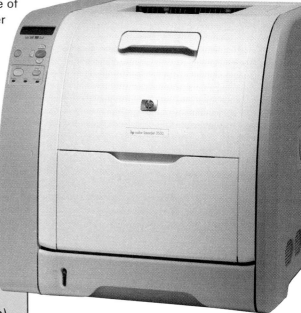

This is a real workgroup laser, though, complete with a 350-page input tray and support for additional capacity up to 850 pages. It's got 64MB of RAM and a fast processor; the time to your first page from idle is about 22 seconds according to the company. It'll even do envelopes and—picture this—if you use specially designed transparencies, you can print them in color for those overhead projector presentations. Huh? Now how much would you pay?

Model: HP Color LaserJet 3500
Manufacturer: Hewlett-Packard (www.hp.com)
Price: $799 (USB 2.0) or $999 ("3500n" includes JetDirect ethernet printer server)

HP Color LaserJet 2550L

What? Another HP? This one has some features worth talking about. First, though, the bad news—it only prints color pages at 4 pages per minute (that's 15 seconds per page, if you want to think about it that way) as opposed to the 20 ppm that it can do in black. It's also a bit smaller than the aforementioned 3500 series, and it's rated at a paltry 30,000 pages per month. Who can keep themselves within these limits?

What it has that makes up for that is some serious Macintosh *cred*—PostScript 3 emulation. It comes with 64MB of RAM and can be expanded to 192MB, which would be nice to have if you're serious about sending your color proofing through this "little laser that could." It's even got an ethernet networking option that adds only $100 to the price.

Model: HP Color LaserJet 2550L
Manufacturer: HP (www.hp.com)
Price: $499 or $599 ("2550Ln" with ethernet port)

Lexmark C510n

It's not as exciting as the HP printers because it costs a bit more, but in this case it may be worth it. The C510 prints at 30 ppm in black and 8 ppm in color; color quality is particularly good according to the reviews and the printer includes PostScript emulation. This printer is also quick to the first page—13 seconds for black and 19 seconds for color. This is a high-speed, high-quality printer that has a slightly higher price as a result. It does have built-in ethernet, 128MB of RAM standard, and a high-speed processor that helps to keep pages moving through the printer.

Model: C510n
Manufacturer: Lexmark (www.lexmark.com)
Price: $1,019

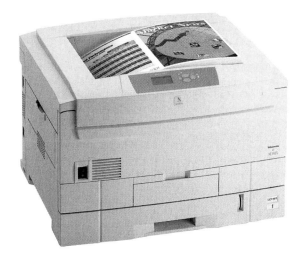

Brother MFC 8840DN Laser Printer

A multifunction printer can be particularly handy for small business networking or in a workgroup setting. If you're going to use that multifunction printer with more than one person, it's a good idea to get one that's laser-based (unless color is incredibly important). Then, you should get one that approaches the top of the line, such as the Brother MFC 8840DN. This printer is fast (21 pages or copies per minute), it offers a flatbed scanner/copier as well as a feeder for copies and faxes. Another trick is that it's a standalone fax machine—it doesn't require a computer for faxing, which you'll find with some less expensive multifunction printers. And it's network ready, supports up to legal-sized paper, and can accept a second paper tray for serious volume. The only caveat with most any multifunction printer is that, invariably, not *every* function is Mac-compatible; in the case of this printer, the Scan To button doesn't scan to anything on your Mac.

Model: MFC 8840DN
Manufacturer: Brother
(www.brother.com)
Price: $649

Phaser 7300 Series

This one is fast, it's extremely high-quality color and it's a workhorse for your workgroup. It's also a standout because it's able to print to tabloid paper (11×17, 12×18 depending on the paper) and, depending on the model you choose, can even print to 12×36 banners using special paper that Xerox offers. True, it's a tad pricey. The printer supports PostScript 3, offers 2400 dpi printing, and has a monthly duty cycle of 83,000 pages per month. It's got 192MB of RAM installed and can be upgraded to 512MB; it can also support an internal hard disk that can be used to store print jobs and fonts. Models ship with just USB and parallel ports, but you can get the printer with ethernet support, extra RAM, support for two-sided printing, and more.

Model: Phaser 7300 series
Manufacturer: Xerox
(www.xerox.com)
Price: $3,499 and up

HP LaserJet 3020
All-in-One

You do need multiple functions, but you don't need a network connection and faxing isn't a big issue. (Or, better yet, you can live with the Mac's built in USB printer sharing.) Fair enough. How about the HP LaserJet 3020, which features a 15 page per minute laser printer with 600 dpi output (not to mention the resolution enhancement). It's got a quick response time; 10 seconds to the first page or copy, and the automatic document feeder makes quick copies of multipage documents easier. Perhaps key is the fact that it has a flatbed scan/copy design so you can copy out of a book, make copies of pages smaller than standard, and so on. (In fact, we can't really come up with a good reason to get a copier that doesn't have a flatbed design; it's too tough to photocopy receipts and checks and all those other little pieces of paper that you inevitably need to copy in the small business world.)

Model: LaserJet 3020 All-in-One
Manufacturer: HP (www.hp.com)
Price: $399

Brother HL-5140

What's the least you can spend on a laser printer? We're getting close. The Brother HL-5140 runs off pages at 21 pages per minute, connects to your Mac via USB, and just plain prints. It's got a 250-page paper capacity and its memory—the standard amount is 16MB—can be upgraded to 144MB if desired. It can handle an add-on 10/100BaseT ethernet server—or an 802.11 wireless server—just in case you ever do decide to upgrade to network capability.

Model: HL-5140
Manufacturer: Brother (www.brother.com)
Price: $199

Inkjet Printers

It used to be that the reason to buy an inkjet printer was extremely cut-and-dry—you wanted a printer that a normal human could afford. Today, inkjet printers have to compete on speed, features, and the fact that they continue to be the most affordable way to print color pages. In the case of many of today's inkjet printers, they can win on these counts.

For the most part, the advantage that laser printers have over inkjet printers is cost per page and the recommended duty cycle for volume printing. In other categories—speed, convenience, affordability—an inkjet printer can be just as good a choice, if not better than a laser. Inkjet technology is used in multifunction printers, for instance, making it reasonably affordable to create your own color copies (along with printouts, faxes, and so on). And many of those multifunction printers can be had for under $200.

If you need a portable printer, an inkjet is your best bet; some printers fit in your laptop case or backpack right along side your Mac portable. Or, on the other side of the spectrum, if you need an affordable way to print ledger-sized or tabloid color proofs, an inkjet is a much more inexpensive choice than a color laser; such an inkjet can be had for hundreds of dollars, whereas a comparable laser costs thousands.

Perhaps the time when inkjets really shine is when you feed them photographs to print. If you're serious about digital photography and you'd like to be able to print photos that rival prints that you would receive from a processing house, then you'll find some inkjet printers that are reasonably affordable and that offer excellent quality. Even standard-issue inkjet printers can print to special coated paper and get impressive results from photos.

Epson Stylus C84WN

Leo's Pick

Epson has made a very solid inkjet entry in this space for quite some time; the C84 is a follow-on to the C80, which was around for quite a while and turned plenty of heads. For an inexpensive printer it's generally got good fit and finish, it's reasonably quiet and it's very versatile; both black text pages and fully glossy photos look good when they are spit out of the C84 series.

Epson pays close attention to the quality of the output, claiming an extraordinary 5760×1440 pixels for output and a 3-picoliter ink droplet; the picoliter (millionth of a millionth of a liter) measurement is used to compare inkjet printers to one another and to generally overwhelm the human brain with their unfathomable smallness.

As with most of the best inkjet printers you can get today, the Epson C84 offers individual ink cartridges for each color; in the "bad old days" you would come across inkjets that had one cartridge for black ink and one for color ink; if your cyan ran out before your magenta, you still had to chunk the cartridge. The C84 does only have four colors; some of the highest-end graphics inkjets offer six.

The C84 is extremely fast for an inkjet; it's rated at 22 pages per minute for black text and up to 12 pages per minute for color printing. It also features "borderless" printing, which enables you to print to the very edges of a piece of paper for the best graphic effects.

The C84 offers a number of different models; the entry model is less than $100 and connects directly to your Mac via USB 2.0. The C84N offers an ethernet connection and a print server so that you can use it on a network; our favorite, the C84WN includes an EpsonNet wireless print server, so that it's both wireless (802.11) and Rendezvous-aware (as is the C84N) so that it is self-discovered by Macs on your network. Too cool.

Model: Stylus C84WN
Manufacturer: Epson (www.epson.com)
Price: $199 (wireless network model) or $99 (USB 2.0 model)

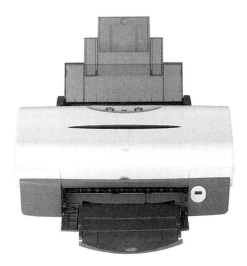

Canon i560

Cheap, fast, and versatile, this is a great printer to pull out of the box and set next to your Mac for the next few years. According to Canon it can print up to 22 pages per minute in black and up to 15 pages per minute in color. It can hold 150 sheets of paper at a time and can handle envelopes as well.

Of course, it wouldn't be a modern inkjet without some photo printing capabilities, and it does a nice job, including the capability to print borderless 4×6 prints as well as printing to glossy paper stocks at 8×10 and larger. The i560 uses four different ink tanks for color, so you can swap one that runs out without wasting any of the other colors.

Model: i560
Manufacturer: Canon
(www.canon.com)
Price: $89.99

HP DeskJet 5850

Because they've already pretty much come up with every sort of feature you can add to an inkjet, the cool ones now sport wireless networking. That's what the 5850 brings to the table, as well as a sleek (if slightly plastic) look and good performance at up to 21 pages per minute in black and 15 pages per minute in color. The 5850 supports 150 sheets of paper or 20 envelopes; you can add a second feeder to increase capacity to 400 sheets. There's also a duplex-printing option to enable you to print to both sides of the page automatically. And, the 5850 offers an option for 4-or-6 ink printing, to improve your color for photos if desired. The wireless networking that's built in to the 5850 makes it a great cross-platform solution. And, heck, there's nothing like a good, cheap, wireless network printer, right?

Model: DeskJet 5850
Manufacturer: Hewlett-Packard
(www.hp.com)
Price: $149

Canon i960

Okay, class, say it together—*photo printer*. Canon is known for having tiny little 2-picoliter drops for its ink, and it has designed this printer to have six different colors of ink, which is part of why it does such a bang-up job with photo printing. If you ever figured you didn't want a digital camera because it would be impossible to get good prints for passing around during holidays, then fret no more. Those ink colors are replaced one at a time, too, so that they don't quite break the bank when you run out of light magenta but you've got plenty of red. (In fact, that's one of the secrets to great photo printing; more colors. The colors that Canon adds to the typical four-color process helps to brighten the prints up considerably.)

Remember we mentioned it's a photo printer? It's so much so that Canon doesn't even tell you what the specs are for printing a page in black text only. (It can do that, however, quite nicely.) It is extremely fast when you're printing a photo; an 8×10 takes about a minute and a half, which is serious speed for a photo inkjet.

Model: i960
Manufacturer: Canon
(www.canon.com)
Price: $199

Epson PictureMate

Epson offers a special printer designed specifically to print 4×6 photos, much as you might expect from the photo lab. The difference is that these photos are printed from digital cameras—in fact, you don't even need to connect the PictureMate to your Mac, although you can; it can print directly from the memory card your camera uses to store images, or it can connect to cameras that use the PictBridge direct connection standard. (It can even connect to cameras that have Bluetooth built in.) Connected to your Mac, you can use the included software to preview images, crop, rotate, change colors, and otherwise prep your photos before printing.

Model: PictureMate
Manufacturer: Epson
(www.epson.com)
Price: $199

HP DeskJet 9600 Series

When you gotta print big, you'll know it. The DeskJet 9600 is a favorite of folks who print their own posters—or designers who need to see color proofs of their tabloid-sized publications. The DeskJet 9600 series offers fast printing for such a large-format printer and it'll handle either 4-color or 6-color printing. The series offers three different models; a low-end, a mid-range with automatic two-sided printing, and a high-end model with duplex printing and PostScript-compatibility.

Model: DeskJet 9600 series
Manufacturer: HP (www.hp.com)
Price: $399 (9650), $499 (9670 with duplex printing), $599 (9680 with duplex and PostScript)

Canon i80

What about a printer that you can take with you? This little guy can print black text pages at up to 14 pages per minute and color at around 10 pages per minute; the resolution is high, the picoliters are low (about 2), and the printer even has an optional Bluetooth upgrade that lets you print to it wirelessly. And, the biggest deal is how little it is—it's only a little larger than a piece of paper, two-inches tall and four pounds. Of course, all this compact technology must cost a lot, right? Well…kinda, yeah. But it's worth it if you need to answer that age old question "Where do I print when I'm in my hotel room?"

Model: i80
Manufacturer: Canon (www.canon.com)
Price: $249

HP PSC 1315

If you need those multiple functions—copying and scanning—*almost* never, but you still want the option, the PSC 1315 offers print speeds up to 17 pages per minute in black and white and 12 pages per minute in color; it has 16MB of RAM, a PictBridge interface for printing directly from digital cameras—oh, and it has a flatbed that can be used for copying (50% to 400%) and scanning. It's not exactly a world-class work-horse for copying (and it doesn't offering faxing directly from the machine), but maybe it'll be nice to have the option around the house.

HP OfficeJet 6110

There are tons of multifunction printers you can choose from and HP makes a number of good ones. The HP OfficeJet 6110 stands out as a small office workhorse that happens to be on the low end of their "professional" series of multifunction inkjets. This one prints at 19 pages/copies per minute in black ink and up to 15 pages/copies per minute in color. It's got an automatic document feeder for faxing, scanning or copying multiple pages, plus a flatbed scanner that can handle legal paper and reductions/enlargements ranging from 25% to 400%. It connects via USB, but you can add a USB-based JetDirect print server to use it on your network.

> **Model:** PSC 1315
> **Manufacturer:** HP (www.hp.com)
> **Price:** $129

> **Model:** OfficeJet 6110
> **Manufacturer:** HP (www.hp.com)
> **Price:** $299

Scanners

Does anybody buy scanners anymore? After all, Mac users now have plenty of multifunction devices to choose from, and these devices have the added advantage of letting you make copies of things.

Your needs may be deeper than that—perhaps you're a graphic designer, or you want a scanner attached to a particular Mac in your office, or you're looking for something a bit more sophisticated than most multifunction devices offer. Whatever floats your boat. Although the standalone scanner isn't quite as prevalent as it once was, there are still plenty of interesting models to choose from.

Another thing that can be nice about getting a standalone scanner is the capability to send slides or transparencies through the scanner; indeed, you may find yourself getting a special scanner (or an attachment for a less than special scanner) that's designed specifically to allow you to scan slides or even film. And if you shoot a lot of photography in 35mm film and you're interested in scanning those images, you'll want to get a specialized scanner that can handle the film.

The other trick to picking a scanner is knowing what you want to use it for. If you'll be using the images for relatively mundane, low resolution tasks—posting to a web site or printing at relatively small sizes on inkjet paper—then a typical scanner should do just fine. If you're interested in scanning film and printing large prints, however, you'll again need a more capable scanner.

By the way, most scanners come with some sort of software that can handle the scanned image and so on, but often you can use your Mac's Image Capture application (in the Utilities folder in Mac OS X) to scan images. The best plan, though, is to scan into a utility such as Adobe Photoshop, where you can also make tweaks and edits to the image.

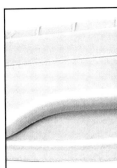

Microtek ScanMaker 6100 Pro

Leo's Pick

The ScanMaker 6100 Pro is a good excuse to buy a scanner, and it's a great all-around performer. For starters, you connect using USB 2.0, which, with a new Mac, means better performance for the scan. And USB 2.0 might prove important, because the ScanMaker can create some large digital images from its scans, given the 6400×3200 dpi resolution that it boasts.

For film and transparency folks, the ScanMaker 6100 Pro has a built in transparency adapter that can handle slides, filmstrips, or 4-inch by 5-inch film. The EZLock Film holders also make it easier to scan and crop images from film. The cover of the scanner serves as an impromptu "lightbox" which enables you to view slides and certain types of film to make sure you're seeing what you want to see.

The 6100 Pro is a true 48-bit scanner, meaning it captures an extraordinary amount of color. That, coupled with its high resolution capabilities, make it good for slide scanning; you can capture a relatively small slide and blow it up for use as a large photo.

The ScanMaker 6100 Pro is good for scanning regular photo prints and images as well. You could certainly use it for the occasional document scan, but it doesn't offer an automatic document feeder, so we wouldn't recommend it for serious document scanning tasks, such as archiving legal documents or serious optical character recognition (OCR), which means turning scanned documents into computer files that you can edit.

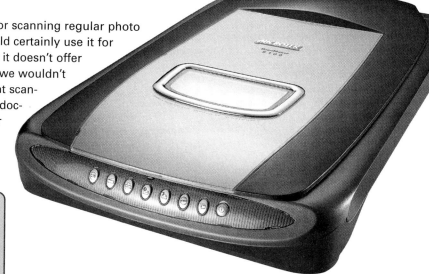

Model: ScanMaker 6100 Pro
Manufacturer: Microtek
(www.microtek.com)
Price: $299

HP ScanJet 4670

The HP ScanJet is making this list because it looks cool, which is exactly why HP built it this way. Don't be fooled! Sure, the upright approach saves a little space (and a traditional flatbed can take up a lot of space on your desk) and the transparent glass makes it possible to see whether there's a document left in the scanner when you're done with it. (That's all we could think of.) But the basic point is to build a document scanner that's decent for photos and OCR and that looks terribly, terribly, cool.

Model: ScanJet 4670
Manufacturer: HP (www.hp.com)
Price: $199

MacAlly BizScan

How's this for a specialty scanner? The BizScan is designed specifically to scan business cards and use OCR to translate what's on the card into something that can be imported into Address Book, Entourage, or a similar program. It even supports the vCard standard, which can be used to import into a variety of programs. Calling it a one-trick pony is almost fair, but it doesn't support color scanning and it can also be used to scan up to 4×5 photographs.

Model: BizScan
Manufacturer: MacAlly (www.macally.com)
Price: $149

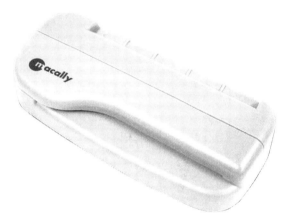

Networking and Wireless

5

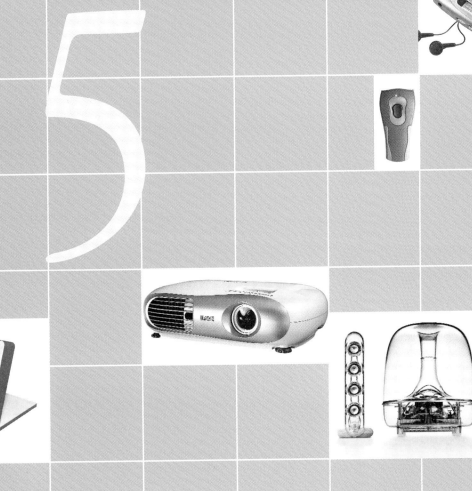

Networking Hubs and Routers

Any Mac made at least in the past five years has an ethernet port built in to it, which was a key feature on the iMac when it first debuted. The idea was (and continues to be) that, even though the iMac was designed as a consumer-oriented computer, it still needs an ethernet port so that it can connect to a broadband Internet connection. Five years ago that was forward-thinking; today it's just a fact of life.

Of course, more and more of us have multiple computers in our homes or small offices, making that ethernet port handy for sharing files and printers. And, as the Internet has become an important part of everyday life, routing Internet access to multiple computers over a network is usually a priority if you've got those multiple computers hanging out.

In this section we'll look at the hubs and routers you'll want to use for creating a wired network in your home or office; wireless options are in the "Wireless Networking" section later in this chapter. For wired networks, we're talking about ethernet. And with ethernet networks, we're

concerned with two types of connecting devices: hubs and routers. A *hub* (or a switch, which is similar, but a bit more efficient) is designed to enable you to connect multiple Macs to one another by connecting each Mac to the device using an ethernet cable.

A *router* also connects to your Mac, but its main purpose is to move a certain type of data from one network to another; often that means getting Internet access to your network. Routers are often combined with the capabilities of a hub, so that you can connect multiple Macs to your router and then share files and connect to the Internet at the same time. But not all routers work that way; some are designed to connect your existing local area network (LAN) to a new network connection such as an Internet broadband modem. In that case, particularly for a larger network, you might end up with both a router and a hub or switch.

Because everyone's situation may be a little different, we'll take a look at a few different options and scenarios.

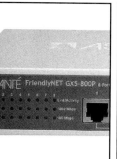    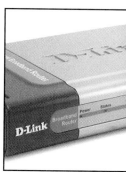

Leo's Pick

Linksys EtherFast Cable/DSL & Voice Router

Whereas this device may otherwise seem to be a mild-mannered and unassuming Cable/DSL router, it offers a cool new gadgety feature that we're just starting to see on the market—a built-in Voice Router. This router is designed out of the box to work with Net2Phone, a service that enables you to make calls over an Internet connection. The advantage of Internet telephony is that you can make long-distance calls very inexpensively; in fact, you can even get flat-rate calling plans for long distance or "minute" plans that resemble plans for mobile service, such as 300 long-distance minutes per month.

What's more, you can make that call using a regular telephone connected to the LinkSys router, which can be a boon over other Internet telephony services that require you to literally make your call from your computer. (That's especially true when you consider that not all Internet telephony services have Mac versions of their software.) So, with this router, the Internet telephony uses a standard telephone—even a cordless phone—and it's computer-independent, so your Mac doesn't even need to be turned on for you to use the phone service. (More on Voice over IP a little later in this chapter.)

Aside from the voice router the EtherFast is a quality Internet router—including a firewall, DHCP server for automatically addressing your networking Macs (or PCs) and, of course, the capability to distribute a single Internet connection to all your connected computers. It's also got a 4-port 10/100BASET switch built in to it, so that you can connect your Macs directly to it; the only other device you need is your broadband modem and you've got a connection for Internet, file/printer sharing, and Voice over IP telephony.

(Note, by the way, that this router isn't considered Mac-compatible by Linksys because the company doesn't offer a Mac-compatible firmware upgrade for the router. However, third-party solutions—such as MacTFTP at http://www.mactechnologies.com—can be used to update Linksys routers. That said, the router is otherwise configurable from a web browser and thus platform independent.)

> **Model:** EtherFast Cable/DSL & Voice Router
> **Manufacturer:** Linksys (www.linksys.com)
> **Price:** $149

D-Link DI-604 or DI-704UP Broadband Router and Switch

If the problem is that you've got three or four Macs that you'd like to connect to one another—and to an Internet broadband connection—then you need a simple device like the DI-604. The DI-604 has four switched ports for devices and an "uplink" port for connecting to your broadband Internet connection. The four ports can accept ethernet connections from your Macs, which are then able to share files with one another—in that way, the device incorporates a router and a switch. If you have an ethernet-capable printer, you could also connect that to the router and access it from the Macs. If you don't have an ethernet-capable printer, then the DI-704UP is a good choice; it includes a USB-based printer server that enables you to make a USB printer available to your network of Macs. Both devices have web browser–based setup and firewalls to keep Internet-based attacks from accessing your network.

> **Model:** DI-604 or DI-704UP
> **Manufacturer:** D-Link (www.dlink.com)
> **Price:** $39 (DI-604) or $59 (DI-704UP)

SMC Barricade 8-Port 10/100 Mbps Broadband Router

If you've got a larger LAN, you'll need more ports; the Barricade 8-port can support eight computers (Macs or PCs) and will switch between 10Mbps and 100Mbps depending on the capabilities of the Mac. (Older—precolorful—Macs are limited to 10Mbps, whereas modern iMacs and PowerMacs and so on are capable of 100MBps or better.) The router can also support an external modem connection (using a PC-style RS-232) that can automatically dial out when the broadband connection goes down; it also offers VPN support for "virtual private networks" or filesharing connections over the Internet.

> **Model:** Barricade SMC7008ABR 8-Port 10/100 Mbps
> **Manufacturer:** SMC (www.smc.com)
> **Price:** $84.99

Asante FriendlyNET 10/100/1000 Switch

Don't need Internet access for your LAN? In that case, you can get away with a 10/100/1000 switch, such as the 8-port Asante FriendlyNET GX5-800P Ethernet Switch. This one supports Gigabit connections for the latest Macs that sport such ethernet ports. (Older or slower Macs and portables can still connect as well.) This is a great way to get high-speed networking accomplished if you've got a room full of PowerMac G5s, for instance; you can still add Internet access via a dedicated router, if necessary.

Model: FriendlyNET GX5-800P
Manufacturer: Asante
(www.asante.com)
Price: $129

Linksys EtherFast Cable/DSL Router

If you've already got a network of Macs connected via a hub or switch (particularly if it's a high-speed switch) you'll probably just want to add a standalone router if you decide that LAN needs broadband Internet access. That's what the Linksys BEFSR11 does, as well as providing Network Address Translation (NAT), which offers a little protection from outside access over the Internet; you might still want to implement some sort of hardware firewall if you don't have one on your network or your individual Macs.

Model: EtherFast BEFSR11
Manufacturer: Linksys
(www.linksys.com)
Price: $49

Setting Up an Internet Router

You've got an Internet router...now what? If the router isn't made by Apple, then it probably has a web-based interface. You'll need to access the router's own IP address and then log in to access the setup options.

With your Mac connected to the router via an ethernet cable, enter the address specified by the manufacturer in Safari, Internet Explorer, or the browser of your choice. For instance, it might be 192.168.0.0 or 192.168.0.1 or something similar. Press Return. If everything is connected and powered on, you'll see a log-in screen; enter the username and password specified by the manufacturer in the router's documentation.

One of the first things you need to do is set up how the router is supposed to communicate with your Internet connection. In some cases, you'll be entering a fixed or static IP address for the connection, along with any gateway addresses that your ISP has specified. In the case of a cable modem, you may simply configure your router to receive an IP address automatically from the modem. For a DSL modem, you may need to set up a PPPoE connection. In that case, you enter a username, password, and some other options.

Next, you'll want to determine how each Mac or PC on the rest of your LAN will receive its individual IP address. In the case of a manual selection, you'll tell the router the range of internal IP addresses (192.168.0.1 through 192.168.0.15, for instance) you want to choose from, then you'll go to each machine and enter a different IP address within that range. That can be handy for certain internal networking applications.

The other option is probably used more frequently in home and small offices—a DHCP server. In this case, you tell the router that you want it to assign addresses when queried by a new machine that wants access to the Internet; the router will assign a unique address and then start sending Internet data to that address. Each Mac or PC will need to be configured for DHCP access, which is easy to do. (In Mac OS X, use the Network pane of System Preferences.)

Aside from those basics, you'll find that your router probably has controls for its security features. For instance, it may have a built-in firewall that you can activate; if so, it may also have a "Demilitarized Zone" (DMZ) feature that lets you designate a certain computer on your network that you allow for access from the Internet—that computer might be a web or Internet server computer. You may also find blocking options that enable you to limit the access that the computers on your LAN have to certain sites, whether they're blocked using an outside surf-watch service or blocked manually by entering disallowed IP addresses.

Oh, and don't forget to change that administrator's password to something a little harder to guess than the one that's printed in the manual!

Wireless Networking

It's tough to get too excited about wired networks and routers—hey, they're nice, but there's nothing terribly "gadgety" about ethernet, which has been around for over 30 years. What is a little cooler is wireless Internet and networking access, something that Apple pioneered and where we've still got some innovative and fun Apple products, as well as some great third-party stuff.

When we talk about "wireless networking" what we're generally referring to is what Apple calls AirPort networking, the PC industry calls WiFi and nerdy types call 802.11, which is the name of the standard on which this type of networking is based. (Actually, it's called IEEE 802.11.) To create a network, you need a computer that's capable of sending and receiving a signal according to this standard and you need a wireless hub that can receive the data and send it to other wireless computers.

Those hubs are often also Internet routers so you can access the web and e-mail while you're

wireless. In fact, that's how it works in coffee shops and other wireless "hotspots"—there's a router hanging out somewhere that your Mac can connect to if it's AirPort-enabled.

Beyond the numbering scheme, you can encounter different flavors of WiFi, including 802.11b—the original AirPort standard—and 802.11g, which Apple calls AirPort Extreme and most other companies somehow try to call "g" or "darned fast." The difference is the amount of data that can be sent through the connection; with 802.11b, the limit is 11Mbps (and often more like 2Mbps); with 802.11g, it's 56Mbps, which feels quite a bit faster than a standard ethernet connection.

For most Macs, you add support for the wireless connection using an Apple AirPort card; every modern Mac supports either an AirPort or AirPort Extreme card. Where you can get a little more creative is with the wireless router or hub that you choose, as the AirPort card is compatible with many of them.

AirPort Express

Leo's Pick

The AirPort Extreme Base Station, discussed next, has its advantages over its younger, cuter sibling, the AirPort Express. But the AirPort Express is simply too much of a gadget not to get top billing.

When introduced, Apple called the AirPort Express the first portable 802.11g router and hub. Designed to look a lot like power adapters that Apple ships with its portable Mac, the AirPort Express isn't any bigger than those adapters, yet it features a fully functional 802.11g router. Plug in a broadband connection to the bottom of the device, connect it to a wall socket, and you'll be able to share the connection with any AirPort-capable Macs.

The AirPort Express has two other ports—a USB port that can be used to share a USB printer wirelessly between multiple Macs and a stereo port. That connection enables you to connect the AirPort Express to your home or other compatible stereo system. (Apple makes a special stereo connection kit for this purpose.) You can then use an AirPort-enabled Mac to broadcast audio from iTunes to your stereo system using AirTunes technology—iTunes can send shuffled tunes, your favorite mix, or what have you; the Mac need only be within AirPort range (about 150 feet).

Finally, if you already have an AirPort Express Base Station on your network, you can use the AirPort Express as a bridge to that network, thus extending the range for the overall wireless network.

What can't you do with it? You can't connect to an existing wired network and use the AirPort Express as a router for ethernet-connected Macs. But that's the most serious drawback—otherwise, this is a seriously fun little device.

Model: AirPort Express
Manufacturer: Apple (www.apple.com)
Price: $129 ($39 for stereo connection kit)

Photo courtesy of Apple, Inc.

Photo courtesy of Apple, Inc.

AirPort Extreme Base Station

The AirPort Extreme Base Station is overpriced, but it's *almost* worth it. Supporting 802.11g and 802.11b protocols, it can be used for high-speed access and can support all your Macs and wireless PCs; it's also got a second port that lets you connect the Base Station to an ethernet hub or switch, thus making Internet access available to your entire network, regardless of whether its wireless. The AirPort Extreme Base Station also offers a modem (in some configurations) that can be used for sharing a phone-line–based Internet connection with your network, if you find that handy. And, although you can get most of this from other broadband wireless routers, the truth is that the AirPort Extreme Base Station works well with Apple's software, it's easier to configure for secure connections with AirPort-enabled Macs and it generally gives you that integrated, "just works" feeling you're used to with Macs.

Model: AirPort Extreme Base Station
Manufacturer: Apple (www.apple.com)
Price: $249.99 ($199.99 without modem and antennae port)

Dr. Bott ExtendAIR

The top-end AirPort Extreme Base Station includes a port that can accept an external antennae, which is what Dr. Bott supplies. Two models are available; the Direct model can be pointed in the general direction where you need access or where you want to place another base station for a longer-range network (up to 500 feet, according to Dr. Bott). The Omni model can be used to simply expand the general range of your Base Station to about 150% of the original range.

Model: ExtendAIR
Manufacturer: Dr. Bott (www.drbott.com)
Price: $149 (Direct) or $99 (Omni)

Belkin USB to 802.11g Adapter

If you're still hanging on to a Power Macintosh G3 or G4—or an older iMac—that doesn't support an internal AirPort card, there are solutions. One is the Belkin USB to 802.11 adapter card, which can work with a software driver to enable the Mac to connect to a wireless network. In most cases—partly because of the limitations of USB—you'd be better off with a wired ethernet connection. But, of course, wireless lets you put computers across the room or otherwise out of reach of ethernet cables—and, well, it's just cooler. (And if you don't need 802.11g speeds, 802.11b adapters are available and usually much cheaper.)

Model: USB to 802.11g Adapter
Manufacturer: Belkin
(www.belkin.com)
Price: $89.99

Belkin Wireless 4-Port 802.11g Cable/DSL Router

With a little bit of everything tossed in, this router isn't as pretty or as Mac-integrated as the AirPort Base Station, but it'll do quite a bit if you have a broadband connection you want to share via 802.11g protocols. Not only does it route Internet data, but you've got four ports that serve as an ethernet switch. Then, on top of that, you've got adjustable antennae that offer, theoretically, better coverage than the AirPort Base Station does without add-ons. You'll configure this guy using a web browser instead of a built-in Mac application and the security features are a little tougher to implement but they'll work—and, it's a great cross-platform solution, as well.

Model: 4-Port Cable/DSL 802.11g Router
Manufacturer: Belkin
(www.belkin.com)
Price: $112.99

Belkin Ethernet to 802.11g Bridge

When you talk about using your Mac's ethernet port to connect to a wireless network, now you're using a *bridge*. Not sure if there's much difference, except that they tend to be more expensive! Actually, you'll get better speeds—at 802.11g speeds, for instance, you'll be fine with a 100BASE-T ethernet connection—and using ethernet doesn't tie up the USB throughput. Also, this may be your only choice on a much older Mac or on some other devices—such as DVRs (Digital Video Recorders) that need access to the Internet and could conceivably do so wirelessly with an ethernet port and the right bridge.

Model: Ethernet to 802.11g Bridge
Manufacturer: Belkin
(www.belkin.com)
Price: $148.99

Kensington WiFi Finder

Of course you wouldn't *steal* Internet access; but sometimes it can be handy, in a pinch, to know where you could borrow some. And, the truth is that there are more and more free, public wireless nodes available out there—if you can find them. I've frequented coffee shops for months before realizing they have a free WiFi connection; but, with this device, that'll never happen again. Just push a button and you'll get a sense of whether there's a signal and an approximate signal strength. Then you'll know whether to whip out your PowerBook or iBook.

Model: WiFi Finder
Manufacturer: Kensington
(www.kensington.com)
Price: $29.99

Bluetooth Wireless

Although it's certainly got an odd name (it's named after a Danish king of the 10th century), the purpose of Bluetooth is both mundane and revolutionary—to be a low-range, low-speed wireless standard for moving relatively small bits of data back and forth without wires. The easiest way to think of it is "wireless USB" although the standards aren't related. Conceptually, they're similar—Bluetooth is a solution for connecting devices to your Mac without actually *connecting* them.

One place where Bluetooth is already popular is in mobile phones—Bluetooth is used both for connecting with computers (for synchronizing data in the contact lists or appointment calendars) and for communicating between the phone and devices such as Bluetooth wireless headsets. Such a headset enables the user to be free from a tether; the mobile phone can sit on your desk or in a charging cradle in your car and you talk into your wireless headset.

The same thing is possible on a Mac; wireless headsets, in some cases, can be used seamlessly between a mobile phone and your Bluetooth-enabled Mac. And the Mac can certainly handle certain Bluetooth-enabled phones to the degree that you can even have information about a caller pop up on your Mac's screen when he or she calls your mobile phone, if the phone is within range of your Mac.

Bluetooth is also useful for keyboards and mice; using Bluetooth for the connection is generally considered superior to Radio Frequency (RF) connections. And Bluetooth can be used for personal digital assistants (PDAs) and for transferring images from some digital cameras. It's becoming more popular all the time for all types of devices. Just be aware that it's *slow*, surprisingly so for a relatively new technology, and that it isn't always the ideal substitute for an actual USB (and particularly a FireWire or USB 2.0) connection when you're dealing with large files. For little bits of data, though, it can't be beat.

D-Link Bluetooth Adapter (also Belkin Bluetooth Adapter)

Leo's Pick

Because they're not really different enough to pick a winner we'll give them both their props here. The Belkin Bluetooth adapter and the D-Link Bluetooth adapter both serve the same purpose—you plug them in to an available USB port, install a driver then they begin looking for Bluetooth devices that they can connect to; when one is found and contacted, you then *pair* that device with your Mac so that they can talk to one another.

These adapters are powered by the USB bus themselves and can be plugged in to any port that has power, including the ports on the side of Apple USB keyboards. (In fact, that's not a bad place to put one, unless the keyboard itself is wireless.) You then use Apple's own internal utilities to access external devices via the adapter—see the discussion that follows this review on page 83.

If there's a difference between the two adapters, it's mostly aesthetics; the Belkin device is a little cooler looking and svelte, while the D-Link device is chunky. Both conform to the Bluetooth 1.1 specification, and both require Mac OS X 10.2 or higher (which is the first version to support Bluetooth.)

In terms of specifications, the Bluetooth 1.1 spec is limited to about 33 feet (10 meters) for the signal to carry and the maximum throughput for asymmetrical (one-way) data transfer is 723Kbps—which is something akin to a mid-range DSL Internet connection. Symmetrical speeds (two-way) are limited to about 434Kbps for any Bluetooth 1.1 device.

> **Model:** Bluetooth Adapter
> **Manufacturer:** D-Link (www.dlink.com) or Belkin Components (www.belkin.com)
> **Price:** $59 (D-Link DBT-120) or $59 (Belkin F8T003)

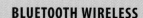

Bluetooth Print Bridge

Once you've got a Bluetooth adapter (or native Bluetooth compatibility) for your Mac, you're able to communicate between your Mac and PDAs or smartphones; but what about printing? The Bluetooth Print Bridge is software that enables you to print out your contacts or appointments or even photos that you've taken with your handheld device. It's compatible with other software from the same company that pretties up those printouts, too.

Model: Bluetooth Print Bridge
Manufacturer: Script Software
Price: $20

Cordless Collector

C'mon. You know you want your own barcode scanner for around the house. The scanner can store scanned items from around your home or office (or classroom or library) until you get near your Bluetooth-enabled Mac, then you sync to the Collection software. For home, you could literally catalog books, games, movies, and CDs. Plus, including software will create barcodes that you can use to inventory your own products or items. The included software is handy for maintaining a personal information database (you scan an ISBN or similar code and it looks up info on the Web). You can even upload your data to a Palm handheld or the Web, and you can use the software to "check out" items and track due dates or returns of loaned items.

Model: Cordless Collector
Manufacturer: Kensington
(www.kensington.com)
Price: $299.99

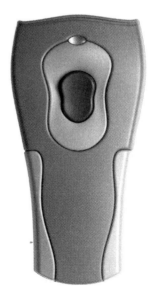

How to Connect with Bluetooth

When you first decide you're going to use a new Bluetooth device with your Mac, you need to set it up, which you can do most easily using the Bluetooth Setup Assistant found in the Utilities folder inside the main Applications folder in Mac OS X. (If you don't see such an application, you may need to update the Mac OS before you can use Bluetooth.) If your Mac's Bluetooth capability (or an installed adapter) is recognized, you'll also see a special menu icon appear in the menu bar that you can use to access the Assistant by choosing Set Up Bluetooth Device from that menu.

Use the Bluetooth menu to access various Bluetooth settings and options.

With the Assistant active, you can choose the type of device to which you want to connect. To use any Bluetooth device, you must first *pair* the devices with your Mac so that they know to pay attention to each other; that keeps you from accidentally updating the Address Book on, for instance, your cubical mate's Bluetooth phone.

Once you have the devices connected, you'll often use Apple's iSync program to synchronize data from Address Book, iCal, and so on. If you're working with a Bluetooth digital camera, you might use Image Capture or iPhoto. Occasionally, however, you'll want to use Bluetooth specifically to exchange files. (You'll do this very occasionally, because Bluetooth is darned slow!) To do that, you can first launch Bluetooth File Exchange, then choose the file that you want to send to the device. Now you'll see menus that enable you to choose the device to which you're going to send the file.

You can also access a number of Bluetooth options, settings, and a different interface for pairing devices in System Preferences by selecting the Bluetooth pane. There you can make all sorts of setting selections such as whether your computer should attempt to discover new devices, whether you require encryption and passwords, how your computer reacts when it's asked to accept a file via Bluetooth, and so on.

Voice over IP: Broadband Telephony

Not only does VoIP have the potential to be another cool use for the Internet, it should also be relatively inexpensive, because you already pay for your Internet connection and that Internet connection is already global.

In fact, all this is true and it seems to be exerting some downward price pressure on other types of phone service. Some of that pressure is from mobile phones, of course, because many plans include long distance. But the long distance companies may also be seeing the future of VoIP, which promises low-priced phone service for anyone with broadband.

Right now there are two basic approaches to VoIP—you can make the calls using your Mac or you can make the calls using a telephone handset. With your Mac, the solution, sometimes called a *softphone*, is similar to audio chat using iChat AV, except that the person you call can be using a regular phone and phone line or a mobile phone. Using the softphone software you'll talk using a Mac-compatible headset or simply the speakers and microphone that your Mac makes available to you. (See Chapter 3, "Video and Audio," **p. 31** for some headset options.)

The other approach to VoIP is using a phone that literally plugs into your broadband connection or to your network. You can do that using a special VoIP telephone, but more often you'll probably opt for a VoIP telephone adapter that enables you to use a standard telephone for the calls. Such adapters are available from many of the VoIP companies or you can get them on their own. Or you can use a special voice router like the LinkSys router discussed at the beginning of this chapter.

In either case, you'll need a VoIP provider. Some calls will be free, if you're calling other computers or VoIP phones using VoIP standards. (SIP, for *session initiation protocol*, is an emerging standard for calling between computers.) Other calls, to regular land-line and mobile phones, should be much cheaper than regular long distance. Mac-friendly softphone-compatible companies include Vonage (www.vonage.com) and Terracall (www.terracall.com), but most any VoIP provider that offers a telephone adapter will work with your Mac on the same broadband connection or network.

ZyXEL Prestige 2000W

If you've got a WiFi (AirPort) network in your home, then you might want to consider a WiFi VoIP phone such as this model, which works over your wireless Internet connection to create a VoIP phone connection. If you're calling someone else's computer (who also has a VoIP solution), then you can simply use the phone for a free call; if you want to call someone who has a land-line or mobile phone, then you'll need a PC-to-Phone carrier such as Vonage or Net2Phone (www.net2phone.com). You then configure the phone to communicate with that service provider (which can actually be a little geeky, but doable). When that's done, you've got a phone that can use an AirPort router or other WiFi network to make a long-distance call using your cheap VoIP phone service.

But that's not all. Because you don't have to make calls only from your own WiFi network—you can use *any* WiFi network. That means you can take the phone with you, if you like, and use it anywhere that you can get a WiFi hotspot. That means you can conceivably take your phone to other offices, or move it between the office and home or stop into your local coffee shop to make VoIP calls. How cool is that?

The phone features a small recharger cradle and, according to the company, you can get about a day's worth of stand-by time and up to four hours of talk time from the phone. As part of the cost you'll need a VoIP provider and you'll want to make sure the phone is compatible with that provider; the phone's instructions walk you through the setup, which includes entering a number of IP addresses and codes to get the phone up and running with your VoIP provider.

Model: Prestige 2000W
Manufacturer: ZyXEL (www.zyxel.com)
Price: $299

HandyTone 286 Adapter

This adapter can be used with any wired broadband connection to enable you to use a regular telephone for VoIP connections. Plug in the ethernet connection to the adapter's ethernet port (either from your broadband modem or from an ethernet router that offers Internet access) and plug in your phone to the phone line port. You then configure the adapter using a web browser or by dialing tones on the phone. If you sign up for service with a VoIP provider you may receive such an adapter as part of the deal; if you'd like a portable adapter or if you simply want the freedom to experiment with different services, then the HandyTone is an interesting option.

Model: HandyTone 286 Adapter
Manufacturer: Grandstream
Price: $79.99

X-Pro Softphone

If you're content to make calls from your Mac—using the built-in speaker and mic, a headset or a compatible USB telephone handset—then you might opt for a softphone to go along with your VoIP service. X-Pro appears to be the most popular Mac-compatible model, as it works with services such as Vonage and TerraCall. X-Pro is an upgrade to X-Lite, which you can download for free from some service providers. X-Pro includes features such as multiple lines, hold and transfer, conferencing, voicemail integration, and other features. Just looking at it starts to make you wonder if the future of managing your calls—particularly your business or home office calls—really might be on your Mac, over the Internet.

Model: X-Pro Softphone
Manufacturer: Xten (www.xten.com)
Price: $50 (discounts for bulk purchase of two or more licenses)

Digital Video and Accessories

6

DV Camcorders

Digital video camcorders are camcorders that use a *charged coupled device* (CCD) to record to tape as a digital, computer-compatible stream of data instead of an analog signal (such as Beta or VHS). The result is that the recording can be immediately fed into a computer for editing by computer software, a step that used to require costly "digitizing" hardware. Because the digitizing process takes place within the camcorder itself, it makes it easier to work with the recording on your computer.

Likewise, a digital recording isn't prone to the same "generational" loss that an analog recording has. When you record from one VHS tape to another, you'll notice that the second recording is worse than the first, due to limitations in cables, VHS decks, tape quality, and so on. Some of the signal's quality is simply "lost."

With a digital recording, however, second generation copies can be made without a loss in quality, as they, in effect, can work like copying any other computer files.

Digital video camcorders are of higher quality than VHS or even certain Beta formats, which have been the professional video standard for years. And the direct and inexpensive access that digital video enthusiasts have to editing software—such as Apple's iMovie and Final Cut products—has fueled a revolution in access to high-quality equipment for editing video projects.

If you've got an interest, you should look into a digital video camcorder and some of the ancillary software and other tools. We'll cover those in this chapter.

Sony DSR-PD170

Leo's Pick

This pick is aimed at prosumers and professionals (or wannabe professionals) who are looking to invest in a camera that will age well for the next few years. The Sony DSR-PD170 is a relatively affordable camcorder that competes toe-to toe with the big guys on image quality, features, and flexibility. But it ain't cheap; if you're looking for a hobbyist's digicam, check out some of the entries on the next few pages.

The PD170 is a great camcorder if you're going to take your digital video work very seriously. It offers a three-CCD approach; one CCD is responsible for gathering the red tones, one for the greens, and one for the blues. Together, that makes up and RGB (red, green, blue) color space that can be used to accurately reflect the colors in the images you capture with your camcorder. Less expensive camcorders use one higher-resolution CCD, which can still offer a great picture, but is a bit compromised overall.

The PD170P happens to be switchable between DV and DVCAM support; DV format (often called "miniDV") is the generally accepted norm for consumer or prosumer cameras, although Digital8 is another competing option from Sony. DVCAM is Sony's professional format, offering much the same advantages as DV, but with slightly more sophisticated technology in the tapes themselves. The DVCAM compatibility can be nice for playing back tapes on professional Sony equipment.

This camcorder offers two other features that excite DV enthusiasts. First, it can shoot in 16:9 format, which is the aspect ratio of typical 35mm films. It isn't always wise to shoot in 16:9, partly because you'll need software that can handle it and that software tends to be the more expensive version of Final Cut Pro and others. (iMovie, for instance, can't edit footage that was captured in 16:9 aspect ratio.)

The second feature is the built-in XLR inputs for professional microphones that accompany the PD170P's built-in boom microphone. This gives you multiple, easy options for adding professional microphones to your setup, while still offering a great deal of portability.

> **Model:** PD170P
> **Manufacturer:** Sony (www.sony.com)
> **Price:** $1,999

Canon Optura Xi

Only slightly lower in the food chain is the Canon Optura Xi, which takes an approach that's popular in high-end consumer camcorders—it also works as a still digital camera. With a single two-megapixel CCD, the Optura Xi can not only take moving images, but snapshots, as well, which can be stored on a removable SD card. And, while it's two devices in one, it's still a very good camcorder, offering an 11x optical zoom and optical image stabilization, both of which are important features. (Stabilization helps to make a handheld video image look less shaky.) There are also *optical* technologies on the Optura Xi, which allows it to standout against cheaper camcorders that use less-effective *digital* zoom and, particularly, digital stabilization. It has also got a nice, large 3.5-inch LCD display that's handy for composing scenes and for reviewing what you've already captured.

Model: Optura Xi
Manufacturer: Canon
(www.canon.com)
Price: $1,199

Canon XL2

Before we move on too quickly from prosumer camcorders, another one deserves a mention. The Canon XL2 is the latest in a series of what are arguably the most popular camcorders for high-end DV shooting—the XL1 and XL1s. The XL2 has two serious advantages over most competitors; you can change the lenses (which is important to professional videographers) and it looks incredibly cool. It's also more expensive than the PD170P, as well as its own little brother, the Canon GL2 ($2,299), both of which are also very good camcorders. Yes, it offers advanced features, a great sound-gathering system and the all-important three-CCD image quality. But the GL2 is the ultimate for shooting on location when you need to *look like* there's a professional shoot going on.

Model: XL2
Manufacturer: Canon
(www.canon.com)
Price: $3,999

JVC GR-D230

Want to go the ultra-compact route? MiniDV enables camcorders to get pretty small; the JVC GR-D230 model is only 3.7 inches tall by 4.4 inches deep—palm sized—and it's nearly dwarfed by its swing-out 2.5-inch color LCD. But it has got a 1.33-megapixel CCD, good enough for digital images for the Web and small prints, and it's packed with features. The lens offers 10x of optical zoom and 500x digital zoom, it has digital picture stabilization and it can support a multimedia card for still images and a USB 2.0 connection for transferring them to your Mac. (It's also FireWire compatible for video transfer, of course.)

Model: GR-D230
Manufacturer: JVC (www.jvc.com)
Price: $799

Sony DCR-PC330

Another camcorder that makes digital photography one of its specialties is the DCR-PC330, which sports a 3-megapixel CCD capable of pretty good snapshots. It's also an upright, palm-fitted camcorder that's nice for vacation footage or small business video, such as a real-estate walkthrough. Features include 10x optical zoom, a 2.5-inch color LCD, and the Sony NightShot Infrared system for getting video in very low-light situations. It even has a 16:9 shooting mode for the adventurous videographer.

Model: DCR-PC300
Manufacturer: Sony (www.sony.com)
Price: $1,399

Samsung SC-D103

Cheaper, you say? This one shoots MiniDV, offers an 18x optical zoom, and has digital stabilization. It has got a FireWire port, a place where you put the tapes, and a start/stop button. It's also got a low-light shooting mode and the capability to take sub-megapixel photos that would work for the Web. But the total outlay is pretty low, and it's a great way to get yourself (or perhaps a youngster interested in video editing) started in the DV game.

> **Model:** SC-D103
> **Manufacturer:** Samsung
> (www.samsung.com)
> **Price:** $349

Canon ZR Series

How about a few camcorders that are a little more inexpensive? The ZR series offers basic camcorders that have good lenses, large optical zooms (18x or better), stabilization features, and the capability to take still images, albeit at just one-megapixel resolution. These camcorders have enhanced night mode, various exposure options, and a very nice feature for an inexpensive camcorder—an analog line-in that enables you to use the camcorder to record directly from an analog source, such as a VCR. In other words, you'd have nothing else to purchase in order to digitize any old VHS footage you might have, along with taking new shots with your ZR.

> **Model:** ZR Series
> **Manufacturer:** Canon
> (www.canon.com)
> **Price:** $399 (ZR80), $499
> (ZR85—1-megapixel photo mode),
> $599 (ZR90—Wide Angle attachment)

Choosing Editing Software

Apple has done a pretty good job of cornering the market on video editing software for Mac users. iMovie is available for free on any new Mac and is one component of the inexpensive iLife bundle; iDVD is also part of that bundle, making it easy to turn movies into DVDs if your Mac has a SuperDrive installed.

Apple has also become well-known and well thought of in the digital video community for its Final Cut Pro, which is capable of some very high-level editing and even special effects tasks. The software, which retails for about $1,000, can be used to edit 16:9 format video (for "filmic dimensions") and it can be used to incorporate a number of different video formats into a single presentation. It's really designed for the video professional, complete with its ties to Apple's SoundTrack audio software and its Shake digital effects package. In other words, you can spend a lot of money on Apple's video editing suite of software.

For the mid-range of editing, Apple's got yet another option—Final Cut Express, which offers prosumer customers a good platform editing DV footage into productions. It's great software for a small-budget independent film, a documentary, or perhaps for some homemade journalism; as long as you're working in standard 4:3 format DV, it's a pretty handy piece of software.

All these offerings have done one interesting thing to the market—scared off some competitors. Adobe used to make Adobe Premiere for Macintosh, but announced that development of the product would cease—it was about a $600 package that came down between Final Cut Express and Final Cut Pro in terms of features. Adobe continues to make Adobe After Effects for Mac—a highly regarded special effects application—but Apple's competition with Shake may change that at some point.

Meanwhile, the only other serious option for Mac is Avid's line of extremely high-end editors, which tend to require a sincere outlay of cash coupled with some additional hardware. All except, that is, for Avid's DV Free product, which is a cross-platform answer to iMovie. It's actually a nice little editor that lets you do pretty much everything you can in iMovie, plus projects can be shared across platforms. Check it out at http://www.avid.com/ on the Web.

Avid's DV Free is an interesting little editor made by someone other than our favorite company, Apple.

Digital Camcorder Accessories

Let's say you want to do a little more than vacation video—you want to be able to take video images that look good enough to put on TV, even if it is just your local public access channel. Or, you'd like to do some work that might one day get your name in lights at a regional film festival, and perhaps take you even further than that down the path of glory to Hollywood or Cannes. Fair enough.

It used to be that you'd need a lot of money to do these things; these days a little money helps, but a lot isn't quite necessary. Aside from your digital video camcorder, though, you will need some important accessories; namely, you're going to need to get some lighting and sound equipment. And the good stuff will cost you a little, although we'll keep the prices down.

The most important equipment you need for a good video shoot is—a good microphone. Did you think we were going to say a good camera? Not as important. Case in point: Blair Witch project. The audio was much more important than the video; as long as people can hear what's being said in your presentation, they'll put up with reasonably bad video. If the audio is garbled, they'll lose interest fast. It's striking, but true.

The other thing you'll need is lighting, particularly when you're ready to take things to a more professional level. With a nice portable lighting kit you aren't limited by the lights in the room or the angle of the moon; you can shoot in different conditions and on your own schedule; to a certain degree. If you're doing documentary or fiction films that you intend to take on the road, you'll definitely want some lights. We'll look at sound, lights, and some other fun stuff in this section.

Beachtek DXA-2
Audio Adapter

Leo's Pick

If your camcorder doesn't have built-in XLR inputs—and only some of the highest-end camcorders do—then you may want to add them yourself using an adapter from Beachtek. The company makes these for a variety of camcorder models; you'll want to check the web site to see whether your camcorder is supported. Adapters have to be designed specifically to fit a particular model (or range of models) so that they can be on-camera and yet out of the way.

Having the Beachtek on-camera adapter is nice, because it gives you the flexibility to work with high-end microphones—and, often, more than one of them—while you are on the move with your camcorder. (Or, even if you're not actually moving, while you're *mobile* and traveling easily with your setup.)

Beachtek offers a number of different models, ranging from lower-priced adapters designed for extremely compact "palm-sized" camcorders to high-end models that include phantom power (to power microphones without requiring batteries in the mics). They even offer a model that has preamps to boost the gain and limiters. This cuts down on "hot" microphones to get richer, more professional sound.

Most of the Beachtek adapters connect to the audio-in port on the side of the camcorder and then screw into the tripod mount, giving you a place to plug in two or four professional microphones or other sound gathering equipment.

Model: Audio Adapters
Manufacturer: Beachtek (www.beachtek.com)
Price: $199–$399

Audio-Technica Pro 88W Series

If you'd like more mobility for your subjects (and you'd like to do it on the cheap) you can get a VHF wireless system for microphones. This particular set has a receiver that you can mount to your camcorder and a transmitter that includes a lavalier microphone and a bodypack that you can strap to your subject's waist. Now you're mobile with the audio, able to hear the subject as they move around and interact with the outside world. This is great for instructional video, documentaries, and so on.

Model: Pro 88W Series
Manufacturer: Audio-Technica (www.audiotechnica.com)
Price: $199

Sony ECM-88

This wired lavalier mic ("lav") is great for interviews or any situation where your talent or subject will be standing relatively still. While a wireless microphone can be handy, it can also be much more expensive to get one that won't cut out, whereas a wired lav can be handy, a little less expensive, and a great way to get some good audio when you need someone's speaking voice to be on a good level. (Don't forget a good set of closed-ear headphones for listening to the quality of your audio while you're shooting.) This microphone has an XLR three-pronged connection, so you'll need a camcorder that supports it or a Beachtek adapter.

Model: ECM-88
Manufacturer: Sony (www.sony.com)
Price: $440 (list)

Audio-Technica AT-897
Shotgun Mic

One of the rules for good sound-gathering is to get your microphone away from your camera and closer to the action. Sometimes that isn't possible, making the next best solution a good shotgun microphone. (Actually, if you have an assistant, putting the shotgun microphone on a boom and allowing the assistant to point it at your subjects is a great idea, too.) With a good camera mount, the AT-897 can be aimed at a subject, allowing you to hear their speech or other sounds while rejecting sounds to the sides or rear of the microphone.

Model: AT-897
Manufacturer: Audio-Technica
(www.audiotechnica.com)
Price: $369

Sony UWP-C1

For higher-end wireless sound gathering, we turn back to Sony—this bundle includes an on-camera UHF receiver that includes 188 selectable frequencies and a camera show mount (so that it can connect to the camera's hot shoe, where you'd often put a flash) and a bodypack transmitter with a belt clip that is attached to a Sony omnidirectional lavalier microphone.

Model: UWP-C1
Manufacturer: Sony (www.sony.com)
Price: $699

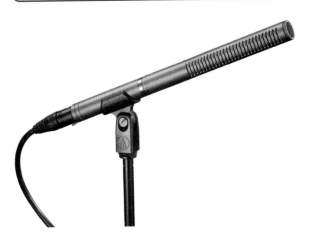

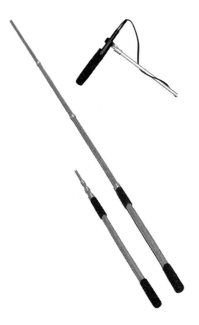

Glidecam 2000 Pro

If you've ever seen a major Hollywood production you know that it's only the rare occasion that the camera is actually held by a person; most of the time, it's dollied, craned, tripoded, and so on. Some sort of expensive machinery is used to keep the camera both steady and moving. With camcorders, you don't have that luxury, but there are devices that help you steady shots as you move, like the Glidecam. With a weighted base and a special carrying handle, the device is one of the least expensive that enables you to move, walk, and pan, while keeping a remarkably steady and smooth look to the video. These counter-balanced devices are fun gadgets to help you improve the look of your videography.

> **Model:** Glidecam 2000 Pro
> **Manufacturer:** Glidecam Industries, Inc. (www.glidecam.com)
> **Price:** $369

Boom Pole

Here's a great example of an extendable boom pole that you can use for connecting a directional microphone (such as a shotgun microphone) and then placing it "in the action" closer to your subjects. With a boom pole, such as this, you can place the microphone up to nine feet away from you, hold it above the camera's visual range and pick up great sound, even as the subjects move around, walk, or confront one another in a penultimate death grip.

> **Model:** Boom Pole with Universal Mounting kit
> **Manufacturer:** K-Tek (www.studio1productions.com)
> **Price:** $119.95

ikelite DV Video Housings

This gadget would make Bond proud. (Particularly the Sean Connery incarnation, who was always spending tons of time underwater.) This housing enables you to take your DV camcorder underwater with you; if you're a certified diver, you're sure to get deep enough to get interesting shots, but even a standard snorkel-strapped ocean jock can get some great shots of coral and fish, assuming you've got the cash for something like this. The bigger the camcorder, the pricier the housing.

Model: DV Video Housings
Manufacturer: ikelite
(www.ikelite.com)
Price: $679.95 (Canon ZR series) to $1,149 (Sony TRV950 and PD series)

S-800 Shoulder Rest

Here's another pro trick—the shoulder rest. If you'd like to be able to use your camcorder to capture shots as you're walking or moving around gathering the news or following your subjects, then the S-800 is a great, inexpensive addition. Simply mount your camcorder to the tripod-like mount, then position the shoulder rest and handle in a comfortable manner; now you can point and walk—not with your hand on the camcorder (which can tend to make noise and cause quick motions)—but with the camcorder rested on your shoulder and pointed at the action.

Model: S-800 Super Pro Shoulder Rest
Manufacturer: Video Innovators
(www.videoinnovators.com)
Price: $106.95

Manfrotto LANC Remote Control

Activating controls on the side of your digi-cam—particularly when it's on a tripod—can cause unwanted shakes and noise. The solution for professional-level stability is a remote control. Bogen Imaging offers special remote controls designed to integrate with a tripod. (In fact, they integrate particularly well with Bogen's tripods!) Many of these models attach to the tilt/pan handle of the tripod, giving you control over focus, zoom, and other choices you might want to make while you're shooting video. These are aimed at prosumer and professional camcorders (which must support LANC connections), with models of the remote for Canon and Sony camcorders.

Model: Manfrotto LANC 522 Remote Control
Manufacturer: Bogen Imaging (www.bogenimaging.us)
Price: $299

Lowel Tota-light Kit

Lowel makes tons of different portable lights and portable light kits, but a favorite is the inexpensive Tota-Light kit. It features two lights—a key light and a fill light—along with umbrellas to disperse the light, light stands to mount and hold the lights at the correct angles, and gels to change the "temperature" (relative warmth and coolness of the colors) of the light. Many of the kits are relatively inexpensive, lightweight, and include its own case for transport.

Model: Tota-light ToGo 95 Kit
Manufacturer: Lowel (www.lowel.com)
Price: $635

Analog to Digital Converters

Okay, so what's the plan for all those old VHS or Super8 tapes that you took of the kids (or pets or grandkids or Mickey)? You'll need to transfer them into digital format if you want to edit them on your Mac—which is pretty much the only chance you'll ever have that *anyone* will feign interest in them. You've at least got to cut out some of the zooms and pans and put a little music in there.

One trick is to use your digital camcorder. If the camcorder has an analog input, then it'll support a connection from your VCR (or your older camcorder) so that the old videos can be transferred from analog tape to DV tape. Then you can import the newly recorded images into your Mac just as if you'd originally shot them using the DV camcorder.

If you don't have a camcorder with analog inputs or if you'd prefer not to use your camcorder for that much video transfer (the mechanisms will wear down after time, which is why many professionals don't like to use their cameras for playback and recording duties), then you can turn to an analog-to-digital converter. These devices generally enable you to plug in your analog devices to them, digitize the signal in the process, and send it through a FireWire connection to your Mac. That signal can then be stored as a file or read directly into programs such as iMovie or Final Cut.

These devices also work in the other direction—you can output digital video to an analog destination, including a VCR or a television. They're a handy add-on to a digital editing suite that isn't totally digital, yet, or one that bypasses your camcorder to save its gears and record heads exclusively for shooting new footage.

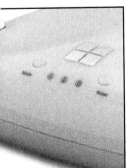

Formac Studio TVR

Leo's Pick

There's a slight premium price for the Formac Studio TVR, but it's highly rated and does a good job of the analog-to-digital-to-analog conversion. It looks a little like a curvy external hard disk, complete with small LEDs that tell you what connections are active and in what direction the data is flowing. With the device connected to your Mac it'll pop up immediately in programs like iMovie; set your VCR to play through it and the footage is digitized and imported into the editing application.

In fact, it's far more than a simple analog-to-digital encoder (assuming such a thing is "simple"). The Formac Studio is also a nice all-in-one "TVR" (Television Video Recorder) product that enables you to tune in and record live TV feeds to your Mac. Like TiVo and similar devices, the Formac Studio TVR enables you to record programs by selecting them on your programming guide. Video plays back in a window or, if you're close to your Mac, you can use the Studio TVR's outputs to connect to a TV monitor and pause live TV or watch recorded shows.

Another thing that's fun about the Formac software is that it's well integrated with your Mac. Because the shows are recorded right on your Mac, the Studio software can work with iMovie to enable you to not only manage and playback the recorded television video, but to even edit it or pull still images. You can take your favorite shows or TV movies and edit out the commercials or edit just the sound bites for playback at parties or with friends. You can also perform some basic edits from within the Studio software.

Then, together with a SuperDrive or Formac's external DVD-R, you can record those recorded shows to DVD for playback on a standard player. You can also export to QuickTime so that you can play back shows on your Mac or—if you compress and crop them enough you can post them to the Web or send them through email. In other words, you've got a flexible video editing solution for a variety of tasks, whether it's analog video or analog television signals.

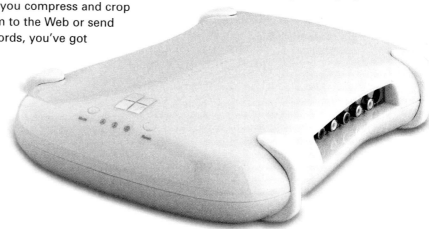

Model: Studio TVR
Manufacturer: Formac
(www.formac.com)
Price: $299

Miglia Director's Cut Take 2

The Director's Cut is similar to the other devices discussed here except that it offers a neat little bonus—it can output to two analog devices at once. While most of the time you think of the analog-to-digital connection going toward the *digital* (so that you can import, say, VHS recordings and edit them), the truth is that you'll often use the device to output video back to a VCR or TV. Why not both? With dual outputs you can send the analog signal to both a VCR and a monitor, so that you can see what you're recording; you could even send to two VCRs at once to make multiple copies. The Director's Cut is also easy to use with iMovie or Final Cut—it appears as a DV camcorder in your editing software, making the import process painless.

> **Model:** Director's Cut Take 2
> **Manufacturer:** Miglia
> (www.miglia.com)
> **Price:** $299

Canopus ADVC-110 Converter

In the same price ballpark, but a bit more utilitarian is the Canopus DV Converter, which offers the same essential function—you can plug analog stuff into it and turn that signal into a digital signal fed through FireWire. The ADVC-110 has an upright appearance and looks a little more like AV equipment of some kind; it's also a lightweight and can be frustrating if you're constantly plugging devices into and out of the box. Still, it serves the purpose of helping you get that older footage into your Mac for editing and sprucing up.

> **Model:** ADVC-110 Converter
> **Manufacturer:** Canopus
> (www.canopus.com)
> **Price:** $319

Digital Cameras and Accessories

7

Prosumer Digital Cameras

Certainly there are purists among us who shoot photos on 35mm film using our favorite camera "backs" and lenses. For most of us, though, the 35mm world is a fleeting memory of expensive chemically developed photos that came slicked together in a bulging envelope—only to reveal more than a few photos that we wouldn't have wanted to pay for.

With digital, you've got two distinct advantages. First, you don't have to develop a photo before you see it. In most cases the images you take appear on a small LCD screen; with the press of a button, you can delete a photo that doesn't look good. Second, you've got no film to worry about.

A digital camera works by bouncing light off one or more *CCDs*, or charged-coupled devices, which are capable of registering the different color levels and brightness of an image and turning that information into digital data—1s and 0s. In a sense, a digital camera is like a compact digital scanner; instead of scanning documents, you use a camera lens to "scan" the landscape, people, or objects in front of you.

The fact that digital cameras capture images to a file is handy; it means you can immediately use that file in computer programs for a variety of purposes. But to get that image, the camera takes some shortcuts. Most notably, the camera's CCD, instead of scanning a perfect reproduction of what it sees through the lens, instead breaks that image up into tiny dots, called *pixels* or picture elements. For the best reproduction, digital cameras generally use many millions of pixels. Exactly how many pixels a camera uses can be one way to judge the quality of images it will produce, so cameras are often advertised according to their *megapixel* rating, which means the number of millions of pixels that are used to store computer images. The more megapixels a camera can boast, the better the image quality is—theoretically. Today's prosumer and professional digital cameras shoot at 5-megapixel or better; 8-megapixels isn't uncommon and 12-megapixel cameras are standard for serious professionals. 2-, 3-, and 4-megapixel cameras are perfectly serviceable for us regular snapshotistas.

For the sake of comparison, even a 1-megapixel camera works fine for images you want to put on a web page or send through email, because a computer screen has relatively low resolution needs. A 2-megapixel camera can create images that would print well at about 3'' by 5''; 3-megapixels is good for a professional-quality 5'' by 7'' or so. We wouldn't use less than a 4-megapixel for decent journalistic work and a 5-megapixel or better camera is necessary for large tabloid-sized images.

Of course, not all digital cameras are made alike. we like to think in terms of three different criteria: price, resolution, and lens selection. And bigger and more expensive isn't always better, depending on your needs.

Strictly consumer-oriented cameras are under $500, with many of them *well* under that mark. These are generally cameras under 5 megapixels, although those are creeping under this mark, too. These cameras tend to be point and shoot—some have a nice zoom feature, but few have full manual settings or the ability to add much in the way of external lens or battery packs. You can get a great camera in this price range, though, and it'll work for a variety of applications—anything from snaps for your web site to images for newsletters, business documents, or desktop publishing. We'll look more closely at these in the next section.

Prosumer cameras—higher-end cameras aimed at hobbyists and people who need quality that approaches professional levels—have really grown as a category. The group features some nice 5-to-8 megapixel cameras that also tend to be loaded down with features such as zoom lenses, manual overrides, and options like the capability to record small bursts of video or audio. These cameras are generally under $1,000; often $500–$750.

Finally, the professional-level brings us *SLR cameras*, such as the ground-breaking Canon Digital Rebel, which actually enable you to look through the lens and, in a few cases, work with interchangeable lenses as would with high-quality 35mm cameras. And the Rebel is actually the bottom of a barrel of high-quality and increasingly expensive digital cameras and camera backs that can accept high-end zoom, wide angle, and specialty lenses. For most of us, the cameras quickly get too expensive to contemplate unless our careers depend on them; at the less-expensive end, though, they're a tempting upgrade to cameras that feel "real," particularly if you're used to the feel and balance of a good 35mm camera.

PROSUMER DIGITAL CAMERAS

Nikon D70

Leo's Pick

Nikon and Canon may trade honors for the best high-end prosumer SLR for a number of years running. The Canon Digital Rebel (EOS-300D) broke the ground and stunned the industry with an interchangeable-lens SLR for under $999 in early 2004; Nikon countered with the slightly more expensive but considerably more capable 6-megapixel D70.

The D70 is a great performer, leaving you with a satisfied feeling as a photographer. In many cases, what makes a good 35mm feel like a high-end camera is its ability to shoot bursts of images so that you can get expressions and life out of your subjects; the D70 is both quick on the trigger and capable of shooting multiple frames quickly (12 frames at 3 frames per second). It offers completely automatic modes, manual modes, and just about everything in between. The automatic modes are flexible for amateur photographers.

The D70 also is a well-designed camera, offering a slick look and feel that's a little smaller than 35mm cameras that you're used to, but it looks like it's wearing a slick business suit—it's a good-looking camera that will get you some respect from the press corps if you're ever pressing up against the speaker's podium trying to get a shot.

As you'd expect from this level of camera, the D70 accepts an external flash via its hot shoe and offers compatibility with a variety of Nikon flashes, as well as support for studio lighting and remote flashes. One complaint, however, is the lack of an accessory battery grip for the D70, an option which is available for the Nikon D100, the D70's older (and slightly pricier) brother. (Among professional photographers we know, there's a slight bias toward the D100 over the D70; they like the D70's pricing, but aren't quite thrilled with the idea that they have to get by without a battery grip and some other features.)

The Nikon D70 can be purchased without a lens at all if you have your own Nikon-compatible lenses; the D70 kit offers a decent 18–70mm lens as a standard part of its bundle (when purchased with a lens) that nudges out the Canon's bundled 18-55mm lens. Of course, the point is to change the lens out as desired, so if you happen to be partial to Canon or Nikon lenses, you might end up making your decision that way.

Model: D70 6-megapixel SLR camera
Manufacturer: Nikon (www.nikon.com)
Price: $999 ($1,299 kit w/lens)
Storage Media: CompactFlash, Microdrive

Canon Digital Rebel

Let it be known to all that the Digital Rebel is no slouch; some of us swear by it. The Digital Rebel was the first digital SLR under $999. Canon crippled a feature or two to keep it from cannibalizing sales of its Canon EOS 10D model, which is a more expensive pro version, but it still holds its own. For less than a grand, it comes with a special lightweight lens, a carrying strap, and a handsome silver case.

The truth is that the Digital Rebel has great automatic modes, the freedom to "go manual," support for Canon's popular EF lenses, some Canon Speedlite EX flashes, and a special external battery grip to give it the look and feel of a serious pro camera. It supports CompactFlash Type II and high-capacity Microdrive memory cards, making it utterly road-worthy for the serious amateur or professional photographer on a budget.

Model: Digital Rebel (EOS 300D)
Manufacturer: Canon
(www.canon.com)
Price: $899 ($999 kit w/lens)
Storage Media: CompactFlash,
Microdrive

Sony DSC-F828

No, it doesn't offer an interchangeable lens, but this high-end, 8-megapixel digital camera offers a wonderful Carl Zeiss fixed lens with 7x optical zoom, making it the equivalent of a professional lens that covers 28mm to 200mm focal lengths. The camera itself is sturdy, hardy, and takes a nice picture. It also offers manual ring controls that can switch between focus and zoom.

The DSC-F828 offers one drawback—the first few months' worth of cameras off the assembly line included photo conversion software for the PC only. Usually that won't be a problem, as you can use iPhoto or Image Capture to get images off the camera (or a CompactFlash or Memory Stick adapter to make things even quicker). But the Sony software is required for editing and converting images in the Sony "raw" image format, which offers the highest quality. As a Mac user, you'll need to get the software from Sony or you'll be forced to stick to shooting in JPEG and TIFF formats.

Model: DSC-F828
Manufacturer: Sony (www.sony.com)
Price: $999
Storage Media: Memory Stick,
CompactFlash

Nikon Coolpix 8800

The Coolpix is the current top-of-the-line for a very capable series of digital cameras that had added up to the 8-megapixel capabilities of the 8800. This model is a compact, high-quality camera capable of images you could use for professional magazine production, yet it also offers point-and-shoot simplicity; it's all a matter of the settings. The Coolpix 8800 is particularly adept at enabling a knowledgeable photographer to dig into exposure settings, which gives you the opportunity to get into the arcane world of aperture and shutter speed settings to achieve more professional results from the camera. It's a high-tech camera, a quick camera (some digital cameras can take a while from power on to ready mode; the 8800 takes about four seconds), and it offers some burst mode settings to help you capture action shots.

As with any fixed-lens digital camera, you're limited by the optics connected to your camera's body; for both sides of this equation, the 8800 is a standout. The Nikkor lens offers 10x zoom as well as a wide-angle settings, giving it the equivalent of a 35mm–350mm range. (Such a lens would cost a few extra hundred dollars for the interchangeable lens cameras discussed at the top of this section.) The flash is a little underpowered, but the Coolpix accepts an external flash. It doesn't take advantage of every feature of Nikon's pro-level flashes, however, making the D70 more attractive if you're planning some add-ons.

Other cameras that are still worth looking at are the Coolpix 5700—similar in overall design, but it only shoots 5-megapixel images and has a couple fewer tweaks than the Coolpix 5000, which is also a capable camera, but has more of an overall point-and-shoot design. Both the 5700 and 5000 are rather heavily discounted in the wake of the 8800's appearance.

Model: Nikon Coolpix 8800
Manufacturer: Nikon
(www.nikonusa.com)
Price: $999.95
Storage Media: CompactFlash, Microdrive

Minolta-Konica Dimage A2

The Dimage series of digital cameras is another one that gets good marks among prosumer users; the Dimage A2 is the more recent 8-megapixel model that includes a 7x wide-to-zoom lens (28mm—200mm) that pleases some photographers because it uses a manual ring instead of buttons to move through the zoom levels. And it's something of a bulky little monster, offering support for battery grip attachments and external flashes. It's also well known for its digital stability features; if you tend to get shaky pictures, this might be the camera for you.

And if the price is a bit stiff, you'll still find the Dimage A1 on the market at a decent little discount or available on the used market at a good price. The A1 is similar in overall features—there have been some solid tweaks, but the 5 versus 8 megapixels is the biggest difference.

Model: Minolta-Konica Dimage A2
Manufacturer: Fuji Photo Film (www.fujifilm.com)
Price: $1,099
Storage Media: CompactFlash, Microdrive

Fuji FinePix S7000

The Fuji FinePix S7000 offers a little less resolution than the other digital cameras discussed here—six megapixels—although that puts it in the same class as the Nikon and Canon digital SLRs that we recommend.

Advantages are a manual ring for zoom, good point-and-shoot features, and a 6x lens that gets good reviews. Detractors note that the images are a bit *noisy*—unexpectedly speckled or blocky—because there isn't a raw mode for storing images; at 6-megapixels, you must save in JPEG mode. The result, however, is a relatively small computer image file. (The FinePix S7000 also has a 12-megapixel *interpolated* mode.)

This is a feature-rich camera that does a good job for the price, which is lower on the street (or eBay) than many of its close competitors. The optics are great as are the heft and ergonomics—it's a great compromise camera.

Model: FinePix S7000
Manufacturer: Fuji Photo Film (www.fujifilm.com)
Price: $799
Storage Media: xD-Picture Card, Microdrive

Consumer Digital Cameras

The flip side of the digital camera market are cameras that are getting lower and lower in price while offering plenty of features and enough resolution for most consumer users. Unless you're looking for a camera that's attached to a PDA or smartphone (or one that looks like a pocket lighter) then you'll want to focus on 3-megapixel or better cameras. You can still find them for surprisingly affordable prices, and they can give you images good enough for printing on special photo paper or using for desktop layouts. (If your *only* goal is photos for the Web or email, then even a one-megapixel camera will work; you'll want to get one with decent optics and features.)

The number of images you can store on your camera depends on the size of the storage media used. While you're shopping for digital cameras, it's worth it to factor in the amount of storage, if any, you're getting with the camera. If you end up needing to immediately buy a larger storage card, you may be paying more for that camera than you realize. You'll also want to think about the *type* of media the camera uses—see the next gadget section for a thorough discussion.

For consumer cameras the considerations are still lens quality, zoom and features such as flash and an accessory shoe. On zoom, particularly, you'll want to be sure you're getting *optical* zoom—the type that changes the focal length of the lens—and not just digital zoom, which blows up a portion of the digital image to simulate zoom. We've seen very few digital zoom features on cameras that were worth using.

The other consideration is really how the camera feels in your hand and how useful and understandable its controls and menus are. Some consumer cameras can be downright confusing in the layers of choices and options; others can be a touch too simple. (Although we'd lean toward the former if given a choice.)

Canon Powershot s410/s500

It's tough to pick just one camera to top this category because we've got a lot of cameras to consider and the idea isn't simply to pick the priciest one. So, we chose two. Granted, they're very similar. The Powershot s410/s500, however, offer a good balance between features, build quality, price, and resolution. The s410 is a 4-megapixel camera with good, fast electronics and a decent lens that features a 3x optical zoom (equivalent to 36–108mm). The s500 adds five-megapixel support.

These models are rather compact, yet the ergonomics and controls are good. It's a Canon, with a good reputation for being a workhorse that takes nice pictures. The all metal case is stylish and tough, with an automatic lens cover that pops closed when the camera is turned off and the lens retracts. It looks great in a shirt pocket or purse, and takes shots good enough for a newsletter, flyer, or a photo that will blow up nicely into an 8 by 11 or larger photograph to give to family. And small extras attest to the build quality, such as an all-metal tripod mount on the bottom of the camera.

These cameras don't offer much in the way of manual controls, with auto focus, auto exposure, and a variety of other items that work on their own. They're very solid performing point-and-shoot cameras. Both do offer exposure options—settings for low light, speed shots, and so on—and they have a flash that can operate in automatic, red-eye and similar modes.

Both cameras offer movie taking functions, they can record audio—either for movies or for short sound memos you can associate with a given photo—and they can shoot in continuous modes up to 2.5 frames per second.

Well designed, well constructed, and they take good photos at high resolution; sure, there's a slight pricing premium, but we think it's worth it.

Model: Canon Powershot s410/s500
Manufacturer: Canon, Inc.
(www.canon.com)
Price: $399/$499
Storage Media: CompactFlash

Olympus C-765 Ultra Zoom

The Olympus makes some great cameras with some annoying names. It can take a while to figure out what "Camedia" means (it's a little 90s-sounding, eh?) or to get a grip on their numbering scheme. But they offer a nice breadth of stylish pocket point-and-shoot cameras (the "Stylus" and "D-series" models) and some quality professional and prosumer models (the "E-series"). Our favorites come in the C-series models, particularly those with "Ultra Zoom"—10x optical zoom lenses that beat most anything you can get from a consumer camera.

We picked the C-765 because it's cheaper than the C-750 (go figure) and it's a compact model with ultra zoom—nice for a variety of tasks. The quality is great on this camera, but be aware that a camera with a long zoom can take fuzzy pictures if it's hand-held; you might look into a monopod or tripod if you're using the zoom lens a lot. And these models come with pretty low-capacity memory cards (xD format), so you'll want to factor in a pricey card if you're going to take lots of shots in one outing.

Model: C-765 Ultra Zoom
Manufacturer: Olympus
(www.olympusamerica.com)
Price: $449.99
Storage Media: xD-Picture Card

Kodak DX7440

Kodak also makes excellent consumer cameras and it's tough to pick a single model to recommend. So, in this case, we chose to go with a representative but slightly less expensive model; the DX7440 offers 4-megapixel resolution and 4x zoom at a recommended price of $349. (Kodak also offers the CX7430 at $249, with a little less zoom lens and fewer manual controls). The DX7440 offers a large LCD display (2.2-inch), a number of shooting modes for various light levels and a very quick auto-focus for a point-and-shoot.

Kodak's consumer cameras are geared around the $79 Kodak EasyShare dock add-on, which isn't mandatory but can be handy for charging the camera's battery and automatically connecting the camera to your Mac for easily transferring photos. There's a Mac version of the EasyShare software that can be used for a variety of editing and presentation tasks; the Kodak cameras also work with iPhoto and, in fact, include a plug-in that enables iPhoto to export photos to EasyShare.

Model: DX7440
Manufacturer: Kodak
(www.kodak.com)
Price: $349
Storage Media: Secure Digital/MMC Card

Konica-Minolta Dimage Xg

Need something in an ultra compact model? The Xg is only a 3-megapixel camera, but it's a great shirt-pocket or pocketbook camera that is sleek enough to be a conversation piece. (You might want to check this out in the store before buying—it's tiny.) You can picture yourself pulling out this camera and taking a snap while riding your scooter around a Mediterranean coastal resort or over a game of baccarat in a swanky hotel.

It comes in colors, has 3x optical zoom, offers quick startup and operation, and uses standard SD memory cards for storage. For such a small camera and lens, photo quality is very good. And the camera can even store digital movies in QuickTime mode and record audio. Note that it uses a proprietary rechargeable battery type that can be expensive to replace, but includes its own recharger. The bundled 16MB card is too small, but it includes Mac OS X software and, well, it's *just darling*.

Model: Dimage Xg
Manufacturer: Konica Minolta
(http://www.minoltausa.com)
Price: $299
Storage Media: Secure Digital (SD)

HP Photosmart 735

Yeah, it comes from a PC company, but this HP camera has a smart little touristy design, takes 3-megapixel snaps, and offers a 3x optical zoom. Picture quality is generally considered more than adequate and it has macro modes, a burst mode for action shots (7 shots in 11 seconds), a number of automatic exposure settings, and a USB 2.0 connection for higher-speed photo transfer. It pops right up in iPhoto with its images ready for manipulation, making it pretty painless for family fun.

Model: Photosmart 735
Manufacturer: HP (http://www.hp.com)
Price: $179
Storage Media: Secure Digital/MMC Card

Digital Flash Cards and Readers

Most digital cameras today offer some sort of removable storage option, most often in the form of a small "card" that stores the digital information. Often the camera comes with a card in a 16 or 32 megabyte format; cards can be had that hold one gigabyte or more of digital information. (This results in much more storage space than that, depending on the technology of the card.)

The type of digital storage you can buy to improve your camera's capability to store photos depends on the camera. Although some cameras support more than one type of storage, most choose one as their standard approach. Although the types of storage all tend to be variations on a theme—some sort of little card or chip on which the photos can be stored—the exact technologies and formats are important to keep track of so that you know you're getting the right card. Here's a quick look:

- **CompactFlash**—An older but extremely popular approach to photo storage. Cards come in two types—Type 1 and the thicker Type 2 cards (sometimes just called *microdrives*), which your camera must specifically support. You can get CompactFlash (CF) cards up to 1GB for more cameras; 2GB or larger cards require cameras that are compatible with them because they use the Fat32 format.

- **SmartMedia**—Also an older standard, it hasn't progressed in storage capacity the way that CF has, and is thus not terribly popular. Older cameras support it, so you'll still see cards around, but they top out at a capacity of 128MB.

- **Memory Stick**—Sony's proprietary standard also is more expensive and more limited than CF; so much so that some of Sony's top-end cameras now support CompactFlash along with Memory Stick. Memory Stick Pro is a newer standard that can get about the 128MB limitation of the original Memory Stick specification, but it only works in Sony's newer cameras.

   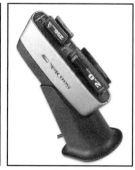 

- **Multimedia Card (MMC) and Secure Digital (SD)**—MMC and SD cards are similar in look-and-feel, and some cameras can support either type of card. They're smaller than the earlier standards, but are quickly approaching their capacities. Some cameras can support both; some support one or the other, so read your specs carefully. MMC/SD is a more expensive technology than CF right now, but it's lighter and smaller and increasingly popular in small cameras.

- **xD Picture Card**—These are also small cards with good capacities and prices, currently made for Olympus- and Fuji-brand cameras.

As with most computing standards, there are a few different options that duel for a while; the result is that one camera supports one standard and another camera a different one. Some support more than one, particularly at the prosumer level. So, read your camera's literature closely to see what it requires.

As for the brands of these cards, that's a tougher call. The well-known names include Kodak (www.kodak.com), Lexar Media (www.lexarmedia.com), SanDisk (www.sandisk.com), Kingston (www.Kingston.com), and many others; we don't really have favorites—it's more important to buy the memory from a shop reputable enough to take back a card if you get a faulty one.

Some flash media cards offer a speed rating, such as 8x, 12x, or even 40x. The number is a multiplier as compared to the original speed of a CD-ROM disc's data transfer, which was 150 kilobytes per second. A 40x flash media card is—theoretically—40 times faster than that. In a practical sense, the number is only important when you're dealing with very large images—those in cameras rated at 5-megapixels or more. With smaller images, the speed isn't as critical.

What is a little more interesting to shop for, however, is a digital media reader. A reader isn't always necessary—you can probably hook up your camera to your Mac using a USB cable included with the camera and transfer pictures that way. A reader can be an interesting addition, however, because it lets you mount the media like an external disk and copy images from the media card without requiring that the camera be connected, which can be convenient for a number of reasons. Readers can also be found in USB 2.0 and FireWire versions, which enable you to transfer images from the media to your Mac more quickly than most cameras.

    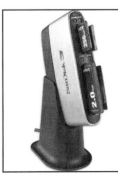

DIGITAL FLASH CARDS AND READERS

SanDisk ImageMate 8-in-1 Reader/Writer

This is an elegant solution if you don't want to connect your camera to your Mac and run down the battery while you're transferring files; it's an even better solution if you have more than one memory card for your camera or even if you have more than one camera or other type of peripheral. The ImageMate 8-in-1 can read from most any type of digital camera media available, including CompactFlash Type I and Type II, Memory Stick and Memory Stick PRO, SmartMedia, xD, MultiMediaCard, and SD.

Of course, the real key is the USB 2.0 interface. If your Mac supports USB 2.0 speeds, then you'll see transfers that occur at the highest possible speed for the media you're dealing with—which, interestingly enough, is no where near the top speed of USB 2.0. Although USB 2.0 can top out at 480 megabits per second (about 60 megabytes per second), the fastest rated CompactFlash cards are only about 10 percent as fast as that. Still, USB 2.0 is much faster than original USB (USB 1.1) connections, so the ImageMate should easily outperform your camera when connected to a USB 2.0 port. (It'll also work with an older USB port if that's all you've got.)

We're focusing on using the ImageMate as a reader, but it's important to note that it's a *writer*, as well. And you can write more than simply digital photos to flash storage cards; you can use them as you would diskettes or removable media. So, if you find it handy to do so, you can copy pretty much any sort of computer file to a flash storage card and then take that card with you for use elsewhere.

With modern Windows PCs and Macs, you can plug in and go with the ImageMate; if you've got Windows 98 or Me (or Mac OS 9) you may need to download and install a driver from the SanDisk web site.

Model: ImageMate USB 2.0 8-in-1 Reader/Writer
Manufacturer: SanDisk (www.sandisk.com)
Price: $49.99

Delkin Devices Reader-24 Firewire

The Reader-24 is a FireWire-based CompactFlash reader that works with Type I, Type II, and Microdrive-style CompactFlash cards. It gets kudos for "just working" out of the box, and it's a favorite among Mac owners, who are a little more likely to be concerned with FireWire peripherals than most PC users. Those users appreciate its speed and its plug-and-go compatibility. The rubberized case is a little generic looking but it's sturdy and functional. If your only reading needs are for CompactFlash-compatible cards, this is your reader.

FireWire, which was invented by Apple, is known as the IEEE 1394 standard. It's commonly used for digital video camcorders, and many PCs support it, although often under the name "1394" or "i.Link," which is Sony's name for the technology.

Model: Reader-24
Manufacturer: Delkin Devices (www.delkin.com)
Price: $49.95

Lexar Media Digital Photo Reader

This one is cool. The idea is that you can take a flash media card—it's compatible with most of the major standards—and play back the images on that card directly on a television set. This is great if you'd like to quickly see what you've got on a card, you want to show the family some of your shots without pulling out the laptop or if you simply prefer to check—and delete—your images using a television screen. Not only is the reader handy and reasonably portable, but it's got a remote control that lets you control a slide show, pan and zoom in on images, and much more. If photos are a big part of your family gatherings, this is a must-have.

Model: Digital Photo Reader
Manufacturer: Lexar (www.lexar.com)
Price: $79.99

Photo Software and Utilities

The point of shooting digital (aside from all the film and processing costs you save) is to be able to the manipulate the image once you get it into your Mac. When a digital camera takes an image, it's generally stored in JPEG format. (JPEG stands for Joint Photographic Expert Group, which is the name of the group that created the standard.) JPEG is a *lossy* compression and file format, which creates files that don't take up a lot of storage space. But, the compression process can introduce *artifacts* into images, usually in the form of tiny blocks that are slightly misshapen or a bit the wrong color.

JPEG is fine for nearly all endeavors—JPEG is one of the main image formats on the Web, for instance, and it's commonly used for all types of professional photography. But many digital cameras offer an even more exact format for storing images, which can be in the form of TIFF (Tagged Image File Format) or a "raw" format which has no lossy compression. The result is a more true image (at least, it's more of what the lens of the camera originally saw, depending on the lens's quality), but a much larger computer file.

Whatever format you eventually store that image in, you'll likely use some sort of image editing software to work with the image. If you're using a relatively new Macintosh with

Mac OS X installed, you'll likely find that iPhoto launches whenever you connect your digital camera—it's likely to be the primary way that you deal with your camera, at least by default.

At the bottom of the iPhoto window (assuming it launched automatically when you connected your digital camera to your Mac and turned on the camera) you'll see a representation of your camera and an indication of how many photos are on it. That's a sign that the camera and iPhoto are communicating correctly with one another. There you'll find the Import button and controls for bringing your photos into iPhoto.

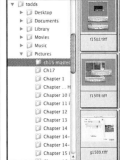

Once a photo is in iPhoto, you can use the built-in controls to view that photo (and others), as well as to touch up the photos, rotate them, and crop them.

Interestingly, iPhoto isn't the only application that Apple includes for dealing with photos; Image Capture is another application that you can use to get at the photos that are stored on your camera. And although iPhoto is a nice program for viewing *thumbnails* (small versions) of your photos, manipulating them and, say, saving them for use on the Web or for publication in special picture books, Image Capture makes it pretty easy simply to get images from the camera stored onto your hard disk in such a way that they are easily accessible by their filenames.

You also might find that your camera comes with software that can be used to work with the images you take; certain manufacturers offer Mac versions of their Image Capture or photo manipulation software, whereas others bundle a copy of an application such as Adobe Photoshop Elements. Elements can be used to make basic edits, translate between file formats (so that you can save TIFFs as JPEGs, or one of many other formats) and to prepare images for printing. For professional-level tasks, the professional version of Photoshop is recommended.

You don't really have to buy additional software in order to work with your photos—particularly if we're talking about digital snapshots in which case iPhoto should work well for what you want to do, offering tools that range from a fix for "red eye" to commands that enable you to post your images on the Web. And if you're not keen on iPhoto's layered approach to managing images in a Photo Library and "albums," you should dig into Image Capture, which has some interesting options of its own, including some automatic features that can crop images, turn them into a slide show, or format them into a web page.

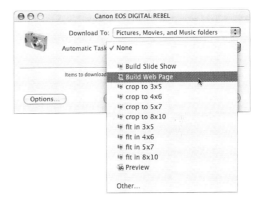

If you need to prepare images for professional use—or if you're a professional or "prosumer" who needs more control over your images, then a commercial application such as Photoshop Elements, the professional version of Photoshop, or GraphicConverter, which is discussed next, might turn out to be more appropriate.

GraphicConverter

For serious, professional-level photo editing you need to get Adobe Photoshop—it's really the only game in town when it comes to preparing images for use in newspapers, magazines, film and other high-end applications. But when your needs aren't quite that serious—or when they *are* but they don't call on the high-level text and painting tools that Photoshop provides—then the solution can be found in the shareware program, GraphicConverter. From Lemke Software, GraphicConverter is most capable at something that seems implicit in its name—converting image files between various computer file formats, ranging from those we've discussed here to obscure formats for all sorts of computing platforms. (GraphicConverter can import about 175 formats and export to about 75.)

Beyond importing and exporting, GraphicConverter enables you to accomplish many important tasks, such as changing the color depth, resolution, size, cropping, rotation, and many filter settings for your images. You can add text, or lines, or do some drawing on your images, although those tools aren't quite the same as they are in Adobe Photoshop or an application like Adobe Illustrator.

GraphicConverter has an extremely powerful *batch* conversion capability, meaning it can convert many images to a new file format or to new settings with one command. And, it includes an image browser that makes short work of viewing thumbnails of images on your Mac, which you can then double-click to launch and edit or convert from within the application. It can even print a folder full of images without requiring you to open each one.

Overall, it's a bit of a geek tool, but GraphicConverter is something that's really worth getting to know if you're going to spend a lot of time working with images on your Mac. It's a superior program with legions of devoted fans who appreciate not only the breadth of features, but the fact that the application has remained inexpensive shareware for years.

Model: GraphicConverter
Manufacturer: Lemke Software
(www.lemkesoft.com)
Price: $30

Photoshop Elements

Often included with digital cameras and scanners, Photoshop Elements is Adobe's version of Photoshop for the rest of us. Its major limitation is that it can only edit images in an RGB colorspace—meaning it's relatively useless to newspaper and magazine professionals, which is probably how Adobe wants it! Elements can perform a lot of the tricks that Photoshop can, however, including capturing photos from your camera, editing and altering those images, improving the color and contrast, and viewing your images in the File Browser, which enables you to preview, sort, and even rename images stored on your hard disk.

In the newest version, there is a Quick Fix workspace that enables you to do a lot of auto corrections that will probably correct most of your image problems, such as correcting photos that are too light or too dark. In the Standard Edit mode, you can get to the real power of Elements, if you want to do a lot of manual manipulation of your images.

Model: Photoshop Elements
Manufacturer: Adobe
(www.adobe.com)
Price: $99.95

Ulead Photo Explorer

One complaint we hear about iPhoto is that it forces its own organization of folders and databases on you instead of enabling you to store photos on your hard disk for easy access. Ulead Photo Explorer is a one-trick pony—it lets you organize, preview, and manage a group of digital images. But it's a handy companion for applications such as Photoshop Elements, as it enables you to import images from your digital camera, and circumvent iPhoto's Library and manage images by accessing them directly on your hard disk. The program also caches image thumbnails to make repeated viewing of a database of images go quickly each time. And the price is hard to beat.

Model: Photo Explorer
Manufacturer: Ulead (www.ulead.com)
Price: $24.95

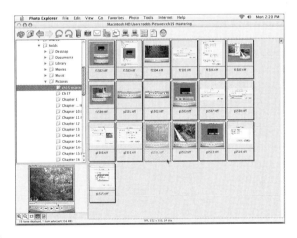

Webcams and Spy Cameras

8

Webcams

Remember when we would know it was the future because there would be picture phones everywhere? In a fascinatingly retro-future scene in *2001: A Space Odyssey*, Dr. Haywood Floyd is on an orbital space station waiting for a ship to take him to view the obelisk on the Moon. After having coffee with acquaintances at the station's Howard Johnson's restaurant, he stops into an AT&T phone booth and makes a video call to his daughter to wish her a happy birthday.

We don't have orbital Howard Johnson's coffee shops, alas, but we do have the video phone—it just isn't attached to the wall in the kitchen the way we all pictured it. (At least, in most cases it isn't.) Instead, that "picture phone" for Mac users is called video conferencing or multimedia instant messaging over the Internet. And it's an option that Apple makes available using its own equipment—the iSight webcam—and its own software and service, called iChat AV. The iSight and iChat are particularly adept at these things and represent most of what you need for re-creating your own "video phone" experience,

assuming the folks on the other line have the capability, too.

The other generic use for webcams is for remote viewing of people or events. I am fond of having cameras pointed at me, and tend to work from my home office on projects like this one, complete with webcams staring at me from all directions. (See http://www.leoville.com/ for Leo's cams.) Webcams are also placed in windows and the tops of buildings to look at roads or the weather or to check out pedestrian traffic in Manhattan or to give people something to wave at (and make other gestures at) on Bourbon Street. And, there's always the handy option of using a webcam for security around your home or office, whether or not you put the images on the Web.

To pull off a webcam setup requires a camera and some specialized software depending on what you're trying to do; we'll look at cameras that work with both iChat AV and other software; we'll look at some of that software as well.

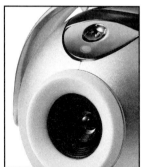
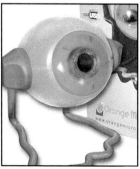

Apple iSight

Well, let's see—it's made by Apple and it's pricier than the competition. That means it has got to be good, right? Actually, it is. It's designed to attach to the top of pretty much any Mac model, including PowerBooks and iBooks. What's more, it sits right on top of your display, making for a more natural looking picture when you're video conferencing. Plus, it looks cool up there.

The iSight isn't just a fixed lens camera—it has an auto focusing lens (to capture you in focus even when you're moving) using a 1/4-inch CCD and a wide aperture that Apple says lets in more light than other webcams. The focus is on a good looking image, which the Apple seems to think will make its camera more popular. (If you look good on it, maybe you'll buy one!)

The iSight has a small green "on air" light and can be turned off with a twist, which ensures it isn't shooting you when you're picking something out of your teeth. (And iChat recognizes that it's turned off, and indicate such to your chat buddies.) The camera is connected via FireWire, which can be a big advantage in terms of the speed and fluidity of motion; the iSight is capable of 30 frames per second, about the same as the North American television standard.

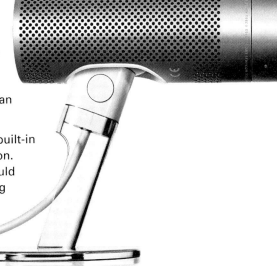

Finally, the iSight isn't just a camera—it also includes a built-in microphone, designed for high-quality audio reproduction. That makes the iSight more than just a webcam; you could actually shoot a little movie using it, if you'd like. As long as that movie is about, say, a person who sits in front of their computer (or in reasonable proximity) the whole time.

Oh, and, just to top things off, from a certain angle, the iSight even looks like the HAL 9000 from *2001*. It's almost a little eerie.

Photo courtesy of Apple, Inc.

Model: iSight
Manufacturer: Apple (www.apple.com)
Price: $149

Orange Micro iBot

The iBot can boast a lot of the advantages that the iSight can, including a FireWire connection and 30 frames per second of video quality. It's also cheaper than the iSight, it still works fine with iChat AV and it even has a little "i" in its name. On the flip side, you either like the little plastic alien-looking design or you don't and the iBot, unlike the iSight, is designed to sit on your desk and look up your nose, particularly when you are sitting at your Mac using it for video conferencing. The iBot has a manual focus, a small stand that adds to its alien appearance and it's nothing less than an affordable alternative to Apple's big gun, particularly for use with Internet video chats over iChat AV.

Model: iBot
Manufacturer: Orange Micro
(www.orangemicro.com)
Price: $99

Logitech QuickCam Zoom Silver

Also designed for sitting on your desk and looking up your nose, the QuickCam has a slightly more conservative appearance than the iBot, although the overall effect is still "mechanical eyeball." The QuickCam uses a USB connection, which means it's slower than the others, although it supports USB 2.0—in which case it's not slower, at least with newer Macs. It's got a special digital zoom feature and "face tracking" technology that Logitech suggests holds you in frame better; it also has a built-in microphone for the audio portion of your communications. All that and the price is right.

Model: QuickCam Zoom Silver
Manufacturer: Logitech
(www.logitech.com)
Price: $79.95

Axis 211 Network Camera

D-Link DCS-1000W Wireless Internet Camera

Here's a fun one—the DCS-1000W offers both a built-in web server and wireless 802.11b support, meaning it can send images to your local network or connect to an Internet connection without requiring an ethernet cable. This is a really interesting option if your goal is an inexpensive security camera, as it offers you the freedom to place the camera anywhere, thanks to the wireless access. The drawback—remote management software is only available for Windows, although you can manage many functions from the web interface. The advantage—it has a pretty decent price for a network-based camera.

Model: DCS-1000W
Manufacturer: D-Link (www.dlink.com)
Price: $229

The more sophisticated route for your Webcam is one that doesn't require a Mac sitting next to it—the Axis 211 Network Camera has a built-in Web server, so the camera can be accessed as a standalone device on the Internet. You simply plug an ethernet cable (one that provides access to the Internet or to your local network) into the camera and turn it on; it can serve images to up to 20 users at once with its built-in Web server. The camera also offers built-in compression, on the fly, to create motion video that offers impressive quality. This is a relatively high-end solution, but a handy one if your goal is security or a standalone cam that is going to encourage viewers to enjoy your business, retail, or tourism web site.

Model: Axis 211 Network Camera
Manufacturer: Axis Communications (www.axis.com)
Price: $449

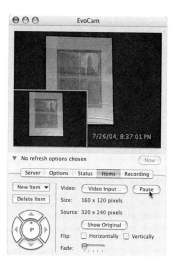

EvoCam

EvoCam is software that periodically takes a photo using your webcam (or a similar device) and then uploads those images to a predetermined destination via FTP. In other words, it's webcam software! EvoCam boasts a built-in web server so that you can access the camera directly on your network to see what it sees; you can also edit the HTML that's used to display the webcam image and there's a user interface that enables you to edit the look of the images themselves, including what graphical badges appear, where the clock goes, and so on. It can also react to AppleScripts, work as a motion detector with your camera, and it will archive the images it takes.

Model: EvoCam
Manufacturer: Evological
(www.evological.com)
Price: $20

ImageCaster

Another solid webcam software solution is ImageCaster, which offers many of the same advantages as those in the previous reviews. ImageCaster includes a full-fledged interface to customize the way each captured image will look, including overlays and text. ImageCaster also offers a graphical schedule for the webcam, so that you can predetermine when images will be captured by the software and when they won't be. You can specify different frequencies (every minute, every few seconds) and even different overlay graphics for different times of the day. Like EvoCam, ImageCaster can sense motion and record images only when that motion takes place, giving you the opportunity to give your webcam a little overtime work as a security guard around your home or office.

Model: ImageCaster
Manufacturer: Econ Technologies
(www.econtechnologies.com)
Price: $30

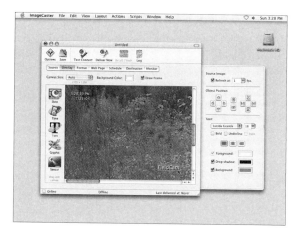

QuickTime Broadcaster

The typical webcam software is designed to take snapshots every so often and upload those images to a web site; the flipside is sending actual video over the Internet. The camera can be either a digital camcorder or a FireWire-based webcam; a USB camera is likely to be slow (although USB 2.0 cameras can work). Then, you need software that enables you to send that signal and make it available online. The mothership's solution is QuickTime Broadcaster, which enables you to use your camera to shoot video, then encode that video "on the fly" so that you can webcast live events. It's designed for QuickTime Streaming Server (which is also free) or a webcasting ISP if you plan for multiple viewers at once. If all you have is a standard-issue web hosting account, you can send the live feed to only one viewer.

Model: QuickTime Broadcaster
Manufacturer: Apple
(www.apple.com/quicktime/)
Price: Free

Wirecast

If Apple's freeware solution doesn't whet your appetite, maybe Wirecast is something you'll want to spend some money on. The software includes not just webcast capabilities, but it integrates live graphic overlays, transition effects, and titling. In other words, it's sort of a miniature live TV studio. It's also a little pricey, so you'll probably want a professional application, but this is a great way to build live video presentations that you stream over the Web. It even integrates with Apple's Keynote software to help you present material in presentation format, using multiple screens, overlays, and so forth. Wirecast works with QuickTime Streaming Server (or the open source Darwin Streaming Server) to complete the webcast over the Internet.

Model: Wirecast
Manufacturer: Vara Software Limited
(www.varasoftware.com)
Price: $599

Spy Cameras

Okay, what's the difference? Most of what we're calling "spy cameras" are small devices that take substandard digital photos—640×480 resolution or worse. That makes them good for little more than posting to web pages or sending through e-mail. But, some of them are pretty snazzy looking and certainly worthy of checking out for their gadget factors.

We'll look at two different types of spy cameras—motion and still. The motion cameras tend to be serious surveillance cameras that can be

used for security, "nanny cams," and similar applications. The still cameras are usually just cool, masquerading as Zippo-style lighters and so on.

Of course, the majority of these cameras are really redundant novelties considering the popularity of mobile phones and PDAs that have cameras attached. But, let's face it, James Bond's "Q" would snicker at a mobile phone camera, but he might take one of these spy cams a bit more seriously.

JB1 Spy Camera

There are two reasons why this little camera is cool. First, it's a camera that's small enough to hide away in a container that looks like a Zippo lighter. Second, it's reasonably affordable, meaning you might actually want to plunk down the cash to play with this gadget.

Leo's Pick

The JB1 is an official, licensed "OO7" product. It's a 640×480 camera with 8MB of built-in RAM, meaning it can store about 150 pictures until you need to synchronize by connecting it to your Mac via USB. (At a lower resolution setting, it can shoot over 310 pictures at 320×240.)

The camera has no flash, but it offers a tiny viewfinder and a fixed lens for shooting. It also has a "quick shot" feature: pop the top open, press a button and snap the top shut and you've just taken a picture. It also has a self-timer that can be set to take an image after ten seconds.

In "surveillance mode," the camera can take images at various intervals, which might be handy if you need photographic evidence of someone with their hand on the cookie jar. (Big Brothers of the world, unite!) According to the company's documentation, you can shoot images for up to 19 days.

Finally, this little guy can even record up to 30 seconds of QuickTime video—with sound! Or, if you record audio only, you can get up to 12 minutes. Just long enough to get your perp to give up the goods and rat out his friends.

Model: JB1 Camera
Manufacturer: Digital Dream (www.jbcamera.com)
Price: $99

Logitech Pocket Digital 130

This one isn't quite as covert as the JB1 Camera but it has the advantage of taking much better photos. That, coupled with the fact that it slides open and closed like a Cold War-era camera from a spy movie, makes it good enough to write up in this section, even though it qualifies as a full-fledged digital camera. It's a 1.3-megapixel camera that can store up to 130 (lower resolution) pictures in its built-in 16MB of RAM; it's also rechargeable via a USB connection, so that you simply drop it in your pocket and go. It's even got a flash, which makes it a great choice for both covert spies and overt party people who simply want a convenient—and cool—little camera for snapshots.

> **Model:** Pocket Digital 130
> **Manufacturer:** Logitech
> (www.logitech.com)
> **Price:** $149

Pen Drive Camera

The Pen Drive Camera is a 64MB to 256MB USB pen drive similar to the keychain, wristwatch, and similar USB drives discussed in Chapter 2, but with a twist—this one has a 2-megapixel camera built into it. It can take images up to 1600×1200 resolution with its tiny lens; there's no flash, but the USB connector is built right into the bottom of the pen, and it can double, clearly, as USB storage for Mac documents, images, or anything else you need to sneak back to headquarters.

> **Model:** Pen Drive Camera
> **Manufacturer:** Add On Technology
> (www.pendrivestore.com)
> **Price:** $110 (64MB), $135 (128MB),
> $190 (256MB)

PDAs and Smartphones

9

Personal Digital Assistants (PDAs)

When Palm Pilots first appeared on the scene, they seemed revolutionary. Not just because they were small devices that could accept input by handwriting and help you manage your address book and to-do list—in fact, Apple had a product, called the Newton, that could do something similar. What made the Palm devices seem revolutionary is that they were very practical for what they offered and they were, at the same time, rather barebones. You used your Palm Pilot for scheduling, contacts, and the occasional quick note; you used your computer for everything else. Like the early Mac, the Palm was also known for its simple and elegant operating system.

Since that time, the concept of what, *exactly*, a PDA should be has morphed considerably. Today's PDAs are a little more like small, all-around computers. They have color screens, many have cameras built in; some are phones, others have wireless Internet or networking capabilities. Many of them can play games or run checkbook management software. Some record audio and snippets of video or act as GPS (Global Positioning System) satellite receivers.

And, interestingly, the PDA market seems to have contracted and consolidated a bit in the past few years. The original Palm company has split into two companies; PalmOne and PalmSource. The latter focused on software; the former still sells PDAs. Sony has left the PDA market at this writing; Handspring was bought by Palm and their remaining products are offered as Palm products.

So, if you'd like a new PDA that's Mac compatible, you're likely looking at a Palm device—unless you decide to check out the darkside—Pocket PC (Windows Mobile) devices! Using special third-party software, you can actually synchronize data with those little devils, so if you like the features you find on a Pocket PC device, they are an option to consider.

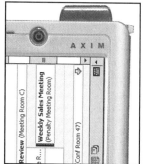

PalmOne Zire 72

Even though your Mac *can* connect to a Pocket PC device, that doesn't quite make a Pocket PC device the best pick—particularly if you're not a purely business-minded cuss. The Zire 72, on the other hand, is probably the most well-rounded of the offerings that sync up nicely with a Mac and, what's more, that sync doesn't require a special purchase. Yes, it's true that Palm Desktop is no longer being actively improved and developed, but the Zire 72 will still sync nicely with iCal, Address Book, and other Mac apps—via Apple's own iSync technology—so it's not really too much of a loss.

The Zire 72 features built-in Bluetooth, meaning you can pair it with your Mac and then sync it relatively easily. (It actually takes a little setup, which includes installing and configuring Palm Desktop a bit, even if you intend to use only iSync with Apple's Address Book and iCal.) The Bluetooth technology built in to the Zire 72 can also be used to access your Mac for file transfers or to access Internet on the device via a Bluetooth-enabled Internet gateway or mobile phone. (You can also use the Zire 72 with a PC that has Bluetooth-enabled Internet sharing; unfortunately, Mac OS X 10.3 doesn't offer that feature.)

Perhaps the most fun you'll have is with the Zire 72's built-in megapixel camera; with a storage card installed, you can get hundreds of small pictures (suitable for sending through email) or even quite a few megapixel (1280 × 960) photos that you can use for Web sites or to make small prints. The camera certainly isn't the most sophisticated, but it does have the same effect as an old Polaroid camera, in that you can snap a picture and then flip the screen around to show it to your victim (er…*subject*).

The Zire 72 has a headphone jack that can be used to listen to RealPlayer compatible movies or to MP3 audio files, which can be transferred to the Zire 72 even from within iTunes. (You may have to translate them to MP3s first, because iTunes' native format is AAC.) Again, support for MP3s is only really limited by the size of memory card you decide to get for your Zire 72. Likewise the Zire 72 has a small built-in microphone that lets you use the device for audio recording; a reporter in the field or student in class can record a conversation or lecture and then either transfer it via Bluetooth or as an email attachment to yourself or others.

Of course, this little device isn't all about fun and games. Bundled with the Zire 72 is Documents To Go, a great little application that lets you read and edit Word and Excel documents on your Palm. And, of course, you can access email and even browse web sites. The appointment calendar now has a nice, colorful overview that includes ToDo tasks and even the subject lines of new email messages that have been received. And, speaking of the color, the crisp, colorful screen is easy to read in low-light and makes the experience of working with a handheld a little different (and more futuristic) than the old days of grayscale screens.

And perhaps one of the biggest advantage of taking the PalmOne route is the abundance of applications that are designed for Palm handhelds and that can synchronize with Palm handhelds. For Mac-based sales people, for instance, the Zire 72 offers the built in Address Book, Calendar and even an Expense function for tracking expenses on the road; that same Zire 72 can also synchronize with Marketcircle Daylite, a full-fledged Customer Relationship Manager (CRM) application that helps you keep up with customers and sales. For all sorts of industries and applications, the Zire 72 can work for you.

If there's a drawback, it's that the Zire 72 has neither a built-in phone nor WiFi access for an Internet connection in hotel rooms, airports, and coffee shops. Instead, you'll need a Bluetooth Internet router or a compatible Bluetooth phone for an Internet connection. (Or, you can share an Internet connection over Bluetooth if you have third-party software such as The Missing Sync, which is discussed a little later in this chapter.) Even with the drawbacks, for the price, Zire 72 is a great, well-rounded little PDA.

Model: Zire 72
Manufacturer: PalmOne (www.palmone.com)
Price: $299

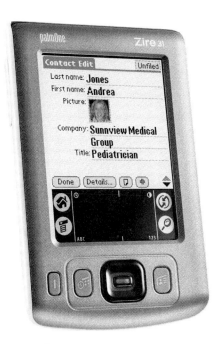

PalmOne Zire 31

The Zire 72's little brother, the Zire 31, offers a nice set of features at a low cost. First and foremost is the color display, which offers less resolution than the Zire 72, but it's fine for contact management, games, and the occasional image, as well as night-viewing. Designed to accept expansion cards, the Zire 31 can play back MP3s as long as you've got a memory expansion card installed. (The base memory is 16MB, which won't hold many songs if you've got contacts and other stuff already stored in there.) And, it comes bundled with a few more applications that the average starter PDA, which makes it pretty attractive for the price.

> **Model:** Zire 31
> **Manufacturer:** PalmOne
> (www.palmone.com)
> **Price:** $149

HP iPaq Pocket PC

Since the world of the Pocket PC is opened up to us Mac users, we might as well take advantage of it. Any Pocket PC PDA is particularly nice if you happen to use a lot of Microsoft applications on your Mac—synching your Entourage mail, contacts, and schedule, along with Microsoft Word, Excel, and even presentation documents. The iPaq H4155 is also WiFi and Bluetooth enabled, making it easy to connect to external peripherals and access the Internet via HotSpots and Internet cafés. It's expandable via a Secure Digital card slot and it has even got a few bundled graphics applications for viewing photos. The iPaq H4355 includes a small thumb keyboard that's nice for tapping out emails and text messages in said Internet café. (Requires third-party software to sync with your Mac. See "Software and Accessories" later in this chapter.)

> **Model:** iPaq Pocket PC
> **Manufacturer:** HP (www.hp.com)
> **Price:** $399 (H4155), $449 (H4355)

PERSONAL DIGITAL ASSISTANTS (PDAS)

Dell Axim

A Dell for a Mac user? It seems like heresy to even consider it but—with the right third-party sync solution—it's perfectly possible to use an Axim with your Mac and synchronize happily between the two. Plus, you'll find that the Axim is an impressive little gadget in its own right, with the Axim X30 offering both WiFi and Bluetooth connectivity, so that you can surf the Internet in a WiFi-enabled café or sync wireless with your Bluetooth-enabled Mac. It's got a fast processor, 64MB of RAM, SD card expandability, and "pocket" versions of Word, Excel, and Internet Explorer. Best of all is the price, which leaves room for PocketMac or The Missing Sync so that you can use it with your Mac.

Model: Axim X30
Manufacturer: Dell (www.dell.com)
Price: $349 (624MHz processor),
$249 (312MHz processor) or
$199 (non-wireless)

Palm Tungsten W

The Tungsten W is not quite a smartphone, but rather a telephony-enabled PDA that can use certain wireless carrier networks for Internet connections; at the same time, it *can* be a phone if you use the included headset or the optional cover. (In the latter case, you're holding a PDA to your face, which may make you feel silly.) With its little nub of an antennae and access to a wireless phone carrier, however, you will have Internet access anywhere that you can get GSM mobile phone access. The Tungsten W is designed to give you "always on" type access making it a mobile Internet tool, including even instant messaging and Palm-style web "clipping" that make for efficient access to popular web sites.

Model: Tungsten W
Manufacturer: PalmOne
(www.palmone.com)
Price: $299–$499 (prices differ based on the mobile phone provider you choose)

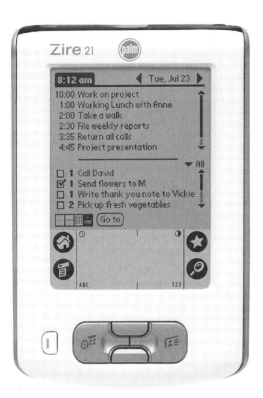

Apple iPod

No, this isn't the only place we'll discuss the iPod—it's got its own chapter, pretty much, which is coming up right after this one. But it's worth noting that the iPod can work as a rudimentary PDA for Mac users who have their contacts in Address Book and appointments in iCal. The iPod's interface is certainly simple, but somehow still effective for quickly swirling through your contacts, for instance, and getting to what you need. (You don't even have to use Address Book; you can manually add contacts by dragging vCard-format files to the Contacts folder on the iPod.) Of course, the iPod has another advantage over most PDAs—it's disk-based, with tons of a capacity, so it can not only hold your contacts and appointments, but also files that you need when you're on the road or moving from home to office. There's even Solitaire. Oh, and rumor has it that you can play music on it, too.

> **Model:** iPod
> **Manufacturer:** Apple (www.apple.com)
> **Price:** $299 (20GB), $399 (40GB), $249 (iPod mini)

Palm Zire 21

So you don't need no stinkin' wireless and you don't need no stinkin' phone—you just want a contact manager that syncs nicely with your Mac and lets you access the occasional Palm OS application. Here's your baby. The Zire 21 is the improved base model that offers a respectable 8MB of RAM, includes a Hotsync cradle and runs Palm OS v5.2.1. It's got a rechargeable battery, a nice little grayscale display and it's a cheap way to get into the Palm thing.

> **Model:** Zire 21
> **Manufacturer:** PalmOne (www.palmone.com)
> **Price:** $99

Photo courtesy Apple, Inc.

Smartphones

Someone came up with the distinction of the "smartphone" instead of the cell phone presumably to make the point that these phones are creeping over into PDA territory. In fact, the future of the standalone PDA concept is probably limited, since most people don't want multiple devices hanging off their persons and a lot of people feel it's important to carry a mobile phone. Enter the "smart phones" that can handle various PDA tasks—contact management, to-do lists and appointments, and even Internet access—while being hip and attractive and compact.

The category "smartphone" is also pretty broad. As you'll see from the picks that follow, there are two general distinctions we can still make about these devices—you've got PDAs that offer phone functionality and phones that offer some PDA functionality.

How you choose a smartphone will likely depend on what you need access to more when you're on the move—your schedule or the Internet. If you're content with having a phone that will synchronize with iCal and Address book, for instance, then you've got plenty of inexpensive (and relatively inexpensive) options that use USB-to-phone cables or Bluetooth to enable you to synchronize that data. (Bluetooth is also nice for adding wireless headsets and other phone-centric accessories.) And you can burn a little extra dough on features such as built-in cameras and music playback.

If you need to run Palm OS or Windows Mobile applications, or if you need serious access to the Internet—browsing, messaging, and email—then a PDA-centric smartphone is the way to go. Smartphones would have been tougher to recommend just months ago, but the latest round are small enough to fit into a pocket, purse, or belt holster and are really just all-around more useful.

The priciest little phones are attractive, multi-functional and offer a number of ways not only to make and receive calls or manage personal information, but also to connect with your Mac and even work as a modem to get your Mac on the Internet. For some of us, a little pocket communicator that offers high-speed data service for our Macs (which usually requires a digital network connection and special Internet service from a provider) and quick access to contacts and appointments is really a move in the right direction.

Samsung SPH-i500

After years of devices hitting the market that struggled to marry the PDA and the phone, the SPH-i500 has finally gotten the form factor right. This flat, small flip-phone fits great in your pocket and looks good sitting on that little table you use for your wallet and keys—but it's a full-fledged Palm OS machine complete with a bevy of Internet features and all the PIM features that you expect.

Leo's Pick

The SPH-i500 runs Palm 4.1 as its operating system and it has a slightly slower processor than you'll get in the latest round of non-phone PDAs. But, it's still pretty good and, more to the point, using Palm 4.1 enables the i500 to continue using Web clippings, the small, efficient web apps (for news, weather, flight info, eBay, and many sites) that Palm used to some success in its i705 and earlier lines of wireless PDAs. The device doesn't offer any of the expandability that you'll find in standalone PDAs (including the Tungsten W) but it'd be hard to imagine too much expandability in this little package.

This is a good phone, which, amazingly, doesn't scrimp on connection power or on options like an actual keypad for dialing numbers. (Again, previous generations of PDA/phones haunt us.) It offers a headset jack, support for voice notes, and you can use voice-based address book entries to dial certain people by simply saying their names. It can even playback MP3s.

The phone doesn't offer Bluetooth for connecting to your Mac; you'll need to use the (rather old-school) Palm-style cradle for synchronizing data. The sync can also happen via iSync and your data can be put in either an aging version of Palm Desktop or in iCal and/or Address Book.

One issue with the i500 is Mac-compatibility; some users have reported early trouble with the phone, which may either require workarounds (one workaround was to turn it off before synching with your Mac, then remove it from the cradle after sync before turning it back on) or a third-party solution such as The Missing Sync for Palm OS (www.markspace.com).

> **Model:** SPH-i500
> **Manufacturer:** Samsung (www.samsung.com)
> **Price:** $499 (check deals from SprintPCS, the exclusive provider)

Kyocera 7100 Series

Competition on the PDA-based smartphone front has heated up quite a bit in the past few years, with Kyocera—which was among the first to make a relatively useful PDA-based phone—now offering the 7100, which, but for its slightly larger size, would give the i500 a clear run for the title of best PDA-based phone. The Kyocera offers Palm 4.1, which supports web clippings for fast info access; you've also got access to your email and other typical PDA functions. The way you dial the phone is a bit clunkier, but the Kyocera responds with a great speakerphone and good Mac compatibility. It's also handy for its capability to work as a high-speed modem on CDMA networks when linked to your PowerBook or iBook and it's offered by a number of network carriers, giving you some freedom in where you buy it. This is a great gadget, but it's also a good sales tool and companion for people who need a little Palm-based computing power on the road.

> **Model:** 7100 series
> **Manufacturer:** Kyocera
> (www.kyocera.com)
> **Price:** $499 (or less; prices dependant on provider and contract)

Samsung SPH-i330

True, this is aging technology, but the i300 still makes the list because it has a color screen, a decent size for a PDA-based phone, and it's going to get nothing but cheaper. (The i300 was also a little bit of a problem child on the Mac synching front, but The Missing Sync (www.markspace.com) software solves that without too many headaches.) The i300 requires you to dial by pressing the touch screen, but it's got voice dial features and some nice built-in applications for recording voice calls and other options that can help some users overcome that nagging feeling that they're holding a PDA up to their ears. No Bluetooth, but with a USB cradle or cable and The Missing Sync software, you can sync photos, email, and more.

> **Model:** i300
> **Manufacturer:** Samsung
> (www.samsung.com)
> **Price:** $299 (Cheaper street prices and packages)

PalmOne Treo 600

This is a definite case of holding a PDA up to your ear when you want to use it as a phone. But, with its small keyboard—which still has a little cachet with the hipsters—this little guy is so handy for wireless Internet tasks, including email and chat that it might be worth it that you have to hold it to your face every so often. If you're more of a typist and less of a talker anyway, then the Treo may continue to be a hip and handy way to take your business on the road and stay in touch. Plus, it's a PalmOne product, so it has all the great apps, offers a nice display, 32MB of RAM and pretty much what you need. It's got a camera built in that takes VGA-quality photos and can playback MP3 audio, if you opt for additional software and an SD-format memory card.

> **Model:** Treo 600
> **Manufacturer:** PalmOne
> (www.palmone.com)
> **Price:** $449 (Cheaper street prices and packages)

Sony-Ericsson T630

When Apple first introduced Bluetooth wireless support and iSync for dealing with such devices, Sony-Ericcson was the lone company on the supported list of products. Coming from a different angle, their phones are phones first, with some PDA capabilities afterward. But, if you're looking for a little less computing power and a little more freedom, these phones can be handy. You'll like the T630 for its friendliness with your Mac; it syncs easily with iSync, carrying your contacts and tracking appointments. Using Bluetooth, it can pop up a contact name on your Mac's screen when a call comes in. And it can work as a wireless modem, enabling you to dial out from your PowerBook or iBook and getting on a CDMA network that, in some cities and locales, can offer you high-speed access. Add to that a camera, support for various wireless services, games, and so on—you can't call this phone anything but fully loaded.

> **Model:** T630 series
> **Manufacturer:** Sony-Ericsson
> (www.sonyericsson.com)
> **Price:** $199 (Cheaper street prices and packages)

Motorola A630

Motorola has been known to hit it out of the park every once in a while and the A630 is no exception. Bridging the gap between phone and Internet appliance, the A630 cleverly unfolds from a compact phone to reveal a QWERTY keyboard for messaging and email. It syncs with your Mac via Bluetooth, can work as a high-speed modem for your wireless-enabled PowerBook or iBook and it has tons of fun features. What's really to like about it, though, is the professional flair; don't ever let any BlackBerry owner tell you they've got anything on you for e-mail or messaging. It doesn't however, have an HTML browser, meaning it's not quite a PDA replacement in that regard.

Model: A630
Manufacturer: Motorola (www.motorola.com)
Price: $499 (Cheaper street prices and packages)

Nokia 6820

Nokia offers phones with classic designs that don't deviate much from a certain look and feel—and those phones seem to range from Spartan in features to positively brimming. This one fits the latter category. It's Bluetooth-based for both data synchronization (it integrates nicely with iSync, and hence Address Book and iCal) and for wireless accessories, such as Bluetooth headsets. It's got an integrated camera for snapshots and advanced support for messaging. It's most unique feature is the fold-out keyboard, which makes emails and instant messaging that much easier to do quickly using a familiar interface. For the serious text-based road warrior, this is an interesting choice.

Model: 6820
Manufacturer: Nokia (www.nokia.com)
Price: $379 (Cheaper street prices and packages)

Software and Accessories

We can't possibly get into all the accessories that you can add to a mobile phone in this section—suffice it to say that there are tons of little doo-dads that you can easily add to any brand of mobile phone. Indeed, if there's anything important to say about such accessories is that they tend to be manufacturer and model-specific; you'll need to know your phone before you order a new battery or phone charger, or even a data kit to connect it to your Mac for file transfers or Internet access. (And, you should check that data kit at Apple's iSync web site at http://www.apple.com/isync/ to ensure that the kit and phone are Mac-compatible.)

If you're considering a Pocket PC–based device, then perhaps the most important add-on is going to be third-party software that actually makes that device useful with your Macintosh. And, increasingly, third-party software is going to be important for users of Palm-based devices, too, because Palm is offering less in-house support for Palm Desktop and certain versions and features of the Palm operating system.

Aside from chargers, cases, and synchronizing software, you may want memory for your PDA; many PDAs accept multiple types of memory cards, although SD seems far-and-away a favorite. The memory card will enable you to store more information on the PDA as well as any multimedia files that the PDA lets you create—photos, audio files, movies or other document types. For more on the different types of media, see Chapter 7, "Digital Cameras and Accessories."

Meanwhile, a few of the other types of accessories we should talk about are devices that enable you to use your PDA more effectively with your Mac, with your local network or with the Internet. There are some interesting options that we can cover quickly that might even make your PDA-to-Mac experience better.

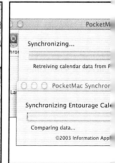

The Missing Sync

Leo's Pick

If you're using a Pocket PC device with your Mac, then software such as The Missing Sync is an absolute necessity; if you're using a Palm device, particularly a newer model, then you'll find that The Missing Sync for Palm OS is a pleasant luxury. In fact, MarkSpace makes a number of different versions of The Missing Sync to help us Mac users participate as full citizens in the PDA world.

The advantage of The Missing Sync for Pocket PC edition is clear; without this software you can't even perform basic synchronization between iCal, Address Book and your Pocket PC device. With this version you can also mount your Pocket PC device on your Mac desktop for quick access to its files, and you can use Bluetooth or WiFi technologies to share an Internet connection from your Mac to the Pocket PC, which can be incredibly handy.

With a Palm device—particularly some Palm-based phones and those running 5.x and later versions of the OS—The Missing Sync for Palm OS makes synchronization easier and it offers additional features, such as synchronization of photos taken with built-in digital cameras and synchronization over a network connection. The Missing Sync is also important for certain devices, such as the Sony Clie line of Palm devices and the Samsung i330 and i500 smartphones, which have special requirements in order to be Mac-compatible. And, as with the Pocket PC version, The Missing Sync for Palm OS enables you to share an Internet connection with your handheld.

So, yeah, it's an additional cost (call it a Mac-user tax) in order to get some of these features that Windows users take for granted, but if you really want to flex your Palm or Pocket PC's strengths, The Missing Sync is close to a must-have.

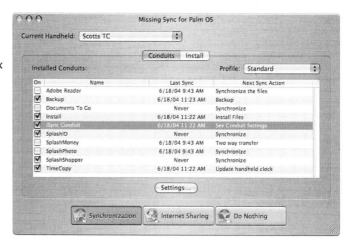

Model: The Missing Sync
Manufacturer: MarkSpace
(www.markspace.com)
Price: $39

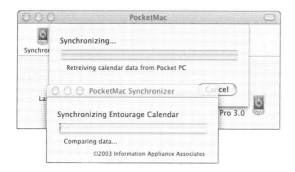

PocketMac

The PocketMac line of software products is specifically designed to synchronize data between various Windows OS-based devices and your Mac, such as Pocket PC PDAs and Microsoft Smartphone operating systems. PocketMac Pro, for instance, can synchronize data to and from a Mac and Pocket PC, including email, contacts, calendar listings, tasks, and documents from a variety of applications, including Microsoft Entourage, Mail, Address Book, iCal, Microsoft Office applications, and others. Other versions of PocketMac support popular smartphones, while PocketMac GoBetween will add capabilities to iSync for devices that are already supported.

Model: PocketMac
Manufacturer: PocketMac
(www.pocketmac.net)
Price: $25–$45 (Depending on version)

Belkin Bluetooth Access Point

If you'd like Bluetooth devices (a PDA or smartphone) to be able to access your network of Macs or the Internet, a Bluetooth Access Point can be handy. This access point can receive an IP address from a DHCP server, allowing Bluetooth devices within the access point's range to do some file sharing and to access Internet sites to the extent of the capability of the device. Some devices (or other computers on the network) can also print to a connected USB printer if desired. The access point offers a web browser interface for easy setup from one of those computers.

Model: Bluetooth Access Point
Manufacturer: Belkin(www.belkin.com)
Price: $199

iRE201 Infrared Access Point

Using the infrared port on your PDA and this device, you can gain access to your LAN and the Internet. The access point connects to your Ethernet router and bridges data from your PDA's infrared port. It can be configured by accessing its built-in Web interface. You wouldn't think that speeds would be terribly high over an IR connection, but you'd be wrong, at least in some cases; IrCOMM, the standard that Palm devices use (and the access point can handle as well), can reach 4Mbps.

Model: iRE201 Infrared Access Point
Manufacturer: Compex
(www.cpx.com)
Price: $79.95

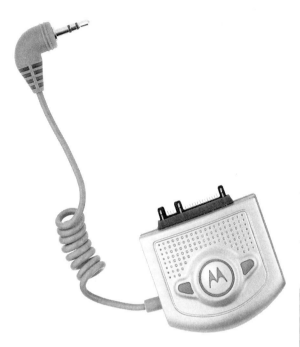

Motorola Bluetooth Wireless Adapter

Motorola has a neat little gizmo—you can add Bluetooth support to a number of Motorola phones that don't offer it. The end result is that you can then connect to your Mac for synchronizing data or file sharing, or you can use your phone to give your Bluetooth-enabled Mac a wireless Internet connection. And even if the Mac-to-phone connection isn't your first priority, you can use the Bluetooth adapter to make wireless phone accessories—such as headsets or speakerphones—an option.

Model: Wireless Adapter DC600
Manufacturer: Motorola
(www.motorola.com)
Price: $39

PalmOne Wireless Keyboard

For Palm-based devices, this keyboard uses infrared—which happens to be built in to all current and many previous models—to communicate keystrokes. The keyboard folds up for easy transport and then folds out to present full-sized keys to make it easier to type emails or take notes; with add-on software, you can even use the keyboard to edit Word documents or do some work in spreadsheets. If you're toying with the idea of taking trips with just your Palm device, then a portable keyboard is probably one way to make that plan work.

Model: Wireless Keyboard
Manufacturer: PalmOne
(www.palmone.com)
Price: $69.95

Presenter-to-Go

If you need another excuse to leave your laptop behind for business trips, having a presentation solution for your Palm or Pocket PC device might be a good answer. The Presenter-to-Go enables you to display your handheld's screen over a VGA connection, which is how the bulk of overhead projectors are connected for PowerPoint-style presentations. This device isn't cheap, but for the businessperson who needs to travel light, it's a neat gizmo. It even includes an infrared remote so that you can walk away from your handheld and still change slides. The device comes in different styles of expansion card (SD, Memorystick, CompactFlash, and so on) in order to work with a variety of handhelds.

Model: Presenter-to-Go
Manufacturer: Margi Systems
(www.margi.com)
Price: $199

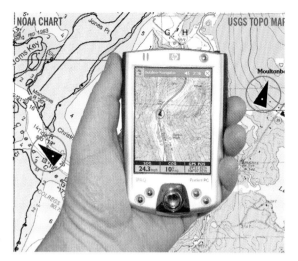

Outdoor Navigator

To get a GPS (Global Positioning System) add-on to work with your PDA, you'll also need software that works with your Mac so that you can download maps to the PDA. Outdoor Navigator is such a software, although it's designed more for camping, hiking, and pleasure boating than it is for driving. With the software installed on your Mac and your PDA, the connected GPS receiver (you do have a connected GPS receiver, right?) can feed data to the maps on your PDA to show you where you are in your travels. The outdoor Navigator can come bundled with an Emtac Bluetooth GPS receiver that lets a Bluetooth-enabled PDA receive GPS data wirelessly.

Model: Outdoor Navigator
Manufacturer: Maptech
(www.maptech.com)
Price: $99 (software and one-year map subscription); $298 (software, subscription, and Emtac Bluetooth GPS receiver)

DataViz Documents To Go

One other software staple for a lot of Palm and Pocket PC users is Documents To Go, which offers you the capability to work with Microsoft Office documents (or AppleWorks and RTF or PDF files) on your Palm device. The Premium edition also enables you to view graphics and photos as well as work with PowerPoint presentation documents. With an external keyboard and an email solution, Documents To Go might conceivably let you leave your PowerBook and home and use only your PalmOne device while you're on the road, even if you need to work with spreadsheet and presentation data.

Model: Documents To Go
Premium Edition
Manufacturer: DataViz
(www.dataviz.com)
Price: $49

Audio Players and iPod Gadgets

10

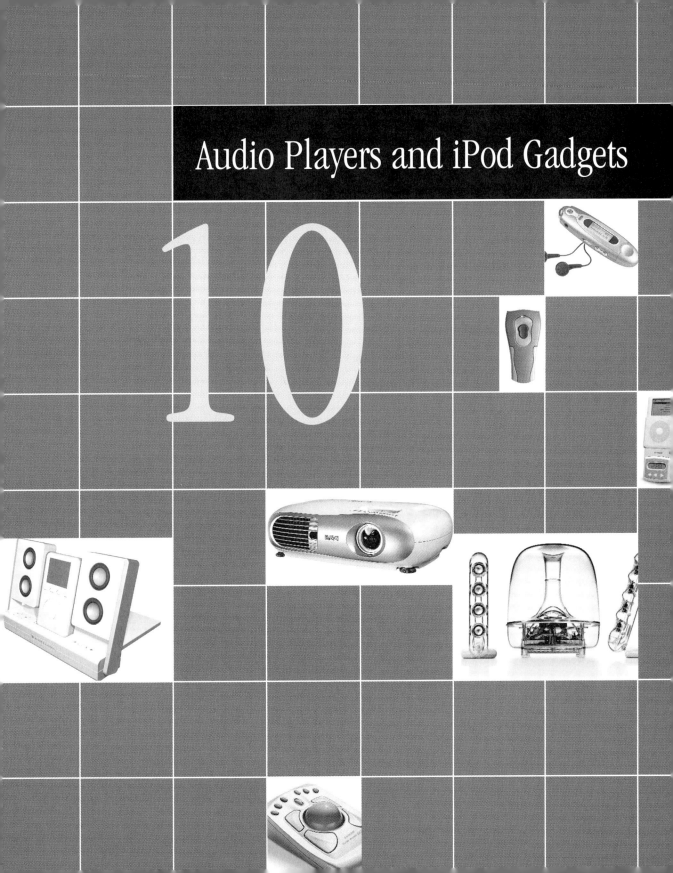

Audio Players

When it comes to digital audio players—by which I mean portable devices that store music as digital files and play back audio that's generally close to CD-quality—there's no doubt that the iPod has stolen the show. Apple's revolutionary device did two things when it arrived on the scene. First, it increased the capacity exponentially compared to the audio players that were available when it first appeared. Second, it worked together with Apple's iTunes player software to make the experience of loading songs onto your iPod—and, eventually, buying those songs and managing the purchase via the Apple iTunes Music store—a satisfying experience for Apple's iPod customers.

There are, of course, other digital audio players, and some of them offer some impressive stats. These days there are two general types of digital audio player—those that use Flash RAM and those that are disk-based. The Flash RAM models generally top out at 256MB or perhaps 512MB of storage, with a few 1GB models now available. The disk-based models, like the iPod, can come in capacities of 40GB or 60GB or more. The main difference is, if a device is disk-based, it needs to

be at least as large as a hard disk, which limits exactly how "micro" it can be.

Flash RAM-based audio players definitely have a huge advantage in that arena, because the memory cards they're based on can be tiny. Depending on a device's Flash RAM capacity, they may only support somewhere between 50 and 150 songs, but if that's all you need, you can get a Flash RAM-based audio player smaller than a credit card or shaped like a pen. And, because Flash RAM players often use the same technology as USB "key" disks and similar devices, you'll find that you can use them for storage as well as for music playback.

The other major issue that differentiates digital audio players is the audio format used for the song files. An iPod, for instance, can play back files stores as MP3, WAV, or AIFF, although the default is the AAC (Advanced Audio Codec) format. MP3 (a shortened version of MPEG Level 3), has been the most popular for years, although AAC and another format, WMA (Windows Media Audio) are beginning to eclipse MP3. All three can create songs that are not only

CD quality, but also compressed files that don't take up much storage space—that lack of high compression is what limited earlier formats, such as the Windows-based WAV and Mac-native AIFF audio formats.

In fact, the battle between AAC and WMA wages on, with Apple having chosen AAC and Microsoft having created WMA. You'll find many WMA-based players on the market that are relatively useless to a typical Mac user; although some will work with third-party software, you can't download or manage songs in the WMA format using iTunes on a Mac, nor can you transfer them or play them back on an iPod.

And while Microsoft can throw its weight around when it comes to standards, the iPod has been tremendously popular, leading to broader acceptance of the AAC format, which offers high-quality, small song sizes, and the ability to encode restrictions into the song file, thanks to the DMA (Digital Music Authorization) built in to AAC. The encoding limits the number of machines that can playback a song bought from iTunes Music Store, theoretically limiting piracy and encouraging song purchases. Again, WMA has a DMA as well, but the two aren't compatible.

In fact, the DMA is the basic reason that the digital music world has moved away from MP3, which was popular in the "free" downloading heyday. With the AAC format and its FreePlay DMA, Apple can offer "rights managed" song files that can't be freely copied and distributed. Indeed, Apple holds the FreePlay DMA close to its vest, so that even other AAC formats—such as the format favored by Real Networks, has a different DMA. That different DMA format technically means the songs can't be used with an iPod, although at this writing, Real has managed to do just that and is selling less expensive songs for the iPod. (Ironically, Real only sells them to Windows-based iPod users.)

With this book in your hands, you're probably a Mac user, so you'll likely opt for a player that can handle Apple's version of the AAC format—meaning an iPod. If you don't want an iPod, then I recommend you look at a player that focuses primarily on MP3, which is an easy-enough format to work with in the Mac OS. A WMA-based player won't be utterly useless to you, but it will be more of a struggle to work with, requiring applications other than iTunes and limiting the songs and online stores that you have access to, because many WMA-centric online options don't have Mac-compatible tools.

iPod

Leo's Pick

Sure, it's clearly the same pick that Captain Obvious would make. But, unlike pretty much any one product that Apple has come up with since the iMac, the iPod has set the industry on its ear. And, in fact, the repercussions of the iPod may be even more widely felt, because they're really helping to add to Apple's bottom line and, to some extent, revitalize interest in Apple's brand name and its other products, such as its desktop and laptop computers.

The iPod is brilliant not because it's the only product that can do what it does, but because it does that thing—organize and play back digital music files—so darned well. Apple has put its legendary research and design efforts into making the iPod's interface great for what it's trying to accomplish. The result is a relatively low-tech display and a very simple, sleek look that nonetheless is extremely clever in its capabilities.

The other thing that's brilliant about the iPod is this: Apple actually made it hip for people to carry a hard drive around with them on their belt loop or in a pocket or purse. What's up with that?! It's at least 50 percent of the secret behind the iPod—because it's hard disk-based, it can hold tons of songs. Of course, that part makes sense.

But what's really cool (to us geeks) are all the other possibilities that having a hard disk means. Like storing gobs of important files that you take from your office to home. Or storing small, standardized vCard (contact-info) files on the iPod and accessing your friends' and colleagues' addresses and phone numbers from the iPod's interface. Or saving standardized calendar files (.ics files) and reporting back your appointments using that same simple interface. Or even allowing a few little games to creep into the interface. No—it's not a PDA. But it is a little portable data device that goes well beyond simply being a music player, and those extra capabilities make it indispensable to any number of Mac users.

Of course, the flip side of the iPod is its integration with iTunes. iTunes is great software that enables you to manage the songs on your iPod—you can "rip" them from your CDs (turning the tracks in to digital audio files) or you can download songs that you purchase from the iTunes Music Store. You can also create playlists for your iPod so that you can play different sets of your songs in easy rotation. iTunes can even translate songs from a few different digital audio formats into the iPod's accepted formats for playback.

Photo courtesy of Apple, Inc.

Photo courtesy of Apple, Inc.

The iPod isn't without its controversy, most of which revolves around the AAC (Advanced Audio Codec) file format that's used for digital audio songs. (AAC is actually a part of the MPEG-4 standard and might not properly be called a "file format" but that's really too nerdy to get into.) AAC is dominant in Apple's sphere of influence because it's a high-quality way to create CD-quality music files that only take up about 1MB of storage space per minute of audio. Apple also likes the format because it includes the copy protection that governs the songs Apple sells in the Music Store.

But, the iPod can't play WMA (Windows Media Audio) files, which is the common format among Windows-focused players. This irks some of the other music services that *also* want to sell $1 songs to owners of iPod, primarily because the iPod is so darned popular. So, you'll see some general grumbling by both Apple and other companies about cross-compatibility and so on.

For now, the iPod works with the iTunes Music Store (as can some other AAC-enabled music players) and other music stores, generally speaking, won't. You won't miss them. Apple has the user experience, the incredible product design and they've made it cool to carry a hard disk. That's all you really need to worry about.

Model: iPod
Manufacturer: Apple (www.apple.com)
Price: $299 (20GB), $399 (40GB)

Photo courtesy of Apple, Inc

iPod mini

The iPod mini gets its own little review (har, har) because it's a slightly different beast. Still hard disk–based and still cute, it's even cuter, offers all the functionality of the iPod and comes in swell colors. There's even an armband that you can buy to strap it to your bicep for jogging. The only caveat—the iPod mini, because it's so mini, only offers 4GB of storage space. Sure, that's plenty. But for $50 more (currently) you get 16 more gigabytes, even if the regular iPod is a little bigger. Still, the iPod mini isn't much of anything if it isn't a status symbol, and there's nothing wrong with giving in to fashion if it suits you.

Model: iPod mini
Manufacturer: Apple (www.apple.com)
Price: $249

Rio Cali

The iPod mini almost makes it hard to recommend any Flash RAM players that are over about $150. The Cali is, however, extremely light and rugged, designed for the "active" type—which you know right off thanks to the included armband. It'll also accept a secondary SD Flash RAM card that can actually increase storage considerably; up to 1GB of additional space, which ups its native 120 song capacity (for the 256MB version) by quite a bit. And, Flash players can't skip, while hard disk-based players can. Digital Networks offers a downloadable iTunes plug-in to make the Cali available in iTunes so that you can load it up with MP3 (but not AAC) songs. And…it's got a built-in stopwatch, which is actually kinda handy, right?

Model: Cali
Manufacturer: Digital Networks (www.rioaudio.com)
Price: $129 (128MB), $179 (256MB)

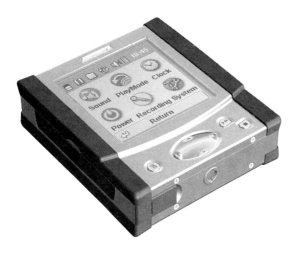

iRock 860

With a name like iRock, it's got to be Mac-compatible, right? Unlike many Flash RAM-based MP3 players, this one trumpets its Mac compatibility and its crossover appeal. It plays MP3s, WMA files, and includes an FM tuner for when you'd like to listen to the radio. It's got 256MB of RAM built in and it's powered by a single AA battery. It pops right up in iTunes with no questions asked; you'll be able to transfer your MP3s (those you create from CDs) but not songs from the iTunes Music Store.

> **Model:** iRock 860
> **Manufacturer:** First International Digital, Inc. (www.myirock.com)
> **Price:** $199 (lower street prices)

Gmini 220

This double-duty hard disk-based device isn't quite an iPod killer—it's a good size, but a little chunky, and it only supports MP3 audio, not AAC. But it does offer a neat little feature the iPod doesn't: it can copy and display images that are stored on a CompactFlash card using a feature it calls the "photo wallet." Sure, it's nice for showing snapshots or family pictures, but it's also nice for previewing the work you've recently done with your digital camera—and downloading it to the 20GB drive so that you can plug the card back into your camera and keep shooting. And it's got a built-in microphone for voice recording and stereo line-in and line-out ports, so it can be used as an audio recorder (in MP3 format) and as a line-level device to connect to your component stereo. Add-on accessories include a handy FM tuner/remote control combination.

> **Model:** Gmini 220
> **Manufacturer:** Archos
> (www.archos.com)
> **Price:** $349

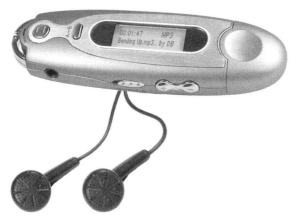

Kanguru Micro MP3 Pro

Again, this one is Flash RAM based and the value is a little tough to sell—for 512MB of storage, you'll pay $200. The advantage is that this thing is incredibly tiny, includes its own little USB port as part of the lipstick-sized device, and it'll double as a USB "key" drive for quickly storing files. Plus, you don't have to get the 512MB model; if you can live with 256MB, then this is a truly tiny little player for about a hundred bucks. Of course, like all the non-Apple players, it's MP3-only, so you won't be able to play songs directly downloaded from the iTunes Music Store.

Model: Micro MP3 Pro
Manufacturer: Kanguru
(www.kanguru.com)
Price: $59.95 (64MB), $74.95 (128MB),
$99.95 (256MB), $199.95 (512MB)

iRiver 300 Series

Here's one more pitch for a Flash RAM-based device. Again, this one is pricey and, again, it's comparable in size to a big lipstick. But it also features an FM tuner, it can record directly to MP3 audio via an external microphone and, if the mood hits you, it can record directly off the radio to an MP3 file. Want to record your favorite radio program and play it back while you're working out at the gym? That's an intriguing option, as is walking around with this little digital amulet on the included neck strap or a more attractive necklace, recording voice messages (up to 72 hours worth at low quality), then plugging in the earbuds before boarding your commuter train (or school bus).

Model: 300 Series
Manufacturer: iRiver (www.iriver.com)
Price: $99.99 (64MB), $129.99 (128MB),
$179.99 (256MB), $279.99 (512MB)

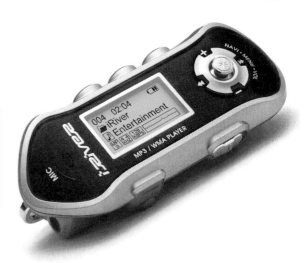

iPod Accessories

Out of its box, the iPod is a relatively simple beast. It's a hard disk with some circuitry that plays back music files; it can also access files designed for contacts, calendar entries, and it can put some simple games on its display. It's got a headset port and it can connect to your Mac via its FireWire port or dock connector, depending on the iPod model.

With Apple and third-party accessories, however, you can get an iPod to do more than almost any of the other MP3 players can do—and often with a little more style. Accessories enable your iPod to transmit a radio signal to a stereo system in your car or home so that you can listen to your digital music through more robust speakers. Others enable you to record audio to the iPod or transfer image files from Flash RAM cards to your iPod's disk. An accessory even enables you to turn your iPod into a universal remote control of sorts.

If there's anything that's a touch infuriating about the iPod, particularly when you decide you want to buy an accessory for the little guy, it's that Apple keeps *slightly* changing the iPod.

Sure, they're upgrades designed to make it thinner, sleeker, and higher capacity, but in a few short years, it's to the point that there have now been four generations of the iPod (plus the iPod mini), all of which have slightly different connectors, dimensions, and specifications. Here's a quick guide:

- Scroll wheel models—The original iPod came in a 5GB version, and a 10GB version, with largely the same technology, was introduced a little later; these have a wheel that literally turns, with small buttons ringing the wheel. These iPods connect directly to the Mac via a FireWire cable, which also recharges the iPod.

- Touch wheel dockless—The next models to appear had a touch wheel, which didn't move, but otherwise looked similar to the first generation. These models still connected directly to your Mac via a FireWire cable and came in 10GB and 20GB capacities, with the addition of a small flap over the FireWire port to keep it a bit cleaner.

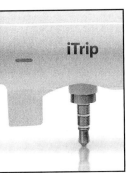  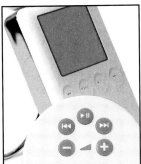  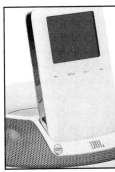

- Touch wheel with dock—These models came in a variety of capacities from 10GB to 40GB, but were otherwise largely similar. These models were thinner and got rid of the FireWire port on the top in exchange for a dock connector on the bottom. You can place the iPod in its dock for transferring files and recharging, or you can plug in a special FireWire cable and use that to connect to your Mac.

- Click wheel models—The most recent generation incorporates the same "click wheel" that the iPod mini offers, which simply allows you to use the same wheel interface for both scrolling between menu items and selecting them. These models are a bit thinner again and are currently available in 20GB and 40GB capacities. They often work with accessories that are compatible with the previous "dockable" iPod models, with a few exceptions.

Sure, those changes tend to be improvements, but it means you need to shop very carefully for accessories that match your particular model. And, of course, there's the iPod mini, which requires its own set of accessories, too.

And, aside from the accessories that add to your iPod's innate capabilities, you've got a slew of possibilities that revolve around boosting the volume or battery life of the little guy. The iPod's popularity and design have inspired a number of speaker solutions, from the portable to outlandish desk-bound models. Aside from improving the sound, accessory speakers may improve the "wow" factor as well.

And, finally, there's some other fun accessorizing you can do in the form of software add-ons for your Mac that enable you to dig a bit deeper into your iPod and make it more functional and perhaps even a bit more fun to use with your Mac.

Griffin iTrip

A number of different solutions have cropped up for getting your iPod to connect to your car stereo. Easily the most elegant is BMW's approach, which is to offer a glovebox-based interface for the iPod. We can't all have BMWs, so the iTrip is probably the next best thing.

The iTrip works by transmitting a relatively weak FM signal that can be received by a car stereo or home stereo system. The result is that your iPod can "broadcast" music to a particular radio station that is then picked up by the stereo receiver and played through its speakers. You can change the playlists and shuffle settings on the iPod, but you still have some control over the volume and equalizer settings via your stereo's controls.

The iTrip isn't the only solution for this sort of connection but it's the most elegant, particularly in terms of styling, as well as being the most flexible—particularly if you want to use it in both your car and near other stereo receivers in your home or office. One advantage is that you can choose any open frequency on the FM dial; some competitors limit you to certain frequencies.

Its one drawback is it draws extra power from the iPod and doesn't offer its own power source. In the car, you may find it handy to buy a separate charger for the power port or cigarette lighter (and if you do, you may want to note the integrated power/transmitter options discussed next). For home or office use, you may want to plug in the iPod's included AC adapter cable.

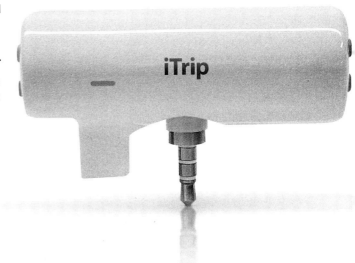

The iTrip offers three models—one for iPods that have a FireWire port, one for iPods with dock connectors, and one for the iPod mini.

> **Model:** iTrip
> **Manufacturer:** Griffin Technology (www.griffintechnology.com)
> **Price:** $34.99 (iTrip), $39.99 (iTrip mini)

DLO Transpod FM

This FM transmitter also requires that it be plugged in to your car's lighter/power port, but it has a special twist—the extending arm that enables you to also see your iPod and manage its controls a little better while driving. (In an ideal world, of course, you'd probably just let your iPod play a long playlist, right?) It's slightly unwieldy, but, at the same time, it cuts down on clutter and gives you an obvious place to put your iPod when you sit down in your car. Models are available for both original and dock-based iPods, including the iPod mini.

Model: Transpod FM
Manufacturer: DLO/Netalog
(www.everythingipod.com)
Price: $99

iCarPlay Wireless

The iCarPlay Wireless adapter combines a cigarette lighter/power port charger with an FM transmitter in a device that's mostly a longish cable, with a small controller box in the middle. Designed for iPods with dock connectors, the adapter plugs in to that dock on one end and the cigarette lighter on the other. The adapter allows you to select from eight different preset frequencies—88.1, 88.3, 88.5, 88.7, 88.9, 89.1, 89.3, 89.5—on the theory that one of them is probably available in any given area. The device requires that it's plugged in to a "hot" port to transmit the iPod's audio, so that should be a consideration if you ever want to use the device when your car is turned off (depending on the way your car powers its lighter/power port).

Model: iCarPlay Wireless
Manufacturer: Monster Cable Products, Inc.
(www.monstercable.com)
Price: $69.95

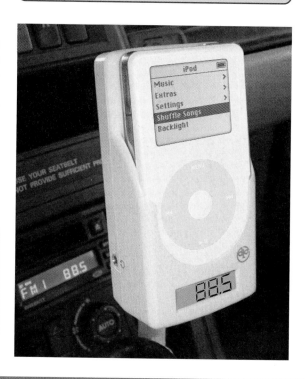

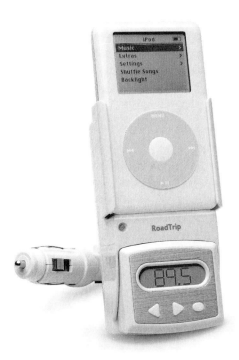

Mobile Cassette Adapter

You might be able to get a better price on a cassette adapter, but would it be in iPod white? A cassette adapter is actually a great choice for iPod owners who happen to have a car that includes a cassette player, whether that's because you've got a cassette/CD stereo in your newer car or you've simply got an old-enough car that all you've got is a cassette player. If that's the case, you can simply leapfrog that silly old CD technology and plug in your iPod directly with a cassette adapter, then listen to your iPod tunes. (After an exhaustive search, however, we've found no iPod-to-8-track adapters. Sorry.)

> **Model:** Mobile Cassette Adapter
> **Manufacturer:** Belkin
> (www.belkin.com)
> **Price:** $79.95

RoadTrip

Similar to the Transpod is the RoadTrip, from Griffin Technology, which also plugs in to a car's power port or cigarette lighter and powers your iPod while it broadcasts the iPod's music to your FM stereo. Using the dock connector for the connection (as opposed to the audio connector, which is what the iTrip uses) can make for a better broadcast signal. As a fun little bonus, the RoadTrip's transmitter can be removed from the unit and plugged into a Mac via USB, enabling you to transmit audio to a home stereo system directly from your Mac.

> **Model:** RoadTrip
> **Manufacturer:** Griffin Technology
> (www.griffintechnology.com)
> **Price:** $79.95

iTalk Voice Recorder

With the iTalk plugged in to the top of an iPod model that includes a dock connector, you can record your voice using either the built-in microphone or an external microphone that you connect to the available input port. You can then record literally hours of spoken audio on the iPod's hard disk, making it a great substitute for the portable microcassette recorder. The device records in MP3, creating relatively small files; connect to iTunes and you'll see your recordings in a playlist called Voice Memos; you can then store them on your Mac, rename them, and call them up at any time. The iTalk includes a pass-through connector for headphones and a built-in speaker, which can be used for any playback; you can even use the iPod Alarm function to turn your iPod into a music alarm.

Model: iTalk
Manufacturer: Griffin Technology
(www.griffintechnology.com)
Price: $39.99

Belkin Media Reader

Remember the iPod is just a hard disk that's cool enough to carry around? With the Media Reader attached, you can quickly transfer anything stored on a Flash RAM card onto your iPod's hard drive, then return it to your digital camera (or whatever else you're using it for). Use the camera's controls to erase the card and you're ready to start shooting again. The reader supports CompactFlash Type I and Type II, SmartMedia, Secure Digital (SD), MemoryStick, and MultiMediaCard (MMC) formats. It's a little bulky and requires batteries, but you can't beat it for photography "in the field" when you don't want to carry your laptop.

Model: Media Reader
Manufacturer: Belkin
(www.belkin.com)
Price: $109.99

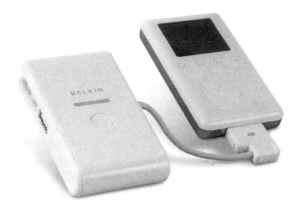

Belkin Digital Camera Link

Belkin offers a different way to go at the transfer-from-camera problem; this devices enables you to connect the camera via USB and transfer images as if your iPod was a Mac. It's got small LEDs that indicate progress, and the iPod itself is already designed to work with such a device. This one's also a little cheaper, too, although it's a bit slower than transferring directly from your camera's memory card.

Model: Digital Camera Link
Manufacturer: Belkin
(www.belkin.com)
Price: $89.99

Navipod IR Remote

This is a nice accessory if you use your iPod in your home stereo system. The Navipod enables you to store the iPod upright and change its settings using a remote control. The stand includes an infrared receiver at the top, which works in conjunction with the remote to enable you to switch songs, go back and forward, change the volume level, or pause playback. Available for both the original form factor and those with the dock connector. It even has a pass-through connector for powered speakers or a line-level connection to your stereo receiver.

Model: Navipod IR Remote
Manufacturer: Ten Technology
(www.tentechnology.com)
Price: $49.95

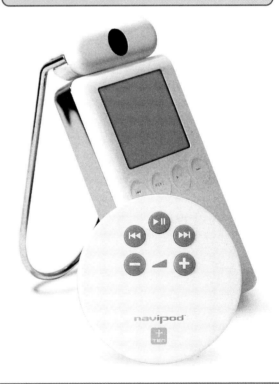

Belkin Battery Backup

If you need your iPod to keep going in the deep jungle or the high mountains—and you happen to have some AA alkaline batteries—you can plug in this puppy and get a few more hours. (If you're eco-guilt kicks in, look for some photo-quality rechargeables.) LEDs on the outside let you know how your battery charge is holding up; it's a nice add-on in a pinch when you need to keep the tunes humming.

Model: Battery Backup
Manufacturer: Belkin
(www.belkin.com)
Price: $69.99

iAir Charger

So, you're on a long cross-country (or international) flight and you realize that your iPod is running down. And, as many of us know, the iPod can be your only link to sanity on a long flight! If you're prepared, you can just whip out your iAir Charger and plug in your iPod to the socket at your seat (if your airline has provided a power port). This one is inexpensive and relatively weightless, so you won't mind having it in your carry-on even if you only use it occasionally. It also includes a cigarette lighter adapter to make it useful in the car, too.

Model: iAir Charger
Manufacturer: Monster Cable
(www.monstercable.com)
Price: $29.95

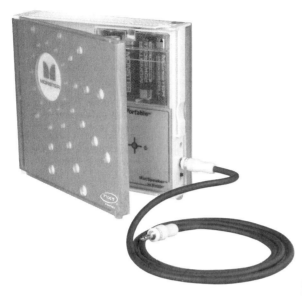

Altec-Lansing InMotion

This portable speaker setup offers digitally amplified sound that with MaxxBass technology to give deep bass response without a sub-woofer. It can run on batteries or an AC adapter, with battery life on four AAs running about 24 hours—perfect for a mobile solution at the beach or park. It's designed for the iPod but offers auxiliary inputs for other devices. The real kicker is that it doubles as a bona fide dock for syncing with your Mac and iTunes, so it's perfect for your desk as well as portable when you need a portable iPod sound system.

Model: InMotion
Manufacturer: Altec-Lansing
(www.alteclansing.com)
Price: $149

Monster iSpeaker Portable

One solution to getting your tunes out of your iPod and into the ether is the iSpeaker Portable, which also happens to fold up nicely for travel. Designed to look like a double-CD case, the iSpeaker offers full stereo sound at two watts per speaker; it can play for about eight hours on four AA alkaline batteries and includes a mini-jack cable that can be used with an iPod or pretty much any other audio device with a headphone jack, including a PowerBook or iBook.

Model: iSpeaker Portable
Manufacturer: Monster Cable
(www.monstercable.com)
Price: $59.95

JBL On-Stage

This is a very cool product, just from the look of it. You'll need a little desk space, but you'll get a lot of sound as a result—the On-Stage includes a tray for supporting your iPod—any generation—or iPod mini. The four small speakers manage to produce a full range of sound, including good (if not wall shaking) bass response, thanks to some premium components and some proprietary tricks of the trade. (JBL is owned by Harman International, the same company that works closely with Apple on its SoundSticks and other audio.) The On-Stage can also charge your iPod and dock it with your Mac, making it a nice addition to your desktop—particularly if your desk has a little room on it.

Model: On-Stage
Manufacturer: JBL (www.jbl.com)
Price: $199

XTremeMac Get Connected Bundle

This is almost the answer to any connectivity question that you have for your iPod. This bundle includes cables that enable you to connect to a home stereo system or computer speakers. It includes a car charger and a cassette adapter to let you play your iPod tunes through a car's cassette deck. Also included is a splitter cable for allowing two people to listen to the same iPod. And, it comes in two flavors—one that connects to older iPods and another that connects to dock-based iPods and the iPod mini.

Model: Get Connected Bundle
Manufacturer: XTremeMac (www.xtrememac.com)
Price: $49.95

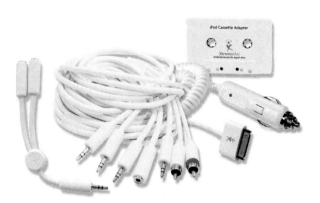

SportsWrap

Forget about the iPod mini—you want all the tunes of a full-fledged iPod, but you'd still like to strap it on and run or dance with it? That's what the SportsWrap is for, the iPod armband that can carry the full weight of a standard issue iPod. It's made of neoprene to keep your iPod dry, offers an expandable strap for larger arms (congrats) and will even strap in your earbuds when you're not using it.

> **Model:** SportsWrap
> **Manufacturer:** XtremeMac
> (www.xtrememac.com)
> **Price:** $29.95

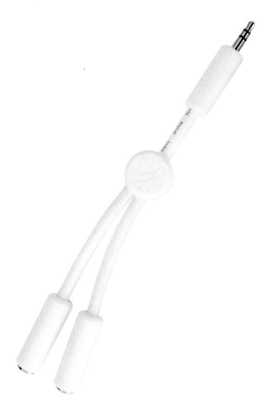

iShare Earbud Splitter

You've got one iPod and two people who need to listen to it in private? The solution is the iShare earbud splitter, which does exactly what you'd expect—lets you use two sets of earbuds or headphones with one iPod. Color coordinated in iPod white to seem like original equipment, the splitter is also very compact, so it doesn't add too much to your cable clutter. And, it uses gold connectors, which may help raise sound quality a notch.

> **Model:** iShare Earbud Splitter
> **Manufacturer:** XtremeMac
> (www.xtrememac.com)
> **Price:** $12.95

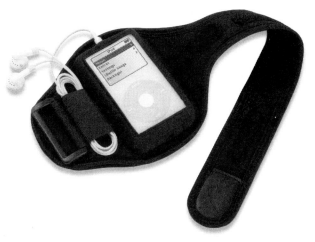

pod2go

Although pod2go is "donationware," this is a great little application to extend your iPod's usefulness as an information appliance. The software will download various items from the Internet, including RSS feeds from your favorite web site or blogs, weather information, movie listings, stock prices, horoscopes, and so on. You can even sync certain text documents to your iPod. Once the sync is complete, you can then use the iPod's interface to view all the information that you've downloaded—most of the news shows up under the Contacts interface. It's a bit of a workaround, but if you keep your iPod synched regularly it's nice to have weather, movie info, and a little something to read between bus stops or while waiting for your sandwich.

Model: pod2go
Manufacturer: Kainjow Software (www.kainjow.com)
Price: Free

PocketMac iPod Edition

This inexpensive program tweaks iSync to turn your iPod into a PDA of sorts. PocketMac iPod Edition makes it possible for you to synchronize not just iCal and Address Book data, but data from Microsoft Entourage as well—that includes Entourage e-mail and notes as well as tasks, to-dos, calendar, and addresses. If you don't use Entourage, you can still sync your Apple Mail e-mail to your iPod. You can also convert your Stickies, and even Word and PDF documents, and display them on your iPod. If you want to quickly access some of this stuff on your iPod—and you're not interested in an all-out PDA—then this is $25 well spent.

Model: PocketMac iPod Edition
Manufacturer: Information Appliance Associates (www.pocketmac.com)
Price: $25

Gadgets for Portable Macs

11

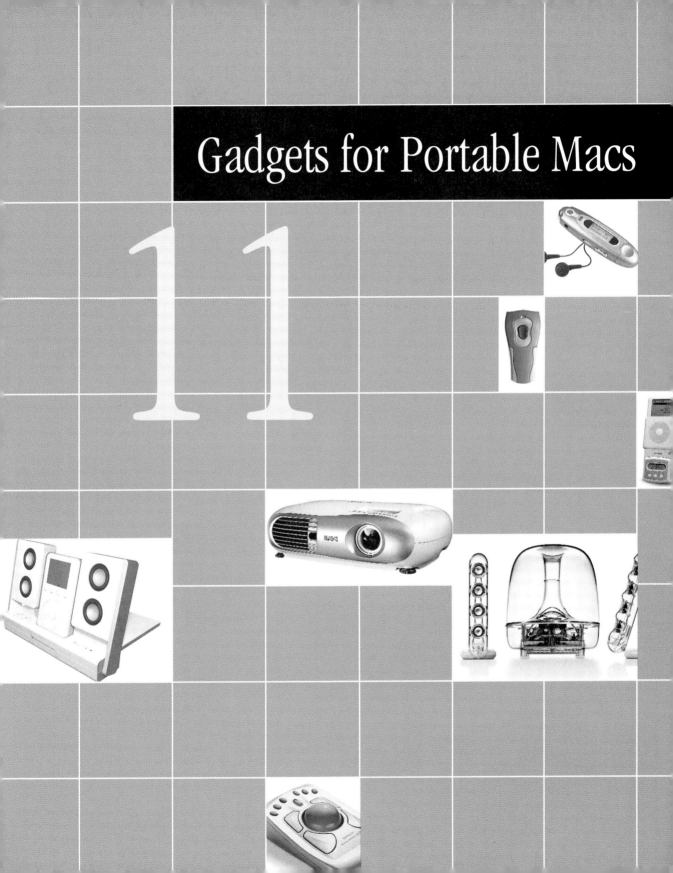

Connectivity and Cards

Apple has sold more and more portable Macs over the past few years, for at least two different reasons. First, and most obvious, is the product design ingenuity that goes into both PowerBooks and iBooks—these are generally gorgeous and practical machines that are often as much status symbols as they are important productivity tools. Toss in the fact that, in recent years, Apple has added different sizes and price ranges for their portables and you end up with a combination that creates a circumstance whereby over 50 percent of Apple's sales are now portables.

The second factor—perhaps just as important—is the connectivity options that are available for portables today. Apple was one of the earliest computer companies to popularize wireless networking via Apple's AirPort technology, which is largely similar and compatible to what the industry calls WiFi. It's that capability that makes it easier to get along with a portable Mac. With all the wireless Internet access that's bouncing around coffee shops, hotels, convention centers, airports, and college campuses, using your portable on the road is easier than ever. That wireless capability also makes it easier to work with your portable around your house or office—you can get up and move around and remain connected to the Internet or your local network.

With the latest round of iMacs and iBooks, you add AirPort support using an AirPort card, which is installed in a special slot that's internal to the portable and that access either under the keyboard or on the undercarriage of the Mac. But that's not the only way you can add wireless connectivity, particularly for PowerBooks.

All recent PowerBook models offer a Cardbus expansion slot that can be used to add various capabilities to your Mac, including Internet or network cards. And, your Mac's USB port can be used for connections as well. Beyond those connections, you can also use the PC Card slot for storage, accessing certain types of Flash RAM cards and for adding ports—FireWire 800, USB 2.0, ethernet—to make your PowerBook a bit more capable.

In this section we'll take a look at AirPort, PC Card, and other expansion options that can help you increase your Mac's connectivity and storage capabilities.

AirPort (Extreme) Card

Okay, so maybe this pick seems obvious. I can't help it! The truth is that a PowerBook or iBook without an AirPort card is only half a machine. I'm sure there are a few folks out there who have no use for wireless connectivity, but the vast majority of portable Macs are made better by adding AirPort.

The original AirPort card conforms to the IEEE 802.11b standard, which is slower than the latest cards. 802.11b is widely compatible, however, and it's still good enough for a lot of wireless tasks, as it can move data at up to 11Mbps, or about 1.5 megabytes per second. Not too shabby. Older AirPort-enabled Macs only support the original card, by the way.

If your Mac can support the AirPort Extreme card—earlier AirPort-enabled Macs require the original AirPort card, while the latest models all require the AirPort Extreme card—then your Mac has the added advantage of conforming to the 802.11g standard, which offers speeds up to 54Mbps, or about 6.75 megabytes per second. That's good enough for all sorts of networking and Internet tasks. And the Extreme card can drop back to 802.11b speeds when necessary, such as when it encounters a wireless network or router that only supports the earlier protocol. (Wireless connections can also drop back in speed because of distance from the router/base station or because of the load on the network.)

Either type of AirPort card can get you up and running on any public WiFi-compatible networks, and you can generally use your Mac with pay-as-you-go services, or services that require a subscription. Although you'll often find coffee shops that still offer free access, many of them are offering access only for members of larger Internet providers; for instance, in Starbucks locations that offer wireless access, you currently have to have a T-Mobile wireless account.

You can also use your AirPort card to access a wireless network in your home or office, which can be routed to your AirPort-equipped Mac via either an AirPort base station or using some other sort of wireless router. Apple's AirPort card is generally compatible with security schemes and features offered by other manufacturers of WiFi routers, so you'll be able to access your network or the Internet with appropriate levels of security and privacy...if you take the time to set them up.

Picture courtesy of Apple, Inc.

Model: AirPort Card
Manufacturer: Apple (www.apple.com)
Price: $99 (Extreme model), $69 (original model, often refurbished or discounted)

Aria Extreme Card

The Aria Extreme card is a 54Kbps WiFi adapter card that uses the Cardbus standard. With a PowerBook G3 or an early PowerBook G4 model, you can plug the Aria Extreme in and get 802.11g speeds for wireless connections. The card works with standard AirPort drivers to give you a seamless experience; you can use the same software tools and Network control panel that is used with actual Apple AirPort devices and you can connect to an AirPort Extreme Base station, AirPort Express base station, or most any third-party WiFi router.

Model: Aria Extreme
Manufacturer: Sonnet Technologies
(www.sonnettech.com)
Price: $79.95

MacSense AeroCard Extreme

This will sound sort of familiar—the AeroCard Extreme adapter can work with Mac or PC; with your PowerBook, it plugs into the Cardbus slot and works directly with Apple's AirPort drivers to give you 802.11b or 802.11g connection speeds for your PowerBook. It's worth noting that, not only can you use the card for wireless connections, but you can actually use the card and your PowerBook to serve an Ethernet-based Internet connection to other AirPort-enabled Macs using Apple's Internet Sharing feature.

Model: AeroCard Extreme
Manufacturer: MacSense
(www.macsense.com)
Price: $89.95

D-Link 10/100 Ethernet Adapter

Here's an option for getting a high-speed ethernet connection for your PowerBook. The card is plug-and-play, meaning you can slide it into the PowerBook while the Mac is up and running and it'll be instantly recognized and added as one of your options in the Networking pane of the System Preferences application. Plug in an ethernet cable, then select the new port in the Network pane, configure it, and you're up and running on your LAN.

> **Model:** 10/100 Ethernet Adapter
> **Manufacturer:** D-Link (www.dlink.com)
> **Price:** $29

D-Link Cardbus USB 2.0 Adapter

Another of the primary uses for the Cardbus slot is adding ports to your Mac for peripherals. Many of us have PowerBooks that lack USB 2.0, for instance, and yet USB 2.0 is nice to have for some cross-platform, high-speed connections. (Digital cameras that lack FireWire ports come to mind; with the latest digital cameras and USB 2.0 connections you get high-speed transfer of your photos.) The D-Link USB 2.0 adapter is affordable, fast, and works well with PowerBooks running Mac OS X 10.2 or higher (along with the downloadable driver).

> **Model:** Cardbus USB 2.0 Adapter
> **Manufacturer:** D-Link (www.dlink.com)
> **Price:** $39

OrangeLink FireWire 800 Adapter

This Cardbus adapter gives many PowerBook users something they don't have access to yet—FireWire 800 ports. With the new double-speed FireWire standard, the latest external hard disks and other peripherals can move data at 800 Mbps or about 100 megabytes per second; you'll need special FireWire 800 cables and devices, although FireWire 400-to-800 adapters and cables are also available and the card is fully backward compatible with the older standard. With an optional power adapter, the card can provide power to FireWire devices, although it doesn't power the bus by default.

Model: OrangeLink
Manufacturer: OrangeMicro
(www.orangemicro.com)
Price: $89

OrangeCombo USB/FireWire Card

Again taking advantage of the flexibility of the Cardbus standard, this card offers both USB 2.0 ports and FireWire ports (4-pin and 6-pin varieties) for your PowerBook. If your PowerBook G3 lacks FireWire ports, you can add them with this card (assuming the PowerBook supports the Cardbus standard; check carefully). Or, you'll find this card handy if you'd like USB 2.0 ports and don't mind an extra FireWire port for convenience and speed. (For instance, you can connect a DV camcorder to one FireWire port and an external FireWire drive to another—they'll be on separate data buses that way, which may increase performance.)

Model: OrangeCombo
Manufacturer: OrangeMicro
(www.orangemicro.com)
Price: $99

Merlin C201 (Sprint PCS Connection Card)

In many locales, you can get relatively high-speed Internet access for a portable computer using a data service from a mobile phone company; Sprint PCS, for example, offers the Merlin C201, a PC Card, as one option for wireless Internet access. (Sprint calls it the Sprint PCS Connection Card.) Although not technically Mac-compatible right out of the box, third-party drivers are available to enable you to use the card with your PowerBook—visit the unaffiliated site http://www.sprintpcsinfo.com/, for example, to search for the drivers. (You also might need a friend with a PC to activate the card initially.) When you're up and running, the C201 will give you speeds of up to 144Kbps, or about three times the speed of a standard modem.

Model: Merlin C201
Manufacturer: Novatel Wireless (www.novatelwireless.com) and SprintPCS (www.sprintpcs.com)
Price: $199.99 (plans and discounts vary)

GC Edge PC Card Modem

Here's another wireless Internet card that offers marginal Mac support; AT&T, Cingular, and T-Mobile all offer a version of the Sony-Ericsson "Edge" card for wireless access. On the right network, certain models of these cards can pull down data at over 245 Mbps; more typical connections net out at around 56 Kbps. Data service isn't yet cheap from any of these providers, but if you don't use too many megabytes of data (save your downloading and e-mail attachments for when you get a WiFi or ethernet connection), then you can really make handy use of the service wherever a compatible wireless network is available. If, that is, you can get the card to work. This one requires third-party software, which is, blissfully, available. (See QuickLink Mobile in next gadget review.)

Model: GC83 Edge PC Card
Manufacturer: Sony-Ericsson (www.sonyericsson.com)
Price: Free–$249 (depending on service agreement)

QuickLink Mobile

QuickLink Mobile for Mac is almost magic software; it enables you to use various cell phones and Sony-Ericsson PC cards with your Mac, including phones with Bluetooth support and Edge PC Cards that are generally considered not to be Mac compatible. You choose the phone or card that you have and the mobile service that you use when you order the software—if appropriate, your package will include both the software and a data connection cable. The software not only lets you manage the mobile Internet connection, but makes it easy to switch between mobile service and WiFi where it's available.

> **Model:** QuickLink Mobile for Mac
> **Manufacturer:** Smith-Micro Software
> (www.smithmicro.com)
> **Price:** $29.95–$49.95 (depending on version and hardware)

Cardbus-to-PCI Chassis

So, you've got a PowerBook but you need to work with a PCI expansion card—or more than one. Believe it or not, it can be done. The Cardbus-to-PCI chassis makes it possible to add a single PCI card that your PowerBook can access or many of them. If you need to do this, you'll usually know—perhaps you want to use a PowerBook as the center of a serious video editing suite or other specialized (medical, military, scientific) solution. Or maybe there's one special card you need to access. In any case, this isn't a cheap solution, but it's flexible and extremely cool.

> **Model:** Cardbus-to-PCI chassis
> **Manufacturer:** Magma Expansion
> (www.mobl.com)
> **Price:** $995 (one slot)
> $1,220–$1,345 (four slot)

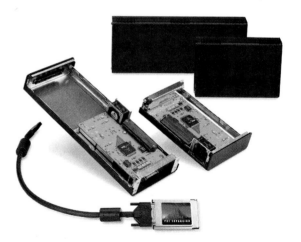

Practicality and Power

If design and connectivity are two great reasons to move to a portable Mac, then the drawbacks—or, at least, occasional reasons for complaints—are practicality and how you get power to the Mac, including a little ancillary issue called "heat." Especially when the heat is applied to the general area of the human body called the "lap."

Yes, iBooks and PowerBooks are pretty portable. But if you really try to use your PowerBook or iBook as a desktop replacement, you'll encounter certain tradeoffs. In this section, we'll take a look at some gizmos that make your portable Mac a bit easier to use in a variety of circumstances, including stands that make them easier to look at on your desk and dock solutions that enable you to connect to external displays, keyboards, and so on when you're in the office.

At the same time, a number of gadgets and accessories can make it more convenient to carry and use your PowerBook or iBook on the road, including carry cases, handles, and clever add-ons that make your portable easier to use in low-light situations or even in inclement weather.

As for power, it's always nice to have a little extra battery time, and although there are no guarantees, you will come across some gadgets to help you manage power consumption, run your Mac's power supply under various conditions, and even recharge its battery in novel ways. We'll also take in some options that help you manage and dissipate heat from your Mac portable.

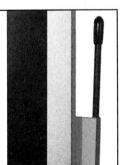    

Bookendz

Leo's Pick

The perfect solution for a "dockable" PowerBook hasn't come along yet—or, more accurately, it hasn't come back since the PowerBook Duo in the mid-to-late 1990s. (The Duo was a subnotebook that slipped into its desktop dock like a VHS tape, enabling you to use external peripherals with it.)

You, can, however, get some of the advantages of such a setup, including the capability to plug in and use an external display, keyboard, and mouse when you're sitting at your desktop with your Mac portable; all those are good ergonomic choices, as sitting hunched over your portable typing on its limited keyboard generally isn't recommended for too many hours of the day.

Instead, the current best thing is a Bookendz dock, which can be used to slide onto the various ports on the back or side of today's PowerBooks and iBooks. The Bookendz enables you to keep desktop items plugged in to the dock at all times—keyboards, ethernet cables, external displays, or hard disks—and then connect or disconnect the PowerBook as desired. When the PowerBook is plugged in to the dock, it works as a desktop computer of sorts; when it's free from the dock, you can use it as you normally would in "portable" mode.

The Bookendz are offered in different models that are specific to your PowerBook or iBook model; the PowerBook models tend to be a bit more substantial if only because you slide the computer onto the device and then plug in the dongles and adapters that fit the PowerBook's built-in ports; for the iBook models, you simply line up the device on the side of the iBook (or a 12-inch PowerBook) and press it into the ports. In either case, though, it can keep you from playing musical cables and fishing around behind (or on the side) of your Mac looking for the right cable and connector every time you sit down at your desk to compute.

Model: Bookendz dock
Manufacturer: Photo Control (www.photo-control.com)
Price: $149.95–$249.95 (depending on model)

PowerBook Handles

QuickerTek touts their PowerBook handles as "strong enough, nay, way too strong" in their effort to gain your trust and help you believe that by installing the handles that even the extra weight—which they claim is "super light"—is something that will be offset by the convenience of having a strong handle by which to lift the PowerBook. And they're probably right. What's more, the handles offer a tilt to your PowerBook when it's sitting on your desk, which may improve the look and ergonomic feel a bit. Models vary for the recent PowerBook G4 models in Titanium, Aluminum, and different display sizes.

Model: PowerBook Handles
Manufacturer: QuickerTek
(www.quickertek.com)
Price: $35–$40

PowerBook Antennas

QuickerTek also offers some creative and innovate (and perhaps slightly unsightly) AirPort antennas for Titanium and Aluminum PowerBooks, including a special model for the 12-inch PowerBook. The antennas improve reception up to double the signal strength (according to the company) over the rather anemic built-in antenna that some of the PowerBook models have become known for. The antenna whip, which is attached via Velcro to your Mac's case, works by threading cable through the PC Card slot (or actually fitting into it, depending on the model) so note that you won't be able to use the slot if you're using the antenna.

Model: PowerBook Antenna
Manufacturer: QuickerTek
(www.quickertek.com)
Price: $89

Targus Coolpad

The Coolpad is designed to lift your PowerBook slightly in order to allow air to flow around it and keep its warm bottom off your legs or other surfaces when you're using it. You simply set your PowerBook on the Coolpad, which has rubber feet to keep it in place. The Traveler Coolpad model is a lightweight version that raises the PowerBook slightly and offers a swivel, which is handy for presentations or for rotating the display to show a colleague something on the screen. The Podium Coolpad also swivels while offering adjustable height, even enabling you to reverse the tilt (so that the keyboard tilts down toward the display), which may have ergonomic benefits.

Model: Coolpad
Manufacturer: Targus
(www.targus.com)
Price: $19.99 (Traveler)
$29.99 (Podium)

Targus Notebook Stand

Another problem with day-to-day use of a laptop is the likelihood that the laptop's display isn't positioned high enough relative to your sightline so that you maintain an ergonomic position. (The top of any desktop display should be level with your eyes when you look straight ahead.) There's not much you can do about that when you're portable, but at your desk, a good plan is to connect an external keyboard and mouse and then raise your PowerBook up closer to eye level; that's what this basic-black Notebook Stand does, plus it's got cubbies and shelves for extra storage.

Model: Notebook Stand
Manufacturer: Targus
(www.targus.com)
Price: $19.95

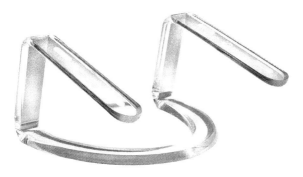

iCurve

Image conscious? Of course we are—we're Mac users! Here's the deal—the iCurve does what any number of little trays and desktop devices can do to elevate your iBook or PowerBook, but the iCurve looks good doing it. It's a particularly nice fit for Apple's Lucite-and-white keyboards, and there's nothing that screams Buck Rogers like an iBook floating above a wireless Apple keyboard and mouse. It's a very chic notebook-as-desktop solution, my friend.

Model: iCurve
Manufacturer: Griffin Technology
(www.griffintechnology.com)
Price: $39.95

Kensington Universal Car/Air/AC Adapter

Sure, Apple includes some nice little AC adapters with its PowerBooks and iBooks, but this one offers the advantage of being easily switched between an AC wall plug, an automotive cigarette lighter/power port, and an Empower-standard power port on an airliner. It comes with a zippered pouch, interchangeable ends so that it will work with various iBook and PowerBook models, and it comes in both black or an attractive white finish that matches the latest industrial designs from Apple.

Model: Universal Car/Air/AC Adapter
Manufacturer: Kensington
(www.kensington.com)
Price: $119.99 ($79.99 for car/air only)

Kensington FlyLight Platinum

Because USB is a powered bus, Kensington can offer this small, flexible light that's powered by the USB port that it plugs into. This light is great for aiming at your keyboard in low-light situations so that you can keep typing; you could also use it on a car, plane, or train to read a map or a book without disturbing the person next to you. Kensington also offers the FlyFan, which is a small personal fan for moving a little air around.

Model: FlyLight Platinum
Manufacturer: Kensington
(www.kensington.com)
Price: $19.95 (FlyFan, $9.95)

Portable Modem and Ethernet Cords

Sure you can ball up the cables that you need to take with you, but how about a sleek retractable solution? Your pick—a modem cable for hotel rooms that have dataports or an ethernet cable if you know you'll be staying (or working) somewhere that offers high-speed access. Or, get both and squirrel them away in your notebook carry-on.

Model: Portable Cords
Manufacturer: Kensington
(www.kensington.com)
Price: $9.99 (modem cord)
$19.99 (Ethernet cord)

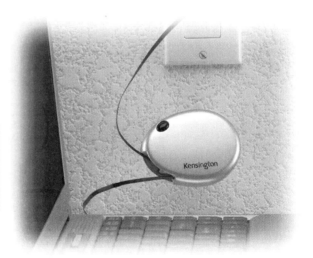

PowerBook Security and Protection

This topic sounds like we're assigning body guards for our portables—yes, we love them that much—but actually what I want to talk about are ways to package and carry your portable—cases, really—as well as some options for securing your portable in situations where you'd like to see it locked down a bit.

Aside from physical security, there are a few software items you can think about, too, that are worth mentioning here. If you're working in Mac OS X, of course, you can assign meaningful passwords to your account, so that if anyone picks up your Mac they first have to sign in to it using your password. Another feature that's worth looking into is Mac OS X 10.3 and later's encryption feature, called FileVault, which enables you to encrypt all the data stored in your home folder, which can include documents, songs, photos, databases, addresses—particularly financial information and any important business items that you tend to carry with your on your Mac portable. Check out the Security pane in System Preferences to learn more about FileVault.

The other important step is a good backup strategy. If you ever lose your PowerBook or iBook, you'll likely be losing a lot of data as well, even if that data is encrypted and password-protected. It's still gone. That's why a deskbound backup solution—at the very least an external hard disk or a rotational plan of backing up to CD-R or DVD-R media—is an important step if the contents of your PowerBook or iBook are of serious value to you. After all, Mac portables are, by definition, a whole lot easier to lose than Mac desktops.

With those caveats out of the way, then, let's take a look at some of the ways to keep your Mac safe and secure while you're moving it around.

The Detour

Leo's Pick

If you're willing to go with a youthful look for your laptop bag, here's a great one. The Detour offers three different carrying options: A top handle enables you to carry it like a briefcase, a shoulder strap gives it a messenger-bag feel, or you can break out the stowable back straps and turn it into a full-on day pack. What I like about it is that it can look both sporty and high-tech and reasonably conservative at the same time—it's a good bag for creative types who end up pulling a PowerBook or iBook out in coffee shops (or presentations).

The Detour seems to be particularly well designed for a biking (or Vespa) lifestyle, with a water-resistent enclosure and rubberized, weatherproof bottom. The top exterior pocket provides quick access, and it's not a bad spot to stow an iPod; the side pockets can accommodate two water bottles. An interior document pocket is separated from the laptop computer compartment, which is padded to keep your Mac secure from scratching and a little light pounding on the bag. (I still wouldn't pick it up and toss it across the room.)

The Detour can accommodate Mac models between the 12-inch iBook and PowerBook and the 15-inch PowerBook, including the 14-inch iBook. That leaves out the 17-inch PowerBook, which is too large for the Detour; Timbuk2 makes the Commute XL series for 17-inch PowerBooks and most widescreen PC laptops.

Model: Detour
Manufacturer: Timbuk2 (www.timbuk2.com)
Price: $100

Data Transfer Messenger Bag

This stylish, urban bag takes a slightly more laid back approach to carrying your laptop, although it still has a floating "nest" design to secure the electronics in case the bag is handled roughly. The design on this one doesn't really scream "laptop case" either, and it has handy side pockets for iPods, PDAs, or small water bottles and snacks. The single strap messenger bag makes for easy treks through city streets or busy airports, while the zippered top allows quick access to small items when the flap is closed. Designed for PowerBooks up to 17-inches (and may be a bit too loose for 12-inch models).

Model: Eagle Creek
Manufacturer: Data Transfer
(www.eaglecreek.com)
Price: $75

Sumdex eTech Messenger Bag

Not planning a trip halfway across the planet? For your daily commute, the eTech Messenger bag is a slim, water-resistant case that holds up to a 17-inch PowerBook securely and still offers room for a book or two, or a sheaf of papers. The styling is clean and crisp and the fold-out organization section offers space for PDAs, CDs, pens, and a loop for keys. This is a lightweight bag that's still good for a trip to the office or for at least one class worth of books and materials when you're taking your portable, too.

Model: eTech Messenger Bag
Manufacturer: Sumdex
(www.sumdex.com)
Price: $49.95

The Acme Slim Bag

These extremely stylish bags (actually you can pay less for only *rather* stylish bags as well) offer, perhaps, minimal protection for your iBook or PowerBook. But they look so good doing it. And, truth is, they're designed to compliment your Mac portable nicely and take care of it with a quilted interior, "splash proof" zippers, and a rear pocket that you can fill with power adapters and cords. The Slim is a cross between a bag and a "sleeve" meaning it can work well inserted into another bag for more serious travel.

Model: Acme Made
Manufacturer: Slim Bag
(www.acmemade.com)
Price: $79.99–$139.99 depending on style/design

Booq BP.3[system]

If you're not afraid to look like a techie type, then the Booq BP.3 System is just about perfect for carrying a laptop around, whether you're biking, hiking, or traveling. Suffice to say that every pocket and cubby has been thought through, with space for electronics, water bottles, flat documents, sunglasses, and so on. There's even a protected iPod pocket that enables you to thread headphones through a hole in the pack! The "[system]" approach includes a fitted laptop sleeve that you can order to fit your portable. Along with the sleeve comes Fonepaq and PDApaq pockets that attach to your shoulder straps for quick access; the amazing BodyHuq strap design makes for great weight distribution—you'll swear by it if you're ever in San Francisco for Macworld Expo, for instance.

Model: Booq BP.3[system]
Manufacturer: Booq
(www.booqbags.com)
Price: $159.95

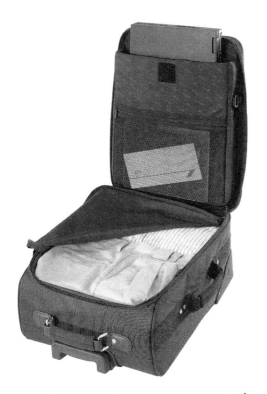

Microsaver Security Cable

Notebook security locks won't necessarily guarantee that your PowerBook or iBook won't come up missing, but it does make your portable a more difficult target. These locks loop through the security hole attached to your Mac and around some relatively immobile piece of furniture. If you handle things correctly, Kensington even offers a replacement guarantee if anyone manages to take your portable when it's properly secured.

Model: Microsaver Security Cable
Manufacturer: Kensington
(www.microsaver.com)
Price: $54.99

Trademark II Overnight Roller

All right, how about a bag that is a bit more corporate? Another way to save your back is to roll your laptop (and other accessories and files and such) around behind you as you walk. But we'll still twist things a bit—the TradeMark II Overnight Roller is both carry-on luggage and a specially designed laptop carrier. With pockets for documents, PDAs, and airline tickets, the TradeMark II separates your clothes and your work materials so that you can even take it into meetings with you.

Model: Trademark II Overnight Roller
Manufacturer: Targus
(www.targus.com)
Price: $99.99

iCover

On many PowerBook and iBook models the oils that the keyboard collects from your fingers ends up smudged onto the LCD display, sometimes causing a permanent streaking. The solution is to place something over the keyboard or display; although there are cheaper solutions, none is more elegant than the micro suede slide-on cover that Acme Made offers. This protector slips over your entire display but leaves enough room for the keys and the latch on your portable so that it closes (and sleeps) properly. Plus it does double-duty of adding some protection from scratches.

Model: iCover
Manufacturer: Acme Made
(www.acmemade.com)
Price: $24.99–$25.99 depending on size

SmartSockets Portable Surge Protector

While your PowerBook or iBook is a little more immune to power outages than the typical Mac (because its internal battery can keep it running) it's still susceptible to power surges and spikes, particularly over phone lines used for modem connections. To protect your Mac in hotel rooms or business centers, the Portable Surge Protector offers protection for laptop power and the modem; it also acts as a splitter in case you stay in a room (motel, bed and breakfast, guest room) that doesn't offer a dataport connection.

Model: Portable Surge Protector
Manufacturer: Kensington
(www.kensington.com)
Price: $14.99

Desktop Mac and Home Gadgets

12

Desktop Mac Add-Ons

When the iMac first appeared in 1999, it hit with such a splash that suddenly there were Bondi Blue colored peripherals all over the market. A little later, when Apple introduced multicolored iMacs, the multicolored peripherals soon followed. Part of that excitement was over the fact that the iMac pushed a new way of connecting to peripherals—USB. The market responded with gadgets that worked for both Macs and PCs. The other part of that excitement was purely esthetic; peripheral manufacturers simply seemed to enjoy churning out colorful components that might look good sitting next to the iMac.

Today, Apple's consumer designs are white plastic or brushed metal, and the designs of the peripherals made by third-party manufacturers often match. But the desire to build peripherals that seemed designed specifically to go with the iMac and eMac is still strong, including some gadgets that truly complement the actual machines and their industrial design, along with some others that simply seem to be along for the ride.

In this section we'll take a look at some gadgets that are designed to work specifically with the iMac G4, the eMac, or specific Power Macintosh models, including a number of items that you haven't seen elsewhere in the book. These are devices designed, ideally, to specifically enhance your experience with these particular models of Macintosh. Because Apple's consumer models lack internal slots for upgradeability, some of these gadgets are clever workarounds for adding peripherals and upgrades.

And while we're talking about upgrades, we'll look at a few that are designed to breathe life into older iMac G3 models in their various colorful "beachball" designs. If you still have an older iMac that you'd like to see stay useful for a bit longer, there are a few options to consider.

iGo

If you've got one of the white iMac G4s, then you probably already feel like you're making a statement with it. Well, you might as well go all out with this unique desk designed specifically to work with that model of iMac. It looks stunning, and offers some practical aspects as well.

The desk (stand?) comes in two different models—a sit-down model and a stand-up model. The sit-down model is sized about right for a desk chair and features rollers that let you move the desk around. This one is just about a perfect fit for a sparsely decorated loft space with modern furnishings. The other is designed without wheels and works when you're standing (for customer service in a retail environment, for example) or on a barstool-height chair.

The iGo enables you to move the keyboard up and down to locate an appropriate height for ergonomic comfort, while the iMac's own swivel arm makes it possible for you to adjust the display. And the unique lamp beneath the base can be used for computing in near dark to illuminate the keyboard and mouse, which can be switched from right side to left side easily.

This desk is designed specifically and completely for the iMac—cables are hidden, translucent white banding is used to press the cables together, and molded speaker pods are designed to hold the iMac's external speakers. There's even a small tray for an iPod or other peripheral device that you'd like to roll around with you.

No doubt this is a luxury, and it won't suit everyone, but just think how great it must be to love that old iMac design so much that you buy a desk specifically for it. It only remains to be seen if the new iMac will get the same treatment.

Model: iGo
Manufacturer: Rain Design
(www.raindesigninc.com)
Price: $399 (direct plus shipping)

Picture courtesy of Apple, Inc.

eMac Tilt and Swivel Stand

Why Apple doesn't include this in the box with the eMac is, I guess, a testament to the fact that they wanted to really keep the cost down. But the tilt and swivel stand adds a lot to the eMac experience by giving you a display at a better ergonomic height and more freedom to angle it the way you need it, in order to avoid glare and get a good look at what's on that screen. It'll even go 360 degrees from side-to-side, enabling you to swing it around (okay...shove it around) and show the screen to someone sitting next to you. That's assuming, of course, that there's room on your desk.

Model: eMac Tilt and Swivel Stand
Manufacturer: Apple (www.apple.com)
Price: $49.95

MacSkate

This cool little device enables you to push a Power Macintosh G4 or G5 around the office a bit easier, which can be handy for moving it around to get at the ports in the back or to open up the side of the case. And, having the skate on the Power Macintosh makes it easier to transport it if you ever need to roll it into a conference room and hook it up for a presentation or if you want to be able to move it around from, say, your home office to the beach house, and back again. This light, but strong, aluminum device installs securely to make your Mac instantly more mobile.

Model: Mac Skate
Manufacturer: Marathon Computer (www.marathoncomputer.com)
Price: $59

Uniriser

The Uniriser is a simple plastic monitor stand for beachball-style iMacs that happens to be both attractive and functional. The clear plastic matches the iMac and doesn't take away from its styling at all; it also features a shelf that's great for external peripherals, such as a removable media drive or an iPod. The Uniriser brings the iMac up off the table and to a better ergonomic height so that you don't lean down or bend your neck over it to look at the iMac.

Model: Uniriser
Manufacturer: Contour Design (www.contourdesign.com)
Price: $24.95

DeskMount

Marathon Computer also makes the very cool DeskMount solution for Power Macintosh G4 and G5 models. The DeskMount enables you to anchor your Power Mac into the bottom of your desk surface, thus raising it up off the floor and at a convenient height for accessing the CD/DVD drive and other front-panel controls. (It's also a little more accessible for banging your knee into it, so watch out for that part.) According to the company's materials you can anchor the DeskMount to just about any surface that stays in solid form at room temperature.

Model: DeskMount
Manufacturer: Marathon Computer (www.marathoncomputer.com)
Price: $59

iDock FireWire Edition

Originally designed to offer legacy ports (serial and SCSI ports) to early iMacs, the last edition of the iDock now offers additional FireWire and powered USB ports along with its swivel base. Aimed at that last round of beachball-style iMac G3s—the slot-loading models with FireWire ports—this little device is a great way to lift the screen and swivel the iMac while enabling you to connect a number of external peripherals.

Model: iDock FireWire Edition
Manufacturer: AddLogix
(www.addlogix.com)
Price: $139.95

G-Dock

Another offering from AddLogix (which was once called CompuCable) is the G-Dock. This amazing little add-on (with an impressive price) offers a number of legacy ports—Mac serial and ADB along with four USB ports—to a Power Macintosh G4, as well as a floppy drive that sits in a special bay that can be "hot-swapped" with other devices, including an ATAPI adapter, a SCSI adapter, and so on. Note that support for a lot of these ports is gone from Mac OS X, so the device works best in Mac OS 9. But if you're sticking with legacy applications and the classic Mac OS for a while longer, you might be able to use your older peripherals and floppies, too.

Model: G-Dock
Manufacturer: AddLogix
(www.addlogix.com)
Price: $199

KVM Switches

How's this for a scenario: You've got two different Macs—or even a Mac and a PC—and you'd like to be able to use one monitor with both of them. But wait…you'd also like to use the same keyboard and mouse to control each computer, and you want to be able to switch between them on-the-fly as the mood suits you. Seem impossible? That's what the entire class of KVM switches is designed to do.

KVM stands for keyboard, video, mouse, and the "switch" part is what you can do between different computers but continuing to use the same K, V, and M. Pretty straightforward. In order to pull this off, though, you need to have a device that's compatible with both machines; if you're working with two Macs, then you shouldn't have much problem as long as they're both modern, USB-based models. If you're trying to switch between a PC and a Mac, then USB is pretty much a requirement; you'll need it in order to use compatible mice and keyboards between the two machines.

Beyond that, KVM is essentially a game of adapters and compatibility. If you're switching

between a Mac and a PC, it's best to have third-party USB keyboards and mice, for instance, as they tend to be a bit more cross-platform than Apple's models. (You'll want at least a two-button mouse for working in Windows, for instance, if you're switching between the OSes.) And the type of display connection you have for your Macs (and PCs) is important, too; most KVM switches are VGA-based, so if you have an ADC or DVI connection between your Mac and your display, you may need to adapt it to a VGA connection in order to send it through the KVM switch, particularly for cross-platform solutions. (As you'll see, it's possible to control two ADC-based Macs from one display with a special KVM.)

So, read carefully, consider your setup and check for the need for additional cables and adapters before leaping into a KVM solution. But if you've ever wanted to use two machines without moving your hands from the same keyboard or your eyes from the same display, here's your chance.

MiniView USB KVM Kit

This kit is both simple and sublime. Your problem: You've got two machines—either two USB-based Macs or a USB-based Mac and a USB-based PC. You want to use those machines with one keyboard, one mouse, one display, and perhaps even one set of audio speakers. You may even have up to two USB peripherals that you'd like to use with each machine—a printer and a scanner, for instance. As long as all those devices are actually compatible with the PCs or Macs in question, then this MiniView USB KVM Kit is all you need to make it happen.

You begin by connecting the keyboard and mouse to the front of the KVM switch and the display you'll be using to the appropriate port on the back. Then, you connect a VGA display cable between each CPU and its corresponding port on the back of the KVM switch (you may need to purchase these cables) and you connect one USB port from each CPU to its corresponding USB port on the KVM switch (these cables are included). If you have additional USB devices you want to share between the two CPUs, connect them to the available USB ports on the back of the device.

Now, connect the switch to its power adapter and fire it up. Select one of the CPUs on the switch and you should see that CPU's operating system and applications fill the display (if that CPU is active). Now, press the switch again and you'll change over to the second CPU—after a moment your display should light up with that CPU's active software and you'll have control over it with the same keyboard and mouse.

Model: MiniView USB KVM Kit
Manufacturer: IOGear (www.iogear.com)
Price: $149.95

OmniView SoHo

The OmniView offers similar functionality to the MiniView, as well as a compact design that manages your incoming cables, although you'll need to buy a few more of those cables as they aren't included. The device is also flash-upgradeable, but not from a Mac; if you happen to be connecting both a Mac and a PC, though, you're in good shape, because you can update the device's firmware from the PC when necessary. The OmniView can also support switching between sound devices (enabling you to use two machines with one set of speakers or a microphone), which is particularly handy if you have third-party speakers; for microphones that switch between PC and Mac, you may need a special adapter for the connection from the KVM to the Mac (see Chapter 3).

Model: OmniView SoHo
Manufacturer: Belkin
(www.belkin.com)
Price: $139.95

MiniView ADC KVM Switch

If you've got two Power Macs (or Power Macintosh G4 Cube models) that have ADC ports on their video cards, then you can use this specialized, self-powered KVM switch to use them both with the same ADC-compatible display. The KVM switch offers power and a digital display signal via two included ADC cables that are connected from the Mac CPUs to the KVM switch; then you connect the display to the KVM switch itself. Now, wire up the keyboard and mouse to the ADC display and you're all set for switching. (Note that this switch will work with a DVI-based Mac or display, too, but you'll need the requisite adapters.)

Model: MiniView ADC KVM Switch
Manufacturer: IOGear
(www.iogear.com)
Price: $199

Surge Protection and Battery Backup

What could be more exciting than a topic like this? Watching paint dry, perhaps? Actually, there are some cool options in the world of surge protection and particularly in battery back-up, which can keep you up and running when the power surges or goes out altogether.

A surge protector is designed to do exactly what it sounds like—protect your Mac from power surges that could damage the Mac's internals. Those surges can occur through a wall plug or over a telephone connection, so it's ideal to protect against both. Surge protectors can be simple and cheap or they can be complex (and, hence, usually more expensive), offering increasing levels of protection and features that enable you to monitor power to your Mac.

A battery backup system—also called a UPS, or uninterruptible power supply—can also range from basic to advanced. While most are also surge protectors, the primary purpose of a battery backup system is to enable you to shut down your desktop Mac gracefully if you ever encounter an extended power outage. The battery will generally offer a limited amount of computing time—15 minutes or so—enabling you to save changes and shut down the Mac.

More sophisticated power systems are available, too, which can be used with "mission critical" systems (computers that you need to keep running if at all possible, for business or other important reasons) to keep them in good working order. Such features include "power conditioning" devices that are able to not only protect against surges or kick in battery power when there's a blackout, but they can also protect against "brown out" problems (where not enough voltage is received, or it "sags" over time) or when "dirty" power is received with spikes and sags in voltage. This sort of protection is ongoing and may not only keep you up and running but also extend the life of your Mac.

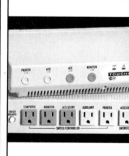

Office Series 750VA UPS with Broadband

Leo's Pick

This middle-of-the-road UPS is designed for home or small offices that need solid power protection and the ability to continue computing for a little while after a complete blackout. The 750VA supports up to 400 Watts of equipment, which should be plenty for a desktop Mac and associated peripherals; it offers six plugs, all with surge protection and four with battery backup. This one is perfect for a consultant or designer with a pricey and important Power Macintosh setup.

That backup battery can offer up to 38 minutes of running time when a blackout situation is encountered and there's no longer power to the device. The device also features what Belkin called Automatic Voltage Regulation (AVR), which conditions the power as it comes into the device and is fed to your Mac so that small sags and spikes are taken out of the stream of electricity and, instead, your Mac encounters only a safe stream of 110 to 120 volts.

The compact, convenient device includes protection for phone lines, so that you can keep a surge from affecting your Mac through its modem port or from messing with your fax, answering machine, or DSL modem. The optional Broadband Protection model will also protect cable modems from surges over coaxial cable.

The device comes with various impressive warrantees, including a $75,000 equipment guarantee and a data-recovery warranty. (Read the fine print on these to get a sense of what they cover and what you need to do to keep the coverage active.) Most importantly, even with its considerable features the 750VA is affordable and a great investment for serious Mac professionals.

Model: 750VA
Manufacturer: Belkin Components (www.belkin.com)
Price: $109.99 ($130.99 including Broadband option)

TrippLite TM500 Under Monitor UPS

Here's a fun one that would go particularly well with an eMac or an old CRT-based iMac. The Under Monitor UPS offers 300 watts of power that will generally enable you to maintain an Internet connection (via phone or broadband) and continue computing for up to 30 minutes during a short blackout. If it's a long one, you can at least safely power down. It includes six outlets; three have battery backup. And, there's a surge protection port for a phone line.

Model: TM500 Under Monitor UPS
Manufacturer: TrippLite
(www.eaglecreek.com)
Price: $179.98

APC Back-UPS LS

This basic, cost-effective unit offers convenient protection from under your desk, including both battery backup and voltage regulation. This taller unit, with plugs on the top, is easy to work with and it comes in different battery capacities which can determine how much backup time you have to work with. It's also available in a stylish black and a "clear" white plastic that seems designed to appeal to Mac users.

Model: Back-UPS LS
Manufacturer: APC (www.apc.com)
Price: $119.99 (500 VA) or
$139.99 (700 VA)

9-Socket SurgeMaster Gold Series

If you're skipping on UPS capabilities, then you want to shop smart for a surge protector. Rule number one—get one with the plugs sockets facing out, not all in a line. That way you can fit blocky AC adapters and still get all six (or however many) sockets filled. Second, get one specifically designed to protect your telephone modem or broadband modem connection type, so that you don't take a surge on any of your equipment that the protector can't handle. Third, get one with a good warranty and read up on how to take advantage of it just in case it does fail. This SurgeMaster meets all these criteria and offers a whopping nine sockets for power; this one is heavy duty, but recommended if you've got a Mac and peripherals that are important to you.

> **Model:** 9-Socket SurgeMaster Gold Series
> **Manufacturer:** Belkin Components (www.belkin.com)
> **Price:** $67.99

ProtectIt! 810N

This TrippLite model offers eight sockets, three that are clearly for large AC adapter transformers, and includes child-safety covers. Surge protection covers the plugs, as well as a phone line, Ethernet connection, and coax connections for your various modem and broadband Internet options, complete with cables for all three included in the box. A lighted switch and diagnostic LEDs let you know at a glance that the surge protector is up and functioning.

> **Model:** ProtectIt! 810N
> **Manufacturer:** Tripplite (www.tripplite.com)
> **Price:** $34.99

USB and FireWire Expansion

Both USB and FireWire have impressive theoretical statistics; each USB bus can handle up to 127 devices and each FireWire bus can deal with 63, total. Of course, those numbers are absurd; you're not likely to have over five USB devices, let alone 127. And, yet, having four or five or three, with some Mac models, can get to be something of a problem when you run out of ports.

The solution when you need to add more USB devices is a USB hub, which you plug into an available USB port on your Mac giving you four or more additional ports that you can use for USB devices. Some USB hubs are tiny, portable things; others offer their own power adapters and can be used to expand your Mac to quite a few more peripherals.

FireWire connections don't require hubs, because you can "daisychain" FireWire devices together. You may find, for instance, that your external FireWire hard disk offers another FireWire port into which you could plug a DV

camcorder or even an iPod. However, both of those are good examples; neither an iPod nor a typical DV camcorder has a second FireWire port of its own. On many iBook and PowerBook models, that means the one available FireWire port is full; on desktop models, having both an iPod and DV camcorder plugged in means there's no room for other devices. You will find that there are FireWire hubs on the market that make it possible to plug more than on FireWire device into a single port on your Mac.

Want more? Most of them are aging, you but you'll still find the occasional adapter that enables you to connect an older Mac or PC peripheral to USB. And recent products have popped up that enable you to share USB devices over a network connection, so that, for instance, a USB scanner or printer can be made available to every Mac on your network.

And you know how USB and FireWire are both *powered* ports? That can make for some interesting gadget solutions, too.

Keyspan USB Server

It was once true that adding network capability to a non-networked printer was expensive and proprietary—you had to hope the manufacturer had a solution for your particular printer. That was less likely for inkjets and specialty printers and more likely for laser printers. Today, it's actually reasonably inexpensive to get an external printer server for many different printer models, and some of them even offer cool features such as wireless access. (In fact, Apple's latest AirPort Base Stations and the AirPort Express offer a USB connection for printer sharing.)

Still, that doesn't take away from the Keyspan USB Server, particularly if you've got more than one USB device you'd like to share. The USB Server can be particularly handy for a household or home office that has more than one Mac (or a PC or two), but not enough daily demand for peripherals to merit multiple printers or scanners laying around. If you've already got a network in place, the solution might be the USB Server, which enables you to share USB devices over an ethernet network.

The USB Server doesn't work with all devices, but it is compatible with printers, multifunction devices, and scanners. (Hard drives and other storage are not yet fully compatible, but the company appears to be working on driver software for some devices, so check the web site.) And as long as you have a wireless router that's connected to your ethernet network, you should be able to access the shared devices via AirPort, too.

Model: USB Server
Manufacturer: Keyspan (www.keyspan.com)
Price: $129.99

Connect 4 USB Hub

The Connect 4 USB hub enables you to connect up to four USB 2.0 devices to a single USB 2.0 port on the side of your Mac; it also can downgrade to USB 1.1 speeds if necessary or appropriate for your devices. This compact hub features full bus power and small LEDs to indicate when devices are plugged in and recognized. It comes in black and in silver.

> **Model:** Connect 4 USB Hub
> **Manufacturer:** Keyspan
> (www.keyspan.com)
> **Price:** $179.98

OrangeLink FireWire Hub

As mentioned, FireWire doesn't require hubs because you can chain together devices. But, with a hub, you can connect multiple devices—and disconnect them—without relying on your devices to have multiple working FireWire ports. You can also use your devices without worrying about whether you're going to "break the chain" and cause some unexpected failure because you tried to remove a device that has other devices connected to it. The OrangeLink FireWire hub includes a power supply and enables you to plug three FireWire devices into a single FireWire port on your Mac. (It also doubles as a FireWire hub for linking together multiple Sony Playstation 2 game stations, just in case that interests you.)

> **Model:** OrangeLink FireWire Hub
> **Manufacturer:** Orange Micro
> (www.orangemicro.com)
> **Price:** $59

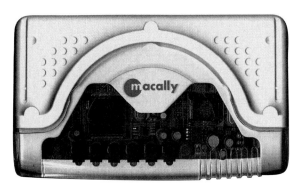

Hub-UF

MacAlly offers several different hubs, but this one impresses us for its usefulness; the Hub-UF offers both four USB 2.0 and two FireWire 400 connections, all in the same "ice"-colored box to match the iMac G4, eMac, and second-generation iBook. The hub has two cables that plug in to your Mac (one for USB, one for FireWire) and it'll work with older Macs that offer only USB 1.1—just slower. It includes its own AC adapter and provides power to the ports.

Model: Hub-UF
Manufacturer: MacAlly
(www.macally.com)
Price: $79

USB-to-Serial Adapter

If you've got an older serial device that you have reason to suspect would work in Mac OS X (or, if you're still running Mac OS 9 but don't have serial ports) then you should look into the USB-to-Serial adapter, which offers two Mac-style serial ports. According to the company it works with a variety of products, including specialty printers, scanners, cameras, printers, and older Mac-compatible PDAs and PDA cradles.

Model: USB-to-Serial Adapter
Manufacturer: Keyspan
(www.keyspan.com)
Price: $79.95

FlexUSB

This little adapter makes it possible to fit a USB connector into your Mac even if you have a tight space in which to squeeze it; the adapter itself can turn at up to a 90-degree angle. The adapter can be particularly handy for USB flash drives and other devices that don't have a USB cable and that are inconvenient when they stick straight off the side or back of your Mac.

Model: FlexUSB
Manufacturer: IDEATIVE
(www.ideative.com)
Price: $12.99

USB Phone Charger

How's this for clever? Because the USB port offers power to USB devices, this little USB-to-phone cord can charge your mobile phone while you work on your PowerBook, iBook, or desktop Mac. Just plug in to a powered port and your phone, then wait about an hour (or so) for a full charge. The cord is available in different configurations with a retractable cable and adapters that fit a variety of phone manufacturers and connector types.

Model: USB Phone Charger
Manufacturer: Keyspan
(www.keyspan.com)
Price: $21.99

X10 and Home Automation

A true gadget geek has a burning desire to at least explore the opportunities of X10—a technology that enables you to send commands to regular household devices via your home's electrical wiring. X10 is a computer language that, in effect, can tell X10-compatible devices what to do automatically. With adapters installed throughout your house, you can cause lamps to turn on and off according to a schedule, you can dim lights, you can turn appliances on and off, change a thermostat's settings, turn on outdoor lighting, control lawn sprinklers, and more.

Whereas much of this can be managed with special switches and remote controls, using your Mac and a USB interface enables you to create some sophisticated routines for your X10 devices, both in the sense that you can set up complicated day-and-time schedules for various devices (turn on your coffee maker at 6 a.m. on weekdays and 8 a.m. on weekends, for instance) and the fact that you can do more sophisticated things, such as respond to *events*.

An event, for instance, might be the triggering of a motion detector; if a motion detector sees motion outside your back door, it could respond with a series of actions; it could turn on an upstairs light, followed up by a downstairs light and so on, simulating a person approaching the back door. It could also illuminate the rear of the house or even turn on a power switch that starts up a CD of a dog barking—you know, if you want to get creative.

Other events can be more computer-centric; for instance, if you send an e-mail to your Mac at home telling it to turn on the hot tub, it could do just that. Or, it could respond to certain logic sequences, such as noticing whether it's day or night and whether the postal mail has been delivered (thanks to a sensor) before turning on the water sprinklers in a certain zone (so you don't soak your mail carrier).

All you need is the software, an X10 interface, and enough interest and money to start putting X10 devices all over your home.

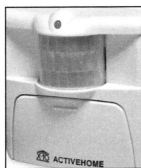

Indigo

Leo's Pick

You won't get too far in the world of computerized X10 automation without the right software, and for too long Mac OS X was without a native solution. That changed with Indigo, from Perceptive Automation, which wrote the software to work with a USB-based X10 interface device. (In order to send signals to your X10 devices, you need a USB-to-X10 interface, such as the PowerLinc USB discussed next.) Now fully up-to-date, your X10 central command can offer up sophisticated controls from any modern Mac.

The fundamentals of X10 software are pretty straightforward—you have devices that you've plugged in all over the house that you'd like to control, and you can control them from your Mac. So, you'll see a list of devices and their current on/off or dimmed position. You can lose a solid afternoon just remotely turning lights on and off and scaring your family.

The next step is to set timers for lights and appliances, which is also built into the basic Indigo interface. Beyond that, you can experiment with triggered actions—those that respond to some stimuli, whether it's an e-mail that Indigo monitors or a reaction to an X10 motion detector. Those actions can take place as a direct result of the trigger or they can evaluate a series of logical steps to decide whether or not to take action.

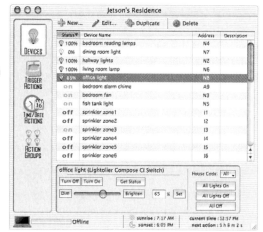

Finally, Indigo offers a number of hooks into AppleScript, meaning you can script it to work with other applications on your Mac or to respond to your own clever programming twists and turns. Or you can use off-the-shelf scripts to get Indigo to work with external devices—remote controls, telephone adapters—that extend and enhance the X10 world.

Model: Indigo
Manufacturer: Perceptive Automation
(www.perceptiveautomation.com)
Price: $89.95

PowerLinc USB

To use Indigo with your X10 devices you'll need the PowerLinc USB interface, which accepts a USB connection from your Mac and plugs into the wall socket in order to send signals to your X10 devices over your home's power lines. Until now, Macs have required USB-to-serial adapters, but the PowerLinc USB makes the connection much simpler; it also has a pass-through plug on its top so that you don't lose access to that plug socket for powering another device.

Model: PowerLinc USB
Manufacturer: SmartHome
(www.smarthome.com)
Price: $34.99

Version II Wireless Motion Detector

There are tons of X10 gadgets you can buy to control lamps, appliances, security cameras, and sprinklers. The coolest addition, though, is a motion detector; with a two-way X10 aware motion device, you can get Indigo to respond to motion. In particular, an interior motion detector can be fun, because you can automatically turn on lights (or other devices) when someone enters a room or, if used for security, you can have the computer respond by turning on lights, activating an alarm, and so on. This wireless model requires an RF base, which receives the wireless signal and transmits it back to the Mac.

Model: Version II Wireless Motionetector
Manufacturer: SmartHome
(www.smarthome.com)
Price: $20.99 (base station: $24.99)

Emulators and Operating Systems

Our final category is designed to turn your Mac itself into an interesting gadget, via software. Thanks in part to its place in the market—as a small but feisty segment of the PC world—a number of emulation and remote access software packages are available for the Macintosh that make it possible to either run different types of software on your Mac (Microsoft Windows or Linux applications, for instance) or to access other computers from the comfort of your Mac's display.

When Apple first switched to the PowerPC processor in the early 1990s, it was touted as a processor that could handle emulation well. At the time, Apple and other manufacturers had experimented with special upgrades to address the "PC" problem, where some Mac users needed to run DOS or Windows programs that weren't available for the Mac. The DOS-compatible Mac models actually had Intel-compatible processors in them, enabling the user to switch between the two processors and use Windows or Mac. Other third-party expansion boards enabled you to add an Intel-compatible processor and get the same result.

That trend died out in the mid-1990s and was replaced by software emulation—the most prominent package was SoftWindows, a program that emulated the Windows environment on a Power Mac. Eventually SoftWindows was overtaken by VirtualPC, software that actually emulated the PC environment and not just Windows; the end result is that you could launch not just Windows, but Unix and Linux operating systems as well. Today, VirtualPC is still the premiere option—even if it is owned by Microsoft!

Other options include MacBochs, an open source emulator for a variety of operating systems, and some screen sharing solutions, such as Apple's Remote Desktop and Netopia's Timbuktu. These last two enable you to work with another physical computer—with its own processor and hardware—but bring it up in a window on your Mac.

And then there's the other option—ditch Mac OS X and run Linux. (OK, you don't *have* to *ditch* Mac OS X.) Yellow Dog Linux offers a great excuse to play Linux nerd on your PowerPC hardware and play with all those goodies you've only read about.

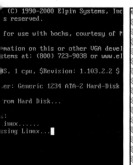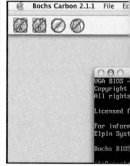

Virtual PC

For a long time, Virtual PC from Connectix was seen as the ultimate nose-thumbing at the Microsoft mothership—even though you had to pay a royalty to Microsoft in order to run Windows on the emulator. At least it *felt* like you were bucking the system by using Windows applications on your Mac.

In the way that things come around, though, Microsoft eventually bought Virtual PC and now gets a full piece of the action whenever you decide to opt for a commercial solution that lets you run Windows applications on your Mac. Oh, well. At least you can still get away with it—Microsoft Virtual PC enables you to run applications that simply aren't offered for the Macintosh, or specialized applications that have been written by your business's IT folks or by consultants. Many a lone designer, PR specialist, or professor has been able to tap into some bizarre Windows-only mainframe access application using Microsoft Virtual PC on his or her beloved Mac, even if the IT people raise their eyebrows.

Microsoft Virtual PC 7 is a long-awaited update that promises compatibility with the PowerPC G5 processor as well as speed improvements and faster graphics. It comes in a variety of different packages that include various versions of Windows—you can also get a version that doesn't include Windows, which enables you to install your own licensed copy of Windows or another compatible operating system.

If you're not too put off by the idea of paying money to Microsoft, this is an easy and effective way to add support for Windows applications—even some games—without being forced to purchase a PC. You'll want a fast Mac, along with tons of RAM and hard disk space, but if you need to run Windows, the extra investment is worth it.

Model: Microsoft Virtual PC
Manufacturer: Microsoft
(www.microsoft.com)
Price: $129–249 (depending on Windows version that's included)

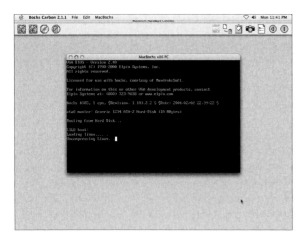

Apple Remote Desktop

Apple's entry enables you to watch other Macs on your network and even take over and control them when you need to help one of your users. Remote Desktop also enables you to install software on their machines and collect information on all the machines on your network in order to better manage them. Remote Desktop is designed for Macs but works with any OS that has Virtual Network Computing (VNC) capabilities; VNC drivers are available for many different platforms. It comes in two flavors—a 10-workstation version (you can administer up to ten remote computers) and an unlimited version. Apple has made it surprisingly inexpensive and it's handy for a local network that you administer or if you simply want to be able to access and control more than one Mac (or PC or Linux box) at once.

Model: Remote Desktop
Manufacturer: Apple (www.apple.com)
Price: $299 (10-workstation),
$499 (unlimited)

MacBochs

Talk about the right price—Bochs is open source software, freely distributed, that you simply download and install. I say *simply*, but this isn't Virtual PC—it isn't a commercial product and it isn't supported in the same way. Indeed, you may at times feel that MacBochs has been developed by Martians for Martians; you'll launch MacBochs using a script and the Terminal, you'll need a configuration text document, and so on. It can get complicated. But, once you've downloaded and configured and scratched your head and figured it out, you *may* have an emulator up and running that works with your Mac to run Windows, DOS, or Unix/Linux variants. (Shown is a small Linux installation.) And if it works you'll certainly have bragging rights.

Model: MacBochs
Manufacturer: Bochs Project
(http://bochs.sourceforge.net)
Price: Free

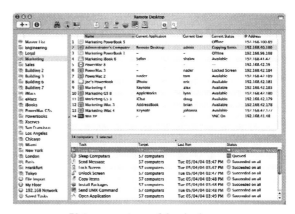

Picture courtesy of Apple, Inc.

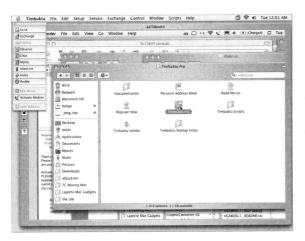

Timbuktu Pro

Timbuktu from Netopia has been around a while doing some of what Apple Remote Desktop does, but specializing in modem-based and Internet connections as well as local network access. Timbuktu is great for consulting work or for helping your grandmother with her Mac—it allows you to chat with the distant user and even send compressed files to them, while still giving you the option to watch what they do onscreen or even take over and control their Mac. Timbuktu works for Windows or Mac but requires a license for each active computer; it can get pricey, but the features for long-distance control and communications can be worth it.

Model: Timbuktu Pro
Manufacturer: Netopia
(www.netopia.com)
Price: $94.95 (single Mac license),
$199.95 (two multiplatform licenses)

Yellow Dog Linux

Linux? On your Mac? It's a fast-growing operating system for all sorts of computers, and Yellow Dog Linux (YDL) is aimed squarely at your Mac's desktop. It runs on PowerPC hardware, has drivers for all popular Mac models, and includes an easy installation, tons of bundled applications, and even OpenOffice (a Microsoft Office "clone") and Mac-on-Linux, which lets you run certain Mac applications in a window. Linux tends to be more resource efficient than the Mac OS, meaning you can run it on older Macs and still see good performance. Plus, the tools and applications for Linux are getting better all the time, including multimedia players, photo editing, development tools, and server applications—in fact, the YDL distribution comes with nearly 1,400 applications! Moving to (or adding) Linux on your Mac is certainly no simple undertaking, but there's no question that YDL is a great way to go about it and a certain answer to the question "How could I blow a weekend playing with my Mac?"

Model: Yellow Dog Linux
Manufacturer: Apple (www.apple.com)
Price: Free Download; $24.95 for CDs,
$59.95 and up for subscription to support and high-end services

Picture courtesy of Apple, Inc.

Home Audio/Video Gadgets

13

Digital Media Hubs

This is one gadget that didn't exist three years ago. A *digital media hub* is a device that lets you play digital audio files on your home audio system. You rip your favorite CDs to hard disk, and the media hub accesses the hard disk to play individual songs and playlists. (Many of these devices are a little PC-centric, so they might focus on WMA—Windows Media Audio—files a bit. That said, nearly any of them will play an MP3, and iTunes can be used to translate songs into MP3 format, so you should find you can work with them and your Mac.)

There are two primary types of digital media hubs. The first type is a self-contained unit that has a built-in hard disk and CD drive. You insert a CD into the drive, burn it to the built-in hard disk, and then play songs from the hard disk. This type of unit typically looks like a regular consumer audio component and connects to your home audio system via digital or analog connections.

The second type of digital media hub doesn't have a built-in hard disk or CD drive. Instead, it connects to your home network, accesses the digital audio files stored on your computer's hard disk, and then streams the music through your home audio system. This type of hub is typically a small and relatively low-cost device

that connects directly to your home audio system; it plugs in to your home network via either wired or wireless connection.

When you're shopping for a digital media hub, take these points into consideration:

- If you get a self-contained unit, how big is its hard drive? (More hard disk space means you can store more CDs.)

- If you get a computer-based unit, how Mac friendly is it? If it works corss-platform, does it connect via ethernet or AirPort? And if it's AirPort (Wi-Fi), is it the slower 802.11b or the faster 802.11g?

- Can you connect multiple units to provide music to other rooms in your house?

- Does the unit have a built-in display or use your TV to display song information?

- Does it play audio only, or can it also stream videos or display digital photos and artwork?

- How much control do you have from the unit itself or via a cross-platform solution such as web interface?

This might be a new type of gadget for you, but if you have a lot of CDs or digital music files, you'll wonder how you ever did without it!

   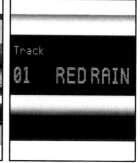 

Wurlitzer Digital Jukebox

Leo's Pick

This is one cool-looking device. The Wurlitzer Digital Jukebox is a free-standing digital media hub, with its own built-in hard disk. It comes in two configurations: the Freestanding jukebox with separate speakers and a Component unit that connects to your home audio system.

The Freestanding unit is the coolest of the bunch. It looks like a high-tech version of a classic jukebox, but a little smaller. Its 145-watt amplifier drives two auxiliary Klipsch speakers, each of which has two 3.5" mid-bass drivers and a 0.5" horn; the main unit has an integrated subwoofer for deep bass.

The main unit also hosts a CD player/burner and an 80GB hard drive that can hold 1,000 CDs when the songs are stored in Windows Media Audio (WMA format). A wireless touch-screen remote control unit snaps into the main unit and features a 3.5" color touch-screen display, a scroll knob for rapid navigation, and dedicated transport buttons.

When you rip a CD to disk, the Jukebox retrieves and displays CD information (artist, album, songs, and genre), CD cover, and additional artist information from the Gracenote CDDB music recognition service. You can browse stored music by genre, artist, album, or song title, as well as create your own playlists. The Jukebox also receives digital Internet radio (when connected to your home network via Wi-Fi) and lets you export music to portable audio players that connect via USB 2.0. You can even send and control music to multiple locations throughout your house, via optional client units.

All this, and it looks cool standing in your living room, too!

Model: Wurlitzer Digital Jukebox
Manufacturer: Gibson Audio (www.gibsonaudio.com)
Price: $1,999 (Freestanding), $1,499 (Component)

Escient FireBall
DVDM-100

This is *the* system of choice for professional home theater installers, unusual in that it's based around both physical and digital media. FireBall manages, catalogs, and controls digital audio files, CDs, DVDs, Internet radio, you name it.

Connect up to three mega-disc CD/DVD changers and have instant access to up to 1,209 physical CDs or DVDs. Or connect one or more optional hard disk music managers to play digital music files. FireBall then taps into Escient's movie databases and Gracenote's CDDB service to retrieve information on more than 15,000 movies and 20 million songs; you can sort your movies and music by CD/DVD cover, category/genre, and more.

Model: DVDM-100
Manufacturer: Escient
(www.escient.com)
Price: $1,995

Yamaha MusicCAST

Yamaha's MusicCAST is a media hub that functions as an audiophile-quality audio component. The MCX-1000 digital audio server serves as the base unit and has a built-in 80GB hard drive that can store up to 1,000 CDs (in MP3 format). Serve music to other rooms with one or more optional MCX-A10 client systems, which connect wirelessly.

The MusicCAST server lets you play music by artist, album, genre, or playlist and incorporates Gracenote's CDDB music database. There's a front panel display for song information; the obligatory wireless remote; and a full complement of analog, digital optical, and digital coaxial outputs.

Model: MCX-1000
Manufacturer: Yamaha
(www.yamaha.com)
Price: $2,200

Slim Devices Squeezebox

Slim Devices' Squeezebox is unique in that it's a Linux-based network music hub that's totally friendly with the Mac and iTunes. It's also capable of playing the widest variety of digital file formats: MP3, WMA, AAC, Apple Lossless, Ogg Vorbis, FLAC, WAV, and AIFF, as well as Shoutcast Internet radio.

The Squeezebox is a low-profile unit with built-in display. It connects to your Mac via wireless Airport or wired Ethernet. You can synchronize multiple players for whole-house audio, and it even has a built-in alarm clock!

Model: Squeezebox
Manufacturer: Slim Devices
(www.slimdevices.com)
Price: $199

Archos Pocket Video Recorder

How about audio *and video* that you can take with you? The Pocket Video Recorder is literally a pocket-sized DVR (digital video recorder) that allows you to take recorded TV shows or movies with you anywhere. You can watch those shows on the 3.5-inch color LCD or hook up to a TV when you reach your destination. Capacities range from 20GB to 80GB, and the Pocket Video Recorder can use that storage for more than simply video; it also works with MP3, WMA, and WAV audio, and it has a slot for CompactFlash media, enabling you to store a memory card's contents on its hard disk, which is great if you need to view photos or clear off a memory card.

The Pocket Video Recorder comes with an iTunes plug-in that enables you to use it as an iTunes-aware MP3 player; when connected to a Mac with USB 2.0 ports, it appears as an external hard disk, giving you access to the video, photos, and audio files directly. It's a little PC-centric—video is in AVI format and standard QuickTime files aren't recognized.

Model: Pocket Video Recorder AV400 Series
Manufacturer: Archos
(www.archos.com)
Price: $549.95—$799.95 (depending on capacity)

Roku SoundBridge

Roku's SoundBridge is a cool-looking network music hub, contained in a slim cylindrical aluminum tube. Its 12" built-in display can be read across the room.

The SoundBridge unit comes in two models (M1000 and M2000) and supports MP3, WMA, AAC, WAV, AIFF, FLAC, and Ogg Vorbis files; streams Internet radio; and has support for Apple's iTunes. It connects to your Mac via wired Ethernet or wireless Airport connection (via an optional adapter). It comes with a wireless remote control and has a variety of audio outputs—analog RCA, digital optical, and digital coaxial.

Model: SoundBridge M1000/M2000
Manufacturer: Roku
(www.rokulabs.com)
Price: $199.99/$499.99

Roku HD1000

Roku's HD1000 is unique in that it's a hub for both music and pictures, designed especially for displaying digital photographs from your Mac on your high-definition TV. The HD1000 connects to your home network or displays photos stored on digital media cards. (Roku even sells prepackaged Art Packs if you don't have enough photos of your own.)

If your normal video source is turned off, the HD1000 automatically kicks in and generates a changing screensaver. Picture quality is terrific; the HD1000 displays photos in true high definition. It also plays digital music files, although it's not as versatile in this respect as Roku's SoundBridge.

Model: HD1000
Manufacturer: Roku
(www.rokulabs.com)
Price: $299.99

DVD Recorders

Toss out your VCR; the latest DVD recorders let you record just about anything to recordable DVD discs—television programming, old VHS tapes, even home movies from your DV camcorder. And you typically get terrific digital video and audio quality, to boot.

To record television or cable programming, make sure the DVD recorder has a built-in television tuner—and, ideally, some sort of electronic program guide. To record from your camcorder, look for a FireWire connection (sometimes labeled as a DV or i.LINK connection); the front panel is more convenient than the rear.

Some DVD recorders also function as personal video recorders (PVRs) thanks to a built-in hard disk. Hard disk recording is great for recording television programming (which you can later burn to DVD) and for pausing and rewinding "live" programming. My favorite unit, the Pioneer DVR-810H, adds a subscription to the TiVo service, which is the ultimate way to program your PVR.

For best playback, make sure your DVD recorder has progressive scan output, typically accompanied by component video and digital audio output jacks. Also look for units that have so-called "chasing playback"; this lets you watch the beginning of what you've already recorded before the complete recording is finished.

Note the five DVD recording formats: DVD-R, DVD-RW, DVD+R, DVD+RW, and DVD-RAM. Most home DVD recorders use the DVD-R/RW formats, although some units are also compatible with the DVD+R/RW formats. Use DVD-R for best compatibility with other players; use the rewriteable DVD-RW format when you want to record over and over again on the same disc.

Finally, if you have a lot of old VHS tapes you want to transfer to DVD, consider JVC's DR-MV1SUS. This is a combination DVD recorder/VCR that lets you make quick DVD recordings of VHS tapes. Just pop in the tape and a blank disc and press a button—it's that easy!

Pioneer DVR-810H

Leo's Pick

Pioneer's DVR-810H is a combination DVD recorder and PVR. It incorporates an 80GB hard disk drive, with recording controlled via the TiVo service. You can even record content to the hard drive while dubbing different content from the hard drive to DVD.

For the purchase price, Pioneer throws in TiVo basic service free of charge—no monthly fees necessary. You can, however, upgrade to the more fully featured TiVo Plus service, on your dime.

The DVR-810H lets you burn to either DVD-R or DVD-RW discs. It features fast 18X DVD recording from the hard disc; you can dub a 1-hour program to DVD in a little over 3 minutes.

Being a rather high-end unit, the DVR-810H features progressive scan playback and all sorts of video niceties, including PureCinema 2:3 technology, a 9-bit/27MHz video digital/analog converter, and Faroudja Direction Correlation Deinterlacing (DCDi). Variable bit rate (VBR) recording provides gentle compression to fit slightly more material on each disc.

You get a bunch of outputs with this puppy, including two composite video, two S-Video, one component video, and both Dolby Digital and DTS Digital connections. In short, there's not much that this gizmo can't do—it's the ultimate DVD recorder for your home theater system!

Model: DVR-810H
Manufacturer: Pioneer
(www.pioneerelectronics.com)
Price: $1,199

Panasonic DMR-E85H

Panasonic's top-of-the-line DVD recorder incorporates a big 120GB hard drive and great editing capabilities. Record your program to the hard drive, edit out the commercials and add chapter stops, then burn to DVD.

This progressive scan unit features the TV Guide onscreen guide—not quite as versatile as TiVo, but it's free. You also get a Flexible Recording Mode that adjusts recording speed/quality to best fit a program on disk, as well as high-speed 32X dubbing from hard disk to DVD.

Model: DMR-E85H
Manufacturer: Panasonic
(www.toshiba.com)
Price: $699.95

Sony RDR-GX7

Sony's RDR-GX7 is a straight DVD recorder, no hard disk built in. Its claim to fame is all the formats it supports—DVD-R/RW and DVD+R/RW.

Naturally, you get progressive scan playback, as well as one-touch dubbing from DV camcorders, via FireWire. There's even a built-in television tuner for recording your favorite programs direct to DVD.

Model: RDR-GX7
Manufacturer: Sony
(www.sonystyle.com)
Price: $699.99

Panasonic DMR-E55

The DMR-E55 gets my vote for best value. It's a good, solid DVD recorder, at an affordable price.

This unit features progressive scan playback and is compatible with DVD-R and DVD-RAM discs. It also has a built-in 181-channel TV tuner for off-air recording.

Model: DMR-E55
Manufacturer: Panasonic
(www.panasonic.com)
Price: $349.95

JVC DR-MV1SUS

Here's a unique unit, a combination DVD recorder/VCR that lets you easily dub your old VHS videotapes onto DVDs. This puppy offers lots of recording options: TV to DVD, VHS to DVD, DVD to VHS, and TV to VHS. You even get twin tuners for dual off-air recording.

The DVD recorder writes to DVD-R, DVD-RW, and DVD-RAM formats and offers progressive scan playback. The VCR is a four-head HiFi unit. You also get front-panel analog and digital (FireWire) A/V inputs for connecting your camcorder or other devices.

Model: DR-MV1SUS
Manufacturer: JVC (www.jvc.com)
Price: $799.95

Home Theater in a Box Systems

If you're setting up a new home theater system and are either confused by or don't want to be bothered with buying separate audio/video components, what you need is a single-purchase solution—a home theater in a box.

Home theater in a box (HTIB) systems give you everything you need for home theater surround sound playback in a single package. You get a single unit that contains a DVD/CD player and audio/video receiver/amplifier, along with matching front and rear speakers, all of which typically have color-coded cables for easy hookup. The only thing missing is the big-screen TV.

Home theater means surround sound, which means you can't just use the tinny little speakers built in to your television set. You need a full array of front and rear speakers, in what is called a *5.1 configuration*. The *5* refers to the bookshelf or floorstanding speakers that deliver the main sound: left front, center front, right front, right rear, and left rear. The *.1* is the subwoofer, which delivers the deep bass punch you need to reproduce bone-shuddering explosions and the like.

All these speakers are driven by a multichannel amplifier built in to an audio/video receiver. The receiver also contains the surround sound decoding circuitry, as well as a switching circuit and (usually) an AM/FM tuner. You control the receiver with a multifunction remote control.

Three main surround sound formats are in use today. Most current movies use either Dolby Digital or DTS, both of which deliver six (5.1, remember) discrete channels of sound. Some older movies use the previous Dolby Pro Logic system, which matrixes the rear channels into the mix and results in a less effective channel separation. Don't worry; almost all of today's HTIB systems handle all three surround sound formats and automatically switch to the correct one when you insert a DVD for playback.

When it comes to choosing an HTIB system, look at the amount of amplifier power offered (more is better) and the size of the speakers. Actually, it's best to listen to the speakers because size alone won't tell you how they actually sound. And check out that remote control— you'll be using it a lot, so make sure it feels good to you!

Panasonic SC-HT920

Panasonic's SC-HT920 is a system that would look great surrounding a wall-mounted plasma television. All the components feature a modern mirror finish and super-thin design, so they look cool while being somewhat unobtrusive.

Leo's Pick

The front left and right Tall Boy speakers come on adjustable stands, so you can position them to match the height of your TV screen. The horizontal center channel speaker sits on your TV, of course, while the rear satellite speakers can be mounted on the wall or hung from the ceiling. The system also includes a stylish diamond-shaped subwoofer, a lot better than the typical boxy subwoofer you find with most other systems.

The receiver can handle all the major surround sound systems: Dolby Digital, DTS, and Dolby Pro Logic. The amplifier delivers 1000 watts total power—170W × 2 front, 260W center, 70W × 2 surround, and 260W sub. The controls are aligned across the top of the main unit, with a small display on the front. There's also a built-in AM/FM tuner, the ubiquitous remote control, and a nifty five-disc DVD/CD changer.

When style matters (and style *always* matters), this is the system to consider.

Model: SC-HT920
Manufacturer: Panasonic
(www.panasonic.com)
Price: $499.95

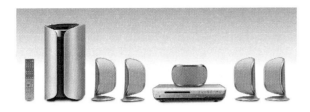

Sony DAV-FC7 DVD Dream System

Sony's DAV-FC7 DVD Dream System provides surprisingly good performance at a very affordable price—just a tad under $400. What you get for the money is fairly impressive—a five-disc progressive-scan DVD/CD/SACD changer, 600-watt amplifier ($100W \times 5$ channels + 100W subwoofer), four satellite speakers, a center front speaker, and a subwoofer. All controlled by remote, of course.

The main unit has the expected Dolby Digital, DTS, and Dolby Pro Logic II surround sound decoding. Color-coded speaker connections make it a snap to set up, and you get an onscreen display for fine adjustments.

Model: DAV-FC7
Manufacturer: Sony
(www.sonystyle.com)
Price: $399.95

Samsung HT-DB390 Wireless Home Theater System

The great thing about this Samsung system is that you don't have to run any wires to the rear speakers—they're wireless! Sound for the rear speakers is beamed to a wireless receiver tower, using 2.4GHz digital technology; the rear speakers then connect to the tower.

The main unit provides 400 watts total power ($60W \times 5$ channels + 100W subwoofer) and supports Dolby Digital, DTS, and Dolby Pro Logic II. Naturally, it plays both DVDs and CDs, for your viewing—and listening—enjoyment.

Model: HT-DB390
Manufacturer: Samsung
(www.samsung.com)
Price: $499.99

Niro 1.1PRO

If two speakers are one too many for you, take a look at the Niro 1.1PRO. This puppy delivers the equivalent of five-channel surround sound with just *one* speaker, which you sit on top of your TV. Niro uses proprietary head-related transfer function (HRTF) and spatial filter network (SFN) technology to deliver a fairly decent surround sound simulation from the single speaker's five computer-controlled drivers. Bass comes from the obligatory (and separate) subwoofer. Naturally, you get DVD/CD playback from the separate receiver unit.

Model: 1.1PRO
Manufacturer: Nirotek America (www.niro1.com)
Price: $799

Bose 3*2*1 DVD Home Entertainment System

Bose's 3*2*1 system is great when space is at a premium—and when you don't want to muck about running wires to rear speakers. That's because this system simulates the full surround sound spectrum from just two main speakers—front left and front right—plus a small sub-woofer.

The media center unit includes a DVD/CD player, an AM/FM tuner, and all the amplification for the speakers. The surround sound effect is surprisingly good, and you can't beat the ease of setup.

Model: 3*2*1
Manufacturer: Bose (www.bose.com)
Price: $999

Universal Remote Controls

If you're like me, you have a coffee table full of remotes. There's one for the TV, one for the A/V receiver, one for the DVD player, and one for the cable box or satellite dish. And that's before you start adding digital music hubs and the like.

How do you get rid of all those remotes?

The key is to combine all your operating functions into a single universal remote control unit. Most universal remotes have codes for the most popular audio/video components preprogrammed; other codes can be "learned" from the old remote. Once you have it programmed, the new remote can control four or more components, just by pressing the right buttons.

The best universal remotes feature some sort of LCD touch screen display. Typically, this display varies depending on which component you're trying to operate. Press the button for TV, and the touch screen changes to display the television controls. Press the button for DVD, and the screen displays the DVD's controls. And so on.

The most programmable remotes are those in Philips's Pronto series. Pronto remotes have become a cult onto themselves, thanks to their almost-complete programmability.

Of course, ultra-programmability is useless if you can't figure out how to use the darned thing. So, don't be seduced by too many whiz-bang features; make sure that the remote is simple enough for everyone in your household to use, without consulting an instruction manual every time they want to change channels.

    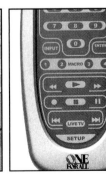

Philips iPronto

The hands-down winner for the most sophisticated consumer-grade remote control today (not counting big whole-house models sold by home theater installers) is the Philips iPronto. This funky unit combines a color touch screen remote control, a wireless Internet browser, and an electronic program guide into a unit that looks a little like a tablet PC.

This is one *big* remote control. The whole thing measures 9.4" × 7" × 0.9" and features a 6.4" color TFT VGA (640 × 480) touch screen display with a fully customizable user interface. You also get eight direct access buttons to navigate screen layouts and five programmable control buttons for volume up/down, channel up/down, and mute. The one drawback: iProntoEdit software is Windows-only, so you can't take advantage of it unless you have a PC available.

But the iPronto is more than a simple remote—it's also your own guide to what's playing. It uses Wi-Fi wireless technology (connected to any always-on broadband Internet connection) to acquire TV programming information for its built-in Electronic Program Guide. That Wi-Fi connection also lets you use the iPronto as a tablet web browser to surf the Internet and send and receive email. Also cool is the fact that the iPronto includes built-in stereo speakers, a microphone, and a headphone jack.

Naturally, the iPronto replaces all the other remotes in your house. It learns infrared codes from other remotes and has an MMC slot and a USB port for future upgrades. (Some firmware updates might require an actual PC.) It's a power hog, as you might expect; good thing it uses a rechargeable lithium-ion battery and comes with its own external charger unit.

Model: TSi6400
Manufacturer: Philips (www.pronto.philips.com)
Price: $1,699.99

ProntoPro NG

Okay, the iPronto is probably overkill for most folks, but you gotta like the idea of a customizable color touch screen remote—which is what you get, for half the iPronto's price, from Philips's ProntoPro NG. This is a sleek unit with a high-resolution 3.8" color LCD touch screen display.

Like the iPronto, you use Philips' proprietary software to create your own screen layouts on a Windows PC and then download them to the ProntoPro NG. And, so you don't have to worry about replacing batteries all the time, it comes with its own docking cradle/charger. Cool!

Model: TSU7000
Manufacturer: Philips
(www.pronto.philips.com)
Price: $899.99

Sony RM-AV3100

Admittedly, color remotes are a little pricey. If you want similar programmability and can settle for a monochrome LCD touch screen display, check out Sony's RM-AV3100. This unit lets you control up to 18 A/V components and is completely programmable.

Also neat is the ability to program macros so you can execute up to 44 consecutive operations at the touch of a button. It comes with a system on/off macro built in for centralized control of all Sony-brand devices.

Model: RM-AV3100
Manufacturer: Sony
(www.sonystyle.com)
Price: $199.95

Harmony SST-659

Harmony's SST-659 differs from other remotes in that it isn't device-oriented—it's activity-oriented. Press a single activity button (such as Watch TV or Watch a Movie) and the SST-659 automatically turns on and switches to the appropriate components.

You set up the activity buttons specific to your home theater system through the online tools at the HarmonyRemote.com website; the remote connects to your Mac via USB. You also can connect to the website every two weeks to download the electronic program guide, which is displayed on the remote's built-in interactive display.

Model: SST-659
Manufacturer: Intrigue Technologies (www.harmonyremote.com)
Price: $199.99

One for All Kameleon 8-in-1 Remote

The Kameleon is one of the coolest-looking remotes on the market. The flexible touch screen display uses a combination of electro-luminescent backlighting and segmented LCDs that intelligently illuminates only the buttons necessary for the currently selected device; some of the buttons are animated.

As the name implies, this remote can control up to eight devices. It also includes a remote finder feature, which helps you locate the unit if you lose the remote. And, for all its coolness, the Kameleon is also a very affordable universal remote; you can find it in most stores for well under $100.

Model: URC-9960
Manufacturer: One for All/Universal Electronics, Inc. (www.uei.com)
Price: $99.99

Satellite Radio

The latest big deal in automobile entertainment systems is satellite radio, where you get high-quality entertainment anywhere in the United States beamed down from a network of satellites. You probably know already that you can get satellite radio in your car, but there are some cool options for home, too. After all, why should you leave all that cool digital programming behind when you lock up your car?

There are two similar but competing satellite radio services: Sirius and XM. Both offer satellite radios for in-home listening and similar programming.

The Sirius satellite radio service has more than 100 streams of music and entertainment—60 commercial-free music streams, plus 40 sports, news, and entertainment streams. The monthly subscription fee is $12.95, and it's the official satellite radio partner of the NFL. Learn more at www.sirius.com.

XM satellite radio is a competing service that offers 120 channels of digital programming—68 commercial-free music channels, 32 news/talk/entertainment channels, and 21 channels of traffic and weather. The monthly subscription fee is $9.99 per month. Learn more at www.xmradio.com.

Which is the better service? As you can tell from the basic specs, they're both pretty similar. XM is a little more adventurous with its music programming; Sirius is a little more attuned to the news radio junkie. Bottom line: They both deliver much more high-fidelity entertainment than you're used to.

Of course, to listen to satellite radio in your home, you need to have a satellite antenna. Although this is a little bit of a bother, you can probably get by with mounting the antenna inside your house, rather than outside. The best location is often on or next to an outside wall. Make sure the antenna cable is long enough to reach to wherever you place the radio.

Delphi SKYFi XM Audio System

Leo's Pick

I tend to like the XM system a little better than Sirius (I like music more than talk), and I really like the SKYFi portable XM receiver. This little gizmo gives you satellite radio on the go—in your car or at home. Combine the receiver with the SKYFi Audio System, and for a little over $200, you have yourself at-home and in-car satellite listening.

Here's the deal: The SKYFi receiver is a palm-sized unit that receives the full range of XM satellite radio signals. In your car, it broadcasts XM signals over an unused FM frequency, so you can listen through your current auto audio system. When you get home, take the SKYFi receiver with you, insert it into the open slot on the front of the SKYFi Audio System, and continue listening to your XM programming through the device's built-in speakers.

Essentially, the SKYFi Audio System turns your SKYFi receiver into a boombox. It integrates a pair of high-quality speakers, a high-gain XM antenna (with a 22.5 ' cable), and a dock for the SKIFi XM receiver. You can place the antenna on your roof, on a table, or wherever works best; for portable use, the antenna attaches to the back of the boombox. The whole thing operates on six D-cell batteries or with the included AC adapter.

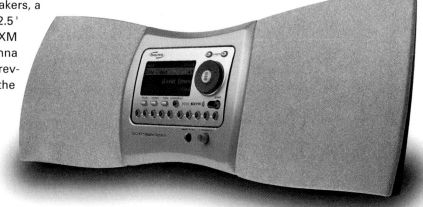

It's a great system for listening to satellite radio indoors or out!

Model: SKYFi Audio System
Manufacturer: Delphi (www.xmradio.com)
System: XM
Price: $99.99 (audio system); $129.99 (portable receiver)

Kenwood DT-7000S Sirius Tuner

Kenwood's DT-7000S lets you listen to Sirius satellite radio through your home audio system. It sits alongside your other audio components and connects to your receiver via a digital optical output.

The unit itself has a built-in four-line scrolling LCD display. And, like any good audio component, you also get a wireless remote control.

Model: DT-7000S
Manufacturer: Kenwood
(www.kenwoodusa.com)
System: Sirius
Price: $300

Tivoli Model Sirius

If you prefer a standalone satellite radio, consider Tivoli's Model Sirius. This is a tabletop radio with an old-school look that can receive Sirius satellite radio signals. It's easy to use, with the big honkin' control dial that's typical of Tivoli's other popular table radios.

The Model Sirius features a classy all-wood cabinet and an easy-to-use digital interface. It also has an AM/FM analog tuner and a built-in alarm clock.

Model: Model Sirius
Manufacturer: Tivoli Audio
(www.tivoliaudio.com)
System: Sirius
Price: TBA

Other Cool Audio/Video Gadgets

Our look at audio/video gadgets concludes with three gadgets that you've probably never thought about but that could be quite useful additions to your home theater setup.

The first of these gadgets, Terk's Volume Regulator, does just what its name implies—it regulates the volume level of your TV. It's great for equalizing the volume between channels or signal sources and for making sure that commercials don't get any louder than the surrounding program.

The second gadget, also from Terk, lets you transmit audio/video signals from one device to multiple televisions in your house. Have one set in the living room, one in the bedroom, and another in the kids' room? You don't have to buy separate DVD players or satellite receivers for each set; use the Terk Leapfrog to beam signals from a single device to all your TVs.

Finally, when you're faced with a multiplicity of video components connecting to a single television, you need some way of switching between them all. JVC's digital video switcher lets you connect up to 13 devices, using a variety of inputs (FireWire, composite video, S-Video, and component video) and outputs. You can even route the signals to a half-dozen TVs and switch between them all with the wireless remote. It's a state-of-the-art version of the simple push-button switchers of yesteryear.

Terk VR-1 TV Volume Regulator

I like this gadget. Terk's VR-1 TV volume regular delivers consistent audio levels throughout abnormally loud or quiet scenes in movie and television programs. It also helps to quiet loud commercials and keep the volume constant when you switch channels or when you switch between different inputs (cable, DVD, satellite, and so on).

The VR-1 uses advanced digital signal processing to automatically adjust the sound level without introducing additional noise. Built-in noise reduction circuitry minimizes audio hiss and provides cleaner, more audible sound from any source.

This gizmo does its job in real time by sampling the audio signal thousands of times per second. The VR-1 has a reaction time of only 0.002 seconds, so even sudden loud noises are automatically adjusted.

You connect the VR-1 between your TV and your home audio system using standard RCA cables. Turn it on and it operates automatically. You'll be amazed at the difference!

Model: VR-1
Manufacturer: Terk Technologies (www.terk.com)
Price: $49.99

Terk Leapfrog Wireless Audio/Video Transmitter/Receiver System

Here's a smart idea. Terk's Leapfrog system lets you transmit audio and video throughout your home from any source. It's great for sending DVD movies from your main home theater system to other rooms, for sharing satellite programming between multiple TVs, or for listening to your CD collection throughout the house.

The system transmits at 2.4GHz, with a range up to 150 feet. It's easy to connect and works with any TV, no matter how old. And it's surprisingly affordable—definitely cheaper than purchasing separate components for every TV in your house!

Model: LF-30S
Manufacturer: Terk (www.terk.com)
Price: $99.99

JVC Digital A/V Switcher

You can buy cheaper switchers, but they won't switch everything this baby does. This is the first A/V switcher with full digital video, component video, and digital audio connections. It's a professional-grade unit, using the highest-quality circuitry for zero signal loss.

Here's what you get. Inputs: eight composite/S-Video/audio, two component video, and two digital optical audio. Outputs: five composite/S-Video/audio, two component video, one digital optical audio. Plus, you get three FireWire DV input/output connections. You control them all via front-panel buttons or with the wireless remote control.

Model: JX-S777
Manufacturer: JVC (www.jvc.com)
Price: $799.95

Mac Gadget Technology Glossary

.AVI Audio Video Interleave; Microsoft's file format (and extension) for Windows-compatible audio/video files; a format to which some digital cameras and camcorders can directly record

.JPEG Joint Photographic Experts Group (pronounced "jay-peg"); a file format and standard for compressing still images. Compression is achieved by dividing the picture into tiny pixel blocks, which are halved over and over until the appropriate ratio is achieved. Because JPEG is extremely effective in compressing large graphics files, it is widely used on the Internet as well as in photo files created by digital cameras.

.MP3 MPEG-1, Layer 3; an audio compression technology that results in near-CD quality sound compressed into one-twelfth the original file size. MP3 music files, played using software or a handheld device, make it possible to download high-quality audio from the Web and play it back on Macs (via iTunes or similar applications) or portable digital audio players. Developed in Germany by the Fraunhofer Institute in 1991.

.TIFF Tagged Image File Format; a common file format for storing bitmapped images. The images can display any resolution, and they can be monochrome, grayscale, or in full color. A common high-quality format for digital camera files.

4:3 The NTSC standard aspect ratio for traditional TVs; a 4:3 picture is four units wide by three units high. Also measured as 1.33:1.

5.1 Dolby Digital produces five separate surround channels plus one subwoofer channel—thus the "5.1" designation.

6.1 Surround format with six separate surround channels plus one subwoofer channel; used in Dolby Digital EX and DTS ES.

7.1 Surround format with seven separate surround channels plus one subwoofer channel.

16:9 The aspect ratio used in HDTV broadcasts; a 16:9 picture is 16 units wide by 9 units high. The 16:9 aspect ratio presents a wider image area than the traditional 4:3 ratio. Also measured as 1.78:1.

802.11b More accurately described as IEEE 802.11b, this is an RF-based technology designed for home and small business wireless networks. Also known as *WiFi*, 802.11b uses the 2.4GHz band. The original AirPort technology was based on 802.11b. The top speed for data is 11 megabits per second.

802.11g Also IEEE 802.11g, this is a higher-speed wireless technology than 802.11g that offers compatibility with older 802.11b devices. Apple markets 802.11g devices as AirPort Extreme cards and base stations, although the AirPort Express base station can also route at 802.11g speeds, which can reach 56 megabits per second.

8mm Recording format for camcorders that uses a videocassette with 8mm tape. "Digital 8" camcorders can record digital data to an 8mm tape.

A

AAC Advanced Audio Codec; Similar to MP3, an audio file format and compression technology used for digital music files. AAC can include a special digital rights management (DRM) technology so that the file's ability to be copied and translated can be limited; Apple uses the AAC format and FreePlay DRM for the audio file it sells via the iTunes Music Store.

ADB Apple Desktop Bus; An older technology for connecting input devices to Macs made prior to the advent of the iMac.

ADC   Apple Display Connector; a special connector designed to transfer video, USB and power from a Mac's ADC port to special ADC-equipped Apple displays.

AGP   Accelerated Graphics Port; a graphics interface specification, based on the PCI bus, designed for three-dimensional graphics.

analog   A means of transmitting or storing data using a continuously variable signal. Prone to signal degradation; does not always accurately reproduce the original.

application   Another word for a computer software program. Common applications include word processors, spreadsheets, and Web browsers.

aspect ratio   The ratio between the width and height of a video display. The NTSC television standard is 4:3, whereas HDTV uses a 16:9 ratio. Some wide-screen movies use an even wider ratio, either 1.85:1 or 2.35:1.

ATA   Advanced Technology Attachment; a standard for internal hard disks often called *IDE*.

ATAPI   AT Attachment Packet Interface; the version of ATA for removable drives such as CD and DVD drives.

audio   Sound.

audio/video receiver   A combination of amplifier and preamplifier that controls both audio and video inputs and outputs. Most a/v receivers include some sort of surround-sound decoder, either Dolby Pro Logic or the newer (and slightly more expensive) Dolby Digital. Also called an *a/v receiver*.

auto exposure   A feature of digital cameras that automatically selects the optimal exposure settings for best image quality.

auto focus   A feature of digital cameras that automatically focuses the camera lens on the main subject in the picture.

B

backup   The process of creating a compressed copy of the data on your hard disk, to be used in case of an emergency.

balanced cable   An audio cable that has two conductive wires, has a ground, and is often shielded. These cables are used to reduce interference and noise.

bandwidth   The amount of data that can be transmitted in a fixed amount of time. For digital devices, bandwidth usually is expressed in bits per second (bps) or bytes per second (Bps). For analog devices, bandwidth is expressed in cycles per second, or hertz (Hz). Specific to audio, bandwidth refers to the range of frequencies a component can reproduce; the larger the bandwidth, the better the sound or picture.

base station   A device that enables AirPort or WiFi-enabled computers to connect to one another and/or access the Internet.

bay   Within a desktop Power Macintoshes' case, the space for installing an internal drive or peripheral.

beam   The process of transferring files or data from one device, such as a PDA, to another device, typically through an IrDA link.

bit   Binary DigIT; the smallest element of computer storage, a single digit (0 or 1) in a binary system; 8 bits equal 1 *byte*. Physically, a bit can be a transistor or capacitor in a memory cell, a magnetic domain on disk or tape, a reflective spot on optical media, or a high or low voltage pulsing through a circuit.

bit depth   The number of bits used to represent colors or tones. 2-bit color is black and white; 4-bit color produces 64 colors or shades of gray; 8-bit color produces 256 colors; 16-bit color produces 32,000 colors; 24-bit color produces 16.7

million colors; 30/32-bit color produces billions of individual colors.

bit rate   The transmission speed of binary-coded data. *See* data rate.

bitmap   A binary representation of an image or font consisting of rows and columns of dots. The broader the color spectrum, the more bits are required for each pixel. For simple monochrome images, 1 bit is sufficient to represent each dot, but for colors and shades of gray, each dot requires more than 1 bit of data, hence "64-bit" graphics.

Bluetooth   The specification for a particular wireless connection technology operating in the unlicensed 2.4GHz RF band. Bluetooth (developed primarily by phone maker Ericsson) was originally intended to be a "wire replacement" technology but has since been expanded to compete somewhat with the more powerful WiFi standard.

board   A device that plugs into your computer's system unit and provides auxiliary functions. Also called a *card*.

bps   Bits per second; the standard measure of data transmission speeds.

break-out box   A box that attaches to a sound card and is used to house additional input/output jacks.

broadband   A high-speed Internet connection, via ISDN, cable, DSL, satellite, or T1 and T3 lines.

browser   Short for Web browser, a client software program that lets a computer or other device access and display HTML pages on the World Wide Web.

burn   The process of writing computer files to a data CD or DVD.

burner   A device that writes data CDs or DVDs.

bus   In the computer world, a common pathway, or channel, between multiple devices. The computer's internal bus is known as the *local bus*, or *processor bus*. It provides a parallel data-transfer path between the CPU, main memory, and peripheral buses. A 16-bit bus transfers 2 bytes at a time over 16 wires; a 32-bit bus uses 32 wires; and so on. The bus is composed of two parts: the address bus and the data bus. Addresses are sent over the address bus to signal a memory location, and the data is transferred over the data bus to that location.

bus speed   The internal speed of a computer's motherboard.

byte   Eight bits, which the computer treats as a single unit. A byte is the unit most computers use to represent a character such as a letter, number, or typographic symbol. One thousand bytes is called a *kilobyte (KB)*, one million bytes is called a *megabyte (MB)*, and one thousand megabytes is called a *gigabyte (GB)*.

C

cable modem   A device that connects your computer to the Internet through cable lines, usually the same lines used for cable television.

cache   A form of temporary storage, either in computer memory or on a computer's hard disk.

cache memory   The area of computer memory that stores the most recently accessed data. When a computer needs data once, chances are it will need it again, soon, so computer designers realized they could speed up the computer by storing the most recently accessed data in a high-speed storage area. Most caches are FIFO (first in, first out), which means that as the cache fills, the older data is thrown out. There are several types of cache on your computer, including application cache, disk cache, hardware cache, and processor cache.

camcorder Video camera and recorder combined into a single unit.

card A device that plugs into your system unit and provides auxiliary functions. You can add video cards, modem cards, and sound cards to your system. Also called a *board*.

Cardbus—A 32-bit standard for PC card devices that makes it possible to move data at higher speeds, making them better suited for interfaces that add expansion ports such as USB and FireWire to Mac portables.

CCD Charge coupled device; a light-sensitive chip used for image gathering.

CD Compact disc; a laser-based digital format for storing high-quality audio programming.

CD-R Compact Disc Recordable; a type of CD drive that lets you record once onto CD discs, which can then be read by any CD-ROM drive and, with proper formatting, by most audio CD players.

CD-ROM Compact Disc Read-Only Memory; a type of CD that stores digital data for computer applications.

CD-RW Compact Disc Rewritable; a type of CD that can be recorded, erased, and rewritten to by the user, multiple times. A CD-RW disc cannot be played in a conventional CD player or in a normal CD-ROM drive.

central processing unit *See* CPU.

CF Compact Flash; a small form factor memory card for removable data storage.

chat Text-based real-time Internet communication, typically consisting of short, one-line messages back and forth between two or more users. Users gather to chat in chat rooms or channels.

chip A small piece of semiconducting material (usually silicon) on which an integrated circuit is embedded. A typical chip is less than a square inch in size and can contain millions of electronic components (transistors). Computers consist of many chips placed on electronic boards called *printed circuit boards*.

chording Typing on special keyboards that requires pressing two or more keys at once in order to type certain letters. This lets you type with one hand, which some people can get to be quite good at.

circuit board A thin plate on which chips and other electronic components are placed. Computers consist of one or more boards, often called *cards* or *adapters*.

client In a client/server relationship between two devices, the client is the device that pushes or pulls data from the other device (server).

CMYK Cyan, Magenta, Yellow, Black; the individual colors used to create color prints.

CODEC COder/DECoder; an algorithm that reduces the number of bytes consumed by large computer files and programs.

color calibration A process that creates or updates information about a device that can be used to match its color capability to other devices.

color depth *See* bit depth.

compact disc *See* CD.

compact flash *See* CF.

component video A video signal that has been split up into its component parts: red (Pr), green (Y), and blue (Pb). Component video connections—found on higher-end TVs and DVD players—reproduce the best possible picture quality, with improved color accuracy and reduced color bleeding.

composite video   A single video signal that contains both chrominance (color) and luminance (brightness) and information. Composite video is typically delivered through a single "video" RCA jack connection and delivers a better-quality picture than an RF signal, but not as good as an S-Video signal.

compression   The process of compacting digital data.

controller   Any MIDI device that can be used to control any other MIDI-capable device. Generally, controllers are in the form of a keyboard, but they can also be drum pads, mixer controllers, and so on.

CPU   Central Processing Unit; a complex silicon chip that acts as a computer's brain, taking requests from applications and then processing, or executing, operations.

cross-platform   Able to work with both Macs and PCs (or with other computing platforms, such as Linux on Intel processors).

CRT   Cathode ray tube; commonly called a *picture tube*. Used in all direct-view, all rear-projection, and some front-projection televisions.

D

D/A converter   Digital-to-Analog converter; the processor on a sound card that converts the analog electrical signal into digital data.

DAMPS   Digital Advanced Mobile Phone System; the American standard for digital mobile telephony. Also known as *TDMA*.

DHCP   Dynamic Host Configuration Protocol; a networking protocol that can automatically assign IP addresses to computers that request from the DHCP server.

dial-up access   An Internet connection via a dial-up modem—*not* via always-on broadband.

digital   A means of transmitting or storing data using "on" and "off" bits (expressed as "1" or "0"). Known for its highly accurate reproduction, with little or no degradation from the original.

Digital 8   Digital recording format for camcorders that uses standard 8mm or Hi8 cassettes.

digital camcorder   A motion video camera that stores images as a computer file, usually on a magnetic tape. The resulting computer file can be copied to a Mac and edited using a special program such as Apple's iMovie. Also called a *DV camcorder*.

digital camera   A still camera that uses a light-sensitive image sensor chip (typically a *CCD*), instead of film, to capture the image.

digital compression   Any algorithm that reduces the storage space required to store or transmit information.

digital zoom   A pseudozoom mode in some digital cameras that operates by cropping the outside of the image and enlarging the center. Typically produces lower-quality images than a comparable *optical zoom*.

digitizer   Also called an *artpad* or *digitizing tablet*, an input device that enables you to move a pen across its surface in order to "draw" in programs and/or control the mouse pointer.

DIMM   Dual Inline Memory Module; a small circuit board that holds memory chips. Unlike SIMMS (Single Inline Memory Modules), you can install memory one DIMM at a time.

disk   A device that stores data in magnetic format. The three main kinds of disks are diskettes, hard disks, and optical disks.

Dolby AC-3   The previous name for Dolby Digital.

Dolby Digital   Surround-sound format, sometimes referred to as *5.1*. Incorporates six discrete digital audio channels: front left, front center, front right, surround left, surround right, and a "low frequency effects" channel for subwoofers.

Dolby Digital EX   Extended version of the Dolby Digital surround-sound format, with 6.1 channels. The extra channel is a matrixed rear surround channel positioned at the rear of the room, behind and between the left and right surrounds.

dongle   A device developed to prevent piracy. It attaches to a port on your computer and works as a key to unlock a particular software application.

download   The process of receiving information or data from a server on the Internet.

dpi   Dots per inch; a measurement of printer resolution. The more dots per inch, the higher the resolution. A 400dpi printer creates 160,000 dots (400×400).

driver   The program support file that tells a program how to interact with a specific hardware device, such as a hard disk controller or video display card.

DSL   Digital Subscriber Line; a new ultrafast Internet connection using standard phone lines. Download speeds can approach 32Mbps. Often preceded by another letter, denoting the type of DSL connection; for example, ADSL stands for Asymmetric Digital Subscriber Line, and SDSL stands for Symmetric Digital Subscriber Line.

DSP   Digital Signal Processor; a chip designed to manipulate analog information that has been converted into digital format. DSP circuitry is used in some surround-sound systems to create different simulated sound fields.

DV   Digital Video; the recording, editing, and storing of video in digital formats. A digital video (DV) camcorder is a video camera that captures and stores images on a digital medium such as a DAT or compact flash card.

DVI   Digital Visual Interface; a connector that sends a digital signal from your Mac's DVI port (or the DVI port on a graphics adapter) to a compatible LCD display.

DVD   A two-sided optical disc that holds a minimum of 4.7GB, enough for a full-length movie. DVDs can store significantly more data than ordinary CD-ROMs can, and can play high-quality videos. (The acronym DVD actually doesn't stand for anything anymore; at one time it stood for Digital Versatile Disk, and at another Digital Video Disk.)

DVD-Audio   New audio-only DVD format that delivers better-than-CD-quality sound; competes with SA-CD.

DVD-R   DVD Recordable; a write-once, read-many storage format similar to CD-R, but for DVDs.

DVD-RAM   DVD Random Access Memory; a rewritable DVD disc format for data recording and playback. DVD-RAM drives typically read DVD-Video, DVD-ROM, and CD media.

DVD-ROM   DVD Read-Only Memory; a DVD disc capable of storing data, interactive sequences, and audio and video. DVD-ROMs run in DVD-ROM or DVD-RAM drives, but not DVD-Video players connected to TVs and home theaters. Most DVD-ROM drives will play DVD-Video movies, however.

DVD-RW   DVD ReWritable; a rewritable DVD format that is similar to DVD+RW but with less capability to work as a random access device. It has a read-write capacity of 4.7GB.

DVD+RW   DVD+ReWritable; one of several competing rewritable DVD formats. Fully compatible with existing DVD and DVD-ROM drives.

DVR   Digital Video Recorder; a device that records programming digitally on a large hard disk. Also known as *personal video recorder (PVR)* or *personal television receiver (PTR)*.

E

email   Electronic mail; a means of corresponding to other computer users over the Internet through digital messages.

email gateway   A proxy server for email.

enclosure   A case designed to hold an external peripheral.

encryption   The process of coding data into a format that can't be read, for security purposes. To read an encrypted file, you must possess the secret key or password that unlocks the encryption.

equalizer   An amplifier that can boost or cut specific frequencies.

ergonomic—Design considerations meant to ease the possibility of pain in the workplace (or when working with workplace machines, such as computers).

ethernet   Perhaps the most common networking protocol. Ethernet is used to network, or hook computers together so they can share information.

F

fast ethernet   The same thing as ethernet, only 10 times faster.

file type   A specific type of file, associated with a specific application.

firewall   Software or hardware that insulates a computer or network from the Internet or other networks. A firewall blocks unwanted access to the protected network while giving the protected network access to networks outside the firewall.

FireWire   A high-speed bus. FireWire is a serial connector, like USB, and allows you to add peripheral devices to your computer very easily, without having to open the box. FireWire, however, can transmit data 30 to almost 40 times faster than USB. That makes it very good for tasks such as getting video off a camcorder. For most devices, you don't need that much speed, but if you wanted to add a very fast hard drive to your PC, FireWire would be an excellent solution. FireWire was originally developed by Apple and is now also sold under the names iLink and IEEE-1394.

FireWire 400   The original implementation of FireWire, which had a top theoretical speed of 400MBps, or roughly 50 megabytes per second of data transfer.

FireWire 800   Newer FireWire standard capable of up to 800Mbps or 100 megabytes per second of data transfer. Unlike USB and USB 2.0, FireWire 400 and 800 have differently shaped connectors.

firmware   Low-level software that runs in a freestanding device (such as a digital camera) and typically controls the functionality and user interface.

floppy disk   Another term for *diskette*.

focal length   A lens measurement that determines the perspective (wide angle through telephoto) viewed through a camera lens.

format   The process that prepares a disk for use.

frame   One single still image that when played in rapid succession with other frames creates a moving picture.

frame rate   The number of video or animation frames that are shown per second. In gaming, frame rate is often as a measure of the Mac's processing and video capabilities. (The better the frame rate, the smoother the animation and the more playable the game is.)

FreeBSD   The Unix-like open source operating system upon which Mac OS X is partly based.

freeware   Computer software distributed at no charge. Unlike open-source software, the author retains the copyright, which means that the application cannot be modified without the author's consent.

frequency hopping   An RF technology that enables a single signal to jump from one frequency to another, to reduce interference and increase security.

FTP   File Transfer Protocol; a series of protocols or rules that define how to transfer files across the Internet. FTP is a very popular way to send files across the Internet, and is not dependent on Web servers and browsers.

full-motion video   The display of movie clips on your Mac in as realistic a form as possible. (Generally in the range of 24-to-30 frames per second.)

function key   One of the special keys labeled F1 to F12, located at the top of your computer keyboard.

G

gateway   A device that connects one or more other devices to an external network.

Gb   Gigabit; approximately 1,000 megabits.

GB   Gigabyte; 1,000 megabytes, more or less (1,024 to be precise).

Gbps   Gigabits per second.

GBps   Gigabytes per second.

GHz   Gigahertz (millions of cycles per second).

GPS   Global Positioning System; a system of 24 satellites for identifying earth locations, launched by the U.S. Department of Defense. By triangulation of signals from three of the satellites, a receiving unit can pinpoint its current location anywhere on earth to within a few meters.

graphics   Picture files. Pictures, photographs, and clip art are all commonly referred to as *graphics*.

grayscale   An image consisting of a range of gray levels, as opposed to a broader range of colors or pure black and white.

GSM   Global System for Mobile (communications); a second-generation (2G) standard for digital cellular transmissions; widely used in Europe and in U.S. PCS 1900 systems.

H

hard disk   A piece of hardware that stores large amounts of data for future access.

hardware   A piece of electronic equipment that you can actually touch. Your personal computer and all its peripherals are hardware; the operations of your PC are controlled by *software* (which you *can't* touch).

HDTV   High-Definition Television; a subset of the new digital TV standard that reproduces pictures in either 780p or 1080i resolution, with a 16:9 aspect ratio and Dolby Digital 5.1 surround sound.

home theater   The attempt to reproduce, as accurately as possible, the experience of watching a film in a movie theater. Typically involves a high-quality video source (such as DVD), audio/video receiver, surround-sound speakers, and a large video display device.

horizontal resolution   The sharpness of a video display, measured in terms of horizontal lines that can be resolved from one side of the screen to the other. Broadcast television has a horizontal resolution of 330 lines; DVDs deliver 500 lines; and HDTV can deliver up to 1,080 lines of horizontal resolution.

host   An Internet server that houses a Web site; any computer on a network that is a repository for services available to other computers on the network.

hotspots   Public places that offer wireless Internet access.

hot shoe   Connector on the top of a camera or camcorder designed to accept accessories.

hot-swappable   A device that can be interchanged with others without powering down your Mac (or, in some cases, without powering down the device itself).

hub (1)   Hardware used to network computers together (usually over an Ethernet connection). It's a small box with four or more RJ-45 connectors that accept cables from individual computers.

hub (2)   A peripheral device that enables you to connect multiple devices to a single expansion port, such as a USB hub or FireWire hub.

Hz   Hertz; a unit of measurement for the frequency of sounds. One Hz is equal to one cycle per second, and the range of human hearing is typically 20–20,000 Hz.

I–J

I/O   Input/Output. The flow of information to and from computers and peripherals.

IDE   Intelligent (or integrated) Drive Electronics; IDE connects mass-storage devices, such as hard drives or CD-ROMs, to a computer.

IEEE   Institute of Electronic and Electrical Engineers.

IEEE 1394   *See* FireWire.

iLife   Apple's popular bundle of multimedia productivity applications that includes iPhoto, iTunes, iMovie, iDVD and GarageBand.

infrared   A means of sending voice or data signals using light transmitted in the infrared range.

inkjet   A type of nonimpact printer that uses drops of ink to form images in a matrix format.

Intel-compatible   Computers that have processors that are compatible with the Intel brand of processors, including those with "true" Intel processors as well as AMD and others, as distinct from Macs, which use PowerPC processors made by Motorola and IBM. *See* Wintel.

interpolation   A way to increase the apparent size, resolution, or colors in an image by calculating the pixels used to represent the new image from the old one.

intranet   A private network inside an organization that uses the same type of software and services found on the public Internet.

IP   Internet Protocol; the protocol that defines how data is sent through routers to different networks, by assigning unique IP addresses to different devices.

IP address   The identifying address of a computer or device attached to a TCP/IP network. TCP/IP networks use IP addresses to route messages to their proper destinations. The IP address is written as four sets of numbers separated by periods.

IR   *See* infrared.

IrDA   Describes both the Infrared Data Association and the standard developed by that organization for infrared-based data connections.

ISDN   Integrated Services Digital Network; a digital communication system that can transmit voice or packet data over a regular phone line at rates between 64Kbps and 256Kbps.

ISP   Internet service provider; a company that connects individual users (calling in using traditional phone lines) to the Internet. Some Internet service providers—such as America Online—also provide unique content to their subscribers.

K

Kb   Kilobit; approximately 1,000 bits (1,024, to be precise).

KB   Kilobyte; 1,000 bytes, more or less. (Actually, it's 1,024 bytes.)

Kbps   Kilobits per second.

KBps   Kilobytes per second.

kernel   The central part of an operating system that oversees all other operations. The kernel loads first and stays in the memory throughout the operation of the OS.

keyboard   The thing that looks like a typewriter that you use to type instructions to your computer.

key drive   A small Flash RAM-based device that can store a relatively small amount of data; the portability of such pocket-sized "drives" cause them to be compared to house keys or keychains.

KHz   Kilohertz (thousands of cycles per second).

KVM   Keyboard, Video, Mouse; refers to devices that can switch between multiple computers using a single keyboard, video display and mouse to control them all.

L

lamp   The light source inside a video projector.

LAN   Local Area Network; a communications network that serves users within a relatively small area. Most LANs serve just one building or a group of buildings. The users' individual PCs are workstations (clients) that access the servers as needed.

LAN access point   A base station used to connect wireless devices to a local area network.

laser printer   A type of nonimpact printer that creates an electrostatic image of an entire page on a photosensitive drum, using a laser beam. An ultrafine coated powder (called *toner*) is applied to the drum, and then transferred to a sheet of paper, creating the printed image.

lavalier   A small microphone that can be clipped to a shirt collar.

LCD   Liquid Crystal Display; a flat-screen display device in which images are created by light transmitted through a layer of liquid crystals.

LCD projector   A type of video projector that generates a picture using a liquid crystal display, which is then projected through a magnifying lens.

legacy   Older hardware that uses proprietary Mac-specific ports (such as the Apple Desktop Bus or Apple serial connectors).

lens   A device, made of ground glass, for focusing light rays onto a CCD or film.

letterbox   A way to display wide-screen images on a standard 4:3 aspect ratio video display, by introducing black bars above and below the picture.

line level   The standard volume level for routing audio signals. For pro audio gear, line level is set at +4dBv and for consumer gear it is −10dBv.

Linux   A Unix-like operating system that runs on many different types of computers. Many different versions of Linux are available, even though it's not necessarily a user-friendly operating system; in fact, it's not recommended for general consumer use (although it does have a cult following among programmers and dedicated Microsoft haters). Linux was created by Linus Torvalds while he was a college student at the University of Helsinki in Finland. Instead of making it proprietary and trying to sell it, Torvalds gave it away, so anyone who wanted to develop for it could do so.

logic board   see *motherboard.*

M

Mb   Megabit; one million bits, more or less.

MB   Megabyte; approximately one million bytes (1,048,576, to be precise).

Mbps   Megabits per second.

MBps   Megabytes per second.

megapixel   A way of measuring image resolution in digital photography. One megapixel equals a million pixels; the higher the megapixel rating, the better quality the picture.

memory   Temporary electronic storage for data and instructions, via electronic impulses on a chip.

MHz   Megahertz; one million hertz. (A hertz is a measurement of frequency; in the case of computers, the speed of a microprocessor is measured in megahertz.)

microprocessor   The chip inside your system unit that processes all the operations your computer can do; a microprocessor includes a CPU and is the brain of any computing device.

MIDI   Musical Instrument Digital Interface (pronounced "middy"); a standard protocol for communication between musical devices such as synthesizers and PC sound cards. At minimum, MIDI defines the codes for a musical event, such as a note's pitch, length, volume, and other attributes, such as vibrato, attack, and delay time. The MIDI standard is supported by most synthesizers, allowing MIDI music to be played by an orchestra of separate MIDI instruments.

Mini DV   Digital video recording format for camcorders that uses an ultrasmall cassette.

modem   Modulator-Demodulator; a hardware device that enables transmission of digital data from one computer to another over common telephone lines via modulating and demodulating. It's the most common way in which people connect to the Internet.

monitor   The thing that looks like a TV screen that displays all your computer text and graphics; monitor generally refers to a cathode-ray tube (CRT) device, while *display* is often used for liquid-crystal display (LCD) devices.

motherboard   The big board that makes up the bulk of the insides of your system unit. The motherboard holds your main microprocessor and memory chips and also contains slots to plug in additional boards (cards). In Macs, sometimes called the *logic board*.

mouse   The handheld device with a rollerball and buttons you use to navigate through Windows and other graphical applications.

multifunction device   A printer that also serves as a scanner and copier, sometimes including faxing capabilities.

MPEG-2   The method of compressing digital video signals used by DVDs, digital broadcast satellites, and digital and high-definition television.

ms   Millisecond.

multimedia   The combination, usually on a computer, of interactive text, graphics, audio, and video.

N

NAT   Network Address Translation; a networking standard that enables a local area network to use one group of IP addresses for internal connections and another series of IP addresses for accessing the Internet, thus hiding the exact addresses of computers on your LAN from the outside world.

Net   Shorthand for *Internet*.

Ni-Cad   Nickel Cadmium (pronounced "ny-cad"); a type of rechargeable battery used in portable computers and devices. To prevent damage to the battery, Ni-Cad batteries should be completely discharged before recharging.

NiMH   Nickel Metal Hydride; a type of rechargeable battery used in portable computers and other devices. Has a longer life than Ni-Cad batteries, and can be recharged at any time without damage.

node   Any single computer connected to a network.

NTSC   National Television System Committee; the industry group that established the current North American analog broadcast TV standard. Sometimes refers to the standard itself.

O

OCR   Optical Character Recognition; the reading of text on paper and translation of those images into a form that computer users can manipulate. When a text document is scanned into the computer, it is turned into a bitmap, or picture, of the text. OCR software identifies letters and numbers by analyzing the light and dark areas of the bitmap. When it recognizes a character, it converts it into ASCII text.

OEM   Original Equipment Manufacturer; a company that buys computers in bulk from a manufacturer, and then customizes the machines and sells them under its own name. The term is a misnomer because OEMs aren't the original manufacturers.

open source   Software for which the underlying programming code is available (free) for users to make changes to it and build new versions incorporating those changes.

operating system   The core system software that lets you (and your software programs) communicate with your hardware.

optical drive   A storage device that uses a laser to read (and write) data to media. CD and DVD-based storage devices are optical drives.

optical zoom   A traditional zoom lens that enables you to move the focus closer to the subject, thus enlarging the image.

OS   Operating system.

P

packet   Part of a larger piece of data. When sent from one device to another (or over the Internet or other networks), data objects are typically broken up into multiple packets for easier transmittal.

PAL   The European broadcast standard.

parallel   A type of external port used to connect printers and other similar devices.

password   A special encrypted "word" (composed of any combination of letters and numbers) that one enters to obtain access to a computer, network, or Web site.

patch   A sound created by a synthesizer. The term comes from the early days of modular synthesis when modules were "patched" together to produce different sounds.

patch bay   An electrical panel that, ideally, contains an input and output for the various devices used in an audio studio. It serves as a central point to connect the various devices together.

PC   Term is sometimes used in the context of the Apple Macintosh to suggestion Windows-compatible (or IBM-compatible) computers, as distinct from Macintosh computers. *See* personal computer *and* Wintel.

PC Card   A credit-card–size memory or I/O device that fits into a desktop PC, portable PC, and some PDAs. Formerly known as a *PCMCIA card*. See also *Cardbus*.

PCI   Peripheral Component Interconnect; a standard for expansion cards used by all Power Macintosh models that have offered expansion card slots since the mid-1990s; originally an Intel standard, PCI slots can be 33Mhz or 66Mhz and can be designed to accept 7-inch and/or 12-inch expansion cards.

PCL   Printer Control Language; the standard for most inkjet and laser printers, originally developed by Hewlett-Packard.

PCMCIA   Personal Computer Memory Card International Association; an industry group formed to promote the adoption of credit-card–size memory and I/O devices.

PCMCIA card   *See* PC Card.

PDA   Personal Digital Assistant; a handheld device that organizes personal information, combining computing and networking features. A typical PDA includes an address book and a to-do list. Some function as cell phones and fax senders. Unlike portable computers, which use a keyboard for input, most PDAs incorporate a stylus and some sort of handwriting recognition capability. PDAs are sometimes called palm, pocket, or handheld PCs.

peer-to-peer   *See* P2P.

peripheral   Add-on hardware device for a computer system, such as a printer or a modem.

personal computer   A multifunction hardware unit that includes a hard disk, memory chips, microprocessor chip, and monitor. Personal computers perform tasks when enabled by *software* entered into memory.

personal firewall   Firewall software designed for a home or small-business computer.

picoliter   A million millionth of a liter. This is a common measurement of the size of an ink droplet that's used to create an image by an inkjet printer.

PictBridge   A specification that enables digital cameras to print directly to inkjet printers without first connecting to a Mac or PC.

PIM   Personal Information Manager; a computer program that manages contact and scheduling data.

pixel   The individual picture elements that make up a video image. The unit of measurement used in measuring the quality of screen displays.

pixelization   The stairstepped appearance of a curved or angled line in a digital image; *see* jaggies.

PlainTalk   As it refers to microphones, a special type of connector longer than a typical microphone's miniplug connector, which fits Apple's line-in audio port.

plasma display   A flat-panel video display that uses plasma gas to "light up" individual pixels in a picture.

port (1)   An interface on a computer to which you can connect a device. Personal computers have various types of ports. Internally, there are several ports for connecting disk drives, display screens, and keyboards. Externally, there are ports for connecting modems, printers, mice, and other peripheral devices.

port (2)   A virtual access point into a computer. Internet services use specific ports on computers used as Web servers.

PostScript   A page description language used by Mac applications and printers (mostly laser printers and high-end inkjets) to "describe" a page to be printed. PostScript is generally used for higher-end desktop publishing tasks because it's the language used by professional printing equipment.

POTS   Plain Old Telephone Service; traditional wired telephone service.

power sag   A condition where less than the optimum amount of electrical voltage is received by your home or office wall plug, which may result in erratic behavior from your Mac.

ppi   Pixels per inch.

ppm   Pages per minute; generally used to measure the speed of an inkjet or laser printer.

PPP   Point-to-Point Protocol; a technical protocol that defines how Internet Protocol (IP) data is transmitted over serial point-to-point links.

printer   The piece of computer hardware that lets you create hard-copy printouts of your documents.

processor   The brains of the entire computer. The processor, which is where a computer's instructions are decoded and executed, performs all of its logical operations.

prosumer   A term meant to suggest a device capable of professional-level results (such as a high-quality camera) but in a package built and often priced for an enthusiast or hobbyist.

protocol   An agreed-upon format for transmitting data between two devices.

PVR   Personal Video Recorder. *See* DVR.

Q

Quicktime   A sound, video, and animation format developed by Apple Computer. A QuickTime file can contain up to 32 tracks of audio, video, MIDI, or other time-based control information. QuickTime is also the name given to the underlying layer of technology in Mac OS X that is responsible for playing back and translating a variety of image, audio and video formats.

QWERTY   The standard layout of an American English (and many other) keyboards.

R

rack   A special type of storage shelf used to house pro audio gear.

RAID   Redundant Array of Independent Disks; a grouping of hard disks that, together with software, either make store the same data to multiple disks (to increase data redundancy) or can write to multiple disks simultaneously (to increase speed).

RAM   Random Access Memory; a common type of temporary computer memory that functions as a machine's primary workspace. The more RAM your computer has, the more efficiently it will operate.

real estate   The visible area on your monitor or display where you can open windows and otherwise work with your computer. A larger screen run at a higher resolution result in more screen "real estate."

receiver   A component that combines a preamplifier, amplifier, and radio in a single chassis. Receivers that include inputs and outputs for video sources and display are called *audio/video receivers*.

Rendezvous   Apple's name for Zeroconf, a specification that allows network devices to be "self-discoverable" on a local area network. Rendezvous-enabled printers, for instance, simply "show up" in your Printer Center when connected to your network.

removable media   Information storage that allow users to remove the stored information if necessary. Examples of removable media include disks and magnetic tapes.

resolution   The degree of clarity an image displays. The term is most often used to describe the sharpness of bitmapped images on monitors, but also applies to images on printed pages, as expressed by the number of dots per inch (dpi). For monitors, screen resolution signifies the number of dots (pixels) on the screen. For example, a 640×480 pixel screen can display 640 dots on each of 480 lines, or about 300,000 pixels. For television monitors, resolution is typically measured in terms of horizontal lines that can be seen or resolved. (*See* horizontal resolution.)

response time   On an LCD display, how quickly pixels are lit and darkened. A slow response time results in "ghosting" of fast-moving images.

restore   The process of returning a backed-up file to its previous location, often from a disk or tape to a hard drive.

RF   Radio Frequency; a means of transmitting and receiving signals via modulated radio waves.

RGB   Red, Green, Blue; the additive color model used in video displays.

right-click   The act of hovering over an item and then clicking your right mouse button; this often displays a pop-up menu of commands related to the object selected. (While the right-click is standard in Microsoft Windows, it's supported with multi-button mice in Mac OS X, too.)

ripping   Copying music from a CD to your computer's hard disk.

ROM   Read-Only Memory; a storage chip that typically contains hard-wired instructions for use when a computer starts up.

root directory   The main directory or folder on a disk.

router   A piece of hardware or software that handles the connection between two or more networks.

S

sampling frequency   The rate at which measurements of an audio signal are taken during A/D and D/A conversion. A higher sampling rate makes for a higher-fidelity audio signal.

scanner   A device that converts paper documents or photos into a format that can be viewed on a computer and manipulated by the user.

SCSI   Small Computer System Interface (pronounced "scuzzy"); the standard port for Macintosh computers, also common in PCs and Unix boxes. SCSI is really a family of interfaces, ranging from the relatively primitive SCSI-1 to the spiffy new Wide Ultra2 SCSI. SCSI hard drives are commonly used for audio applications because they generally can read and write data faster than can an IDE drive.

serial   A type of external port used to connect communication devices, such as modems and PalmPilots.

server   A central computer on a network that responds to requests for information from one or more client computers. On the Internet, all Web pages are stored on servers; in a client/server relationship between two devices, the server is the device that is controlled by commands from the other device (client).

shareware   Computer software distributed free, but requiring purchase to use beyond an initial period of time (or to use the full feature set).

shutter   That part of a camera that opens and closes to control how long the film or CCD is exposed to light.

shutter speed   The length of time the shutter remains open when shooting an image.

shuttle   An input device that enables you to move quickly "back and forth" along a media timeline.

SIP   Session Initiation Protocol; an Internet protocol that standardized how Internet-based audio conferencing sessions are begun and ended.

SLR   Single Lens Reflex; a film-based camera that enables you to look through a viewfinder and see through the lens.

SM   SmartMedia; a small memory storage card, similar to *Compact Flash*.

smart phone   A next-generation (3G) digital cellular phone that offers enhanced data and communications capabilities.

SmartMedia   *See* SM.

sneakernet   Whimsical term meant to suggest a "network" that requires you to get up and move data from one computer to another using a floppy diskette or removable disk.

sound card   The card that processes audio data on a PC. It's often a PCI card, but it can also be USB or FireWire based—or it can be built into the computer's motherboard.

static IP address   An IP address that doesn't change when you reinitiate a broadband Internet connection; static addresses are necessary in order to turn a computer into an Internet server.

storage   A catch-all to refer to fixed and removable disks and other devices used to save computer files.

streaming   Refers to the continuous transmission of data, typically audio or video, so it can be processed as a steady stream. With streaming, the client browser or plug-in can start displaying the data as sound and pictures before the entire file has been transmitted.

stylus   A penlike device used to operate the touch screen on a PDA.

subnet   A smaller pool of network nodes within a certain range of IP addresses that is part of a larger network.

subwoofer   A speaker specially designed to reproduce a range of very low frequencies—typically 20Hz–200Hz. Subwoofers are common in home theater systems to enhance the reproduction of low bass in movie soundtracks.

suite   A set of applications designed to work together. A suite typically includes word processing, spreadsheet, presentation graphics, and database programs.

SuperDisk   A portable storage medium from Sony that can hold up to 120MB of data; SuperDisk drives can read and write information to and from older 3 1/2-inch disks.

surge protector   A device that protects your system from unwanted power-line surges.

surround sound   The experience of being surrounded by sound from a video or audio source. Typically achieved with a surround-sound decoder (either Dolby Digital or Dolby Pro Logic) and multiple speakers.

switch   A network device similar to a hub, but that intelligently moves data packets from one network node to another.

S-VHS   Super VHS; a variation on the standard VHS format that delivers sharper pictures (400 lines of resolution versus 240 lines for standard VHS).

S-Video   A four-pin connection that transmits the chrominance (color) and luminance (brightness) portions of a video signal separately, for improved color accuracy and reduced distortion.

SVGA   Super Visual Graphics Array; a graphics display of 1280×1024 pixels, using 16 million different colors.

synching   The process of linking two devices together to exchange data or work from the same documents. For example, a DAT can be synched to a PC and be used to store audio data while still being controlled by the PC.

T

T-1   A leased-line connection capable of carrying data at 1.5Mbps; typically used for fast Internet connections to large corporations.

T-3   A leased-line connection capable of carrying data at 44.7Mbps.

TCP/IP   Transmission Control Protocol/Internet Protocol; the protocol used for communications on the Internet. It coordinates the addressing and packaging of the data packets that make up any communication.

telecommunications   How your computer talks to other computers, using a modem.

telephoto lens   A camera lens with a focal length greater than 50mm; makes far subjects appear closer than through a standard lens.

terabyte   One thousand gigabytes.

third-party software   Software written and/or published by one company to augment the ability of a product made by another company. For instance, software written by a third party might be designed to make a PC-compatible device work with a Mac.

thumbnail   A miniature representation of a page or image. Thumbnails often take considerable time to generate, but provide a convenient way to browse through multiple images before retrieving the one you need. A number of programs let you click on the thumbnail to retrieve the item it represents or view the picture at a larger size.

toner   Ultrafine coated powder, typically stored in some sort of cartridge, used by laser printers to create printed images on paper.

touch screen   A display that allows you to input information or move a mouse pointer by touching the display's screen.

trackball   A device designed to control your Mac's on-screen mouse pointer by moving a ball with your fingers, almost as if controlling an upside-down mouse.

trackpad   A device used to control your Mac's on-screen mouse pointer by sliding a finger across its surface; this is the device built into modern PowerBooks and iBooks.

TrueType   A scalable font technology that renders fonts for both the printer and the screen. Originally developed by Apple, it was enhanced jointly by Apple and Microsoft.

U

Unix   A computer operating system. Unix is designed to be used by many people at the same time and has TCP/IP built in.

USB   Universal Serial Bus; an external bus standard that supports data transfer rates of 12Mbps (12 million bits per second). One USB port can connect up to 127 peripheral devices, such as keyboards, modems, and mice. USB also supports hot plugging and Plug-and-Play installation.

V

VCR   Video Cassette Recorder; a device that records audio and video signals on videotape cassettes.

VGA   Video Graphics Array; a graphics display of 640×480 pixels with 256 colors.

VHS   Today's standard videocassette format.

VNC   Virtual Network Computing; a standard that enables one computer to remotely control another computer over a network connection.

VoIP   Voice over IP; any of a number of technologies that lets you use an Internet connection to initiate a voice conferencing session or phone call.

VPN   Virtual Private Network; a network in which some parts are connected via the public Internet, but encrypted, so that the network is "virtually" private.

W

WAN   Wide Area Network; a connection between two or more local area networks (LANs). Wide area networks can be made up of interconnected smaller networks spread throughout a building, a state, or the globe.

WAP   Wireless Application Protocol; a standard for providing cellular phones, pagers, and other handheld devices with secure access to email and text-based Web pages. WAP features the Wireless Markup Language (WML), a streamlined version of HTML for small-screen displays. It also uses WMLScript, a compact JavaScript-like language that runs in limited memory.

Web   *See* World Wide Web.

Web browser   *See* browser.

WEP   Wireless Equivalent Privacy; the encryption and security protocol for WiFi networks.

wide screen   A picture with an aspect ratio wider than 4:3 or 1.33:1.

wide-angle lens   A camera lens with a focal length less than 50mm; it gives a wider field of view than normal lenses.

WiFi   The 802.11b wireless networking standard; short for "wireless fidelity."

WinTel   Computers that are compatible with Microsoft Windows and Intel-brand processors. Meant to suggest personal computers other than Macintosh computers.

WLAN   Wireless LAN; a local area network composed of wireless connections between devices.

woofer   A driver within a speaker enclosure that uses a large cone to reproduce bass frequencies.

X

XLR   A connector that's used to carry balanced audio signals.

Y–Z

Zip drive   A portable storage medium from Iomega that can hold between 100MB (originally) and 250MB of data.

Index

M

N

O

P

W